An Introduction to th
Psychology of Paranorr
?elief and Experienc

An Introduction to the Psychology of Paranormal Belief and Experience

TONY JINKS

McFarland & Company, Inc., Publishers
Jefferson, North Carolina, and London

LIBRARY OF CONGRESS CATALOGUING-IN-PUBLICATION DATA

Jinks, Tony, 1970–
    An introduction to the psychology of paranormal belief and
experience / Tony Jinks.
        p.   cm.
    Includes bibliographical references and index.

    ISBN 978-0-7864-6544-6
    softcover : 50# alkaline paper ∞

    1. Parapsychology.   2. Psychology.   I. Title.
BF1031.J56 2012   130.1'9   dc23   2011036677

BRITISH LIBRARY CATALOGUING DATA ARE AVAILABLE

Front cover design by David K. Landis (Shake It Loose Graphics)

Manufactured in the United States of America

McFarland & Company, Inc., Publishers
  Box 611, Jefferson, North Carolina 28640
    www.mcfarlandpub.com

Table of Contents

Preface

At the start of this book, I believe a disclaimer is in order. Although I teach a paranormal subject at a university and have written the occasional scientific paper on paranormal topics, I do not attend conferences or meetings with paranormal experts. Nor do I actively investigate mysterious events as a pastime. I think that makes me somewhat of an outsider — and certainly not a prominent authority on all things paranormal. Nevertheless, being an outsider has its advantages, because it has allowed me to scrutinize the field without pressure or expectation. That is a nice position from which to write a book about the psychology of paranormal belief and experience.

However, one cannot be completely impartial about paranormal events — if I was, then I surely would not have the interest or the motivation to write a book in the first place. Briefly, I will describe my position, so as to put the content of this book into perspective.

When someone admits to seeing a strange object hovering in the sky, the reaction from those who hear the story is largely one of ridicule. The witness saw a spacecraft full of little green men, did he? What has he been smoking? These rejoinders are considered by the listener to be clever, snappy. We all have probably used them at some time or another to express our incredulity. Similarly, other strange experiences — from telepathic hunches to seeing angels or ghosts — are treated as though the witness is drunk, or stupid, or gullible, or overly emotional... The list is almost endless.

I believe these retorts are facile, and display no wit at all. They are also based on psychological theory, whereby a witness's experience stems from a problem in his or her "mind." And to be perfectly honest, it's general practice for educated skeptics to make similar statements, although frequently (but not always) the skeptic uses more sophisticated, scientific language to make the explanation sound impressive.

So, if the arguments used to discount paranormal claims have such a strong psychological basis, it makes sense to want to understand this psychology in greater depth. That is the purpose of this book — to scrutinize the psychological theories that are used to explain paranormal belief and experience. Most commonly, these theories dismiss the paranormality of an encounter, but on occasion they are actually supportive of its anomalous nature. Suffice it to say, the latter theories are not widely appreciated, but this does not make them any less interesting, or important.

My primary objective is to try and comprehend the ideas of the paranormal experts and write about them in a way that *I* can understand. Then I can relay the knowledge I have gained to others who can benefit from my years of study and deep reservoir of scientific research. The book is therefore directed at a general readership who do not possess a background in psychology, or even science for that matter, in the hope that they can get still a sense of how the field of psychology views the paranormal. I simply do not have the background to write a book on the paranormal for experts in the paranormal but that's not necessarily a problem, because there are lots of articles written by the experts for experts, but not many for everyone else.

A secondary purpose for the book is to create a type of "investigative manual" so that any reader who reads or hears about (or personally experiences) something paranormal can assess the event from a variety of psychological perspectives. Perhaps this will allow him or her to draw a conclusion that is more sophisticated and balanced — and dare I say it, "intelligent" — than laughing a claim off as a product of "craziness" (be it that person's craziness, or someone else's).

So I apologize in advance to the professional researchers if I have left out any of their findings, or missed an interesting topic. It would take a much larger book to cover it all. And to the average reader, I hope I do not lose you with any of the technical stuff.

Finally, while I have tried to make the book as balanced as possible, it is hard to sit on the fence. If anything, I have tended to sway towards acceptance of the paranormal because I have never come across a supporter of the paranormal who has pushed his beliefs on me. On the other hand, I have met plenty of skeptics who assume, because I lecture on a paranormal subject, that what I teach must be critical of strange beliefs and encounters. If I do not teach with a hardcore, skeptical attitude (the horror!) then it suggests there is something wrong.

It is this attitude I find rather distasteful, and I do take it personally. Consequently I have more than a little sympathy for the paranormal enthusiast who generally takes these spiteful attacks with dignity and humor. Then again, the skeptics mount some persuasive arguments, too. So, whatever side you are on, the paranormal is worth studying, and the psychology of the paranormal is a good place to start.

Introduction:
What Is the Paranormal?

For over a century, many thousands of books, journal articles and opinion pieces have been written about the paranormal, and thankfully they all tend to define the term with reasonable consistency. Sociologist Marcello Truzzi suggests this consistency is one of separating events that are *paranormal* from events that are *supernatural*. Paranormal events are extraordinary, but natural, occurrences that are ultimately explainable scientifically. Supernatural events, on the other hand, fall outside the natural order therefore cannot be rationally understood by mere humans (Truzzi 2001).

The arch-skeptic and magician James Randi takes a similar line, explaining that the word paranormal has ancient Greek origins and means *beside or beyond what is normal*. To Randi, "paranormal" is an adjective that identifies events not yet defined or explained by science, but he believes such events and abilities could be explained if enough information was available to the researcher. In contrast to Truzzi, however, Randi considers the terms "paranormal" and "supernatural" to mean essentially the same thing. Anything and everything mysterious can be understood scientifically when the right amount of information becomes available (Randi 1997).

The less-skeptical author Stuart Gordon similarly defines the paranormal as beyond the range of normal experience (Gordon 1992). However, he further suggests that this normal experience is assumed to be Western (or scientific) in outlook. In non–Western cultures, what a Westerner considers paranormal might be considered perfectly normal.

So what exactly is a scientific outlook? Moreover, is "the paranormal" a scientific pursuit or not, considering the conflicting definitions just provided? Simplistically, "science" is a word describing a method of hypothesizing about a state of affairs in the real world (perhaps from everyday observation), systematically collecting the relevant material information, and reaching a conclusion about the accuracy of that hypothesis. Furthermore, if we take the view that only through such empirical observation and testing can truths about the world be known, then one might be said to support a scientific world view. This is the type of "science" that Randi practices, and for convenience I'll call these individuals "scientists."

Paranormal topics such as ghosts and psychic powers frustrate scientists because they are frequently difficult, or more likely impossible, to test empirically. For example, how could your next door neighbor's startling hunch about the following week's winning lottery numbers be experimentally evaluated if she only tells you those numbers after the lottery has been drawn? (Naturally, she forgot to buy a ticket!) Similarly, how can the strange goings-on in the creepy old house down the street ever be appraised if the alleged ghost never performs on cue when scientists turn up to investigate? Much to these scientists' chagrin, a surprisingly large number of people accept theories about these types of paranormal events that certainly aren't based on empirical evidence and fall outside the fixed boundaries of what science thinks is legitimate. For example, the premise that ghosts can be explained in terms of a transcendental world containing the souls of deceased humans.

Scientists reject such premises as meaningless, hence the subjective data that makes up most paranormal experience is conveniently "defined out" of scientific concern (Twemlow 1994). It's simply not worth taking seriously.

Scientists also apply the scientific perspective to all cultures and historical periods, so just because you might not "believe in science," or come from a place where science isn't the primary world view, doesn't mean the paranormal is real. It might be real to you, but it's still not really *real*.

Although most scientists don't concern themselves with studying anything remotely paranormal, a few busy themselves with answering the question of why people still believe in paranormal events, and perhaps experience them on occasion, when such events are scientifically impossible. These scientists are usually psychologists, and the psychology they practice is a brand that is universally taught and applied in schools, universities and in the wider community.[1] It is scientific psychology, with a strong rationalist and empirical foundation. I refer to it throughout the book as "mainstream psychology" or "scientific psychology." Not surprisingly, within the parameters of this discipline are hypotheses that explain paranormal *beliefs* as judgmental errors and paranormal *experiences* as ordinary events that the witness has mistaken as extraordinary.

Nevertheless, this mainstream psychological approach is not indisputable and folklorist Eddie Bullard suggests it has its own, obvious flaws. For instance, it's not uncommon for mainstream psychologists to argue that people claim to experience paranormal events in order to fulfill a function, such as the need for belief in higher powers, or to provide entertainment because life is boring. However, describing an object or event's function isn't an adequate explanation of that object or event. Bullard argues the scientist would never resort to this type of *functionalist* approach to explain the workings of something serious, like antibiotics or the weather. The difference is that paranormal topics aren't considered scientific in the first place, so the customary respect given to the process of explanation doesn't seem to apply (Bullard 1991). Indeed, even the psychological functions attributed to an alleged paranormal event can be quite ridiculous, or require further clarification. For example, if a bystander claims to have seen a ghost, a skeptical mainstream psychologist might attribute the sighting to the witnesses' "attention-seeking personality type." Yet surely this function itself needs further elucidation? What is an "attention-seeking personality type," and what evidence is there that this person possesses one?

With this criticism in mind, the purpose of this book is to present a balanced evaluation of the conventional (mainstream) psychological hypotheses applied to paranormal belief and paranormal experience. This doesn't mean there aren't plenty of non-psychological theories explaining the paranormal. In fact, these non-psychological theories are far more widely known and written about than the corresponding psychological ones. How many people would be aware of, let alone be interested in, some of the complicated psychological explanations for ghostly apparitions that will be explored in later chapters? To most people a ghost is the wandering spirit of a dead person, simple as that!

It's also important to realize that not all psychology is mainstream and skeptical. As we explore these mainstream theories throughout the book, we also need to pay attention to the viewpoints of other psychologists and researchers who don't necessarily adopt a conventional outlook with regard to the paranormal. These psychologists by and large still use strict psychological research methods and theories to explain paranormal processes — but in ways that don't necessarily discount the legitimacy of these processes. A convenient term to describe these psychologists is *parapsychologist*, and much of the first half of the book explores the distinct approaches both mainstream psychologists and parapsychologists take in explaining the paranormal, and the sometimes heated arguments they indulge in.

Towards the end of the book we'll also examine extreme alternate psychological theories that have been proposed to account for paranormal experiences — theories developed over many years by psychologists, psychiatrists and an assortment of other academic researchers. Some of these theories are seriously unconventional, and many mainstream psychologists wouldn't be caught dead even considering them. Consequently, the attitude of mainstream psychology to these fringe theories will rarely be discussed, because there the attitude is universally one of derision. Nevertheless, the theories still fit within the broad definition of psychology, and need be included to achieve the balance we're seeking. Before we start, however, an examination of the various paranormal topics will help to illuminate what they are, and why they do not conform with the scientific principles so beloved of the mainstream psychologist.

Established Topics of the Paranormal

Life After Death

Arguably, the premier paranormal topic is "life after death" (LAD). The earliest formal scientific studies of paranormal events occurred in the 19th century and centered on LAD — the inspiration being a fashionable craze known as *table-turning*. During a table-turning session, participants would sit around a table under the direction of a psychic medium, and perhaps feel it move beneath their hands in ways other than through (apparent) human intervention. The assumption at the time was that such movement was caused by the actions of either the souls of the dead, or other types of non-human spiritual beings inhabiting a realm distinct from the physical world. This is how table-turning evolved into *Spiritualism*, a practice that began as a fun pastime, but eventually ended up a religion (Inglis 1986). In truth, Spiritualism involved more than just turning tables, and when practiced in a séance environment any number of extraordinary events might occur, ranging from the obtainment of spirit messages to the materialization or "apporting" of assorted objects (such as vases or photographs, or even the spirits themselves). Ectoplasm, the white stringy stuff you often see in Victorian-era photographs of mediums in trances (sometimes awkwardly emanating from their mouths or nostrils), is an example of an apported material. Furthermore, the medium or the medium's guests might also be levitated — a common feature in the séance and historically associated with high spiritual states such as religious ecstasy.

Such was the popularity of Spiritualism that early paranormal researchers focused solely on experiences said to be evidence for LAD. Particular interest was paid to the ghostly appearance of dead people (also known as *discarnates*), reincarnation (or "past life") memories, and the extraordinary, spirit-induced powers demonstrated by a medium whist in a trance.

Despite the prevalence of deceased human spirit guides in the history of mediumship, there have been mediums who claim to have psychical contact with discarnate beings that aren't necessarily "former humans." Some of these guides have even been extraterrestrials. As far back as the late 19th century, Hélène Smith spoke of a Martian civilization she'd encountered while in a trance-state, and wrote in a Martian alphabet while channeling the conversations of aliens with names such as Astané, Ramier and Esenale. According to the author and investigator John Keel, these Martians possessed the oriental facial features, long hair and long fingers that later came to characterize many of the beings who purportedly fly around in UFOs (Keel 1971).

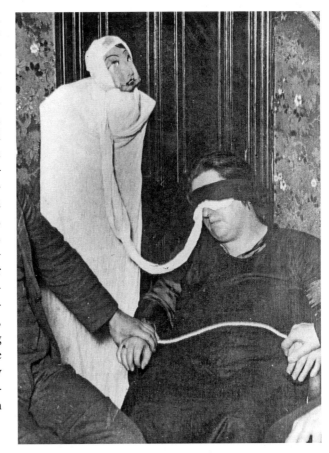

Medium Helen Duncan allegedly materializes her child guide "Peggy." From a glance at the photograph, taken in the 1930s at her home, it might not be a surprise to learn that Duncan appeared in court on more than one occasion in her career, and spent time in jail for fraud. Apparently, she was very good at hiding the objects she would "apport" in séances by swallowing them, then secretly regurgitate them at the appropriate moment (Mary Evans Picture Library).

Extraordinary Perception

By the early 20th century, certain psychical researchers were unhappy with applying LAD to all accounts of extraordinary events and experiences, and explored alternative paranormal possibilities. Thus began the study of *extraordinary perception*, also known as *extrasensory perception* (ESP). Simply put, ESP encompasses four abilities:

(1) *Telepathy* is said to occur when an individual gains knowledge of another person's thoughts without recourse to normal channels of information processing, such as through a verbal conversation.

(2) *Clairvoyance* refers to a perceiver's knowledge of events occurring in a place remote from the perceiver, again without recourse to conventional channels, for example a telephone call. Most correctly, clairvoyance is the knowledge of a visual nature (hence the term clair*voyance*). If someone claims to hear something in a distant place they are displaying *clairaudience*, and if they feel something at that location they are displaying *clairsentience*.

(3) *Precognition* involves a person gaining knowledge of events before they happen through methods other than the normal cognitive (thinking) processes, such as reasoning about what *should* happen in the future based on previous experience.

(4) *Retrocognition* is the knowledge of past events, once again through ways other than normal cognitive processes, for example reading or being told about a historical incident. By definition, *reincarnation* experiences are a category of retrocognition, because people can claim retrocognitive experiences that do not arise from personal memories of a "past life."

A distinct, and often-overlooked, form of ESP is *dowsing* (or divining). This is the ancient technique of finding underground water (and perhaps substances of more contemporary importance, such as oil) using a variety of basic instruments such as sticks or metal rods. Pendulums are also popular. When dowsing for water or minerals, the dowser might walk across a field, allowing the sticks in their hands to wobble and point to the underground location of the dowsed substance. One controversial theory that supports the legitimacy of dowsing proposes that the dowser "reacts" to the earth's magnetic field through the dowsing rod because they not only possess heightened sensitivity to "earth forces," but also enjoy a physiological makeup that mimics a battery. This battery effect allows an electric charge to be generated in the dowsing rod, which can then detect magnetic field through small deflections (Cosh 1996).

In contrast, skeptics of dowsing see it as no more than a manifestation of the psychological *ideomotor effect*, whereby the dowser performs imperceptible and involuntary body movement (such as twitching) which are influenced by their subconscious expectations of what should happen (Randi 1998). This idea isn't Randi's. Its origins go back at least as far as William James, one of the founders of modern psychology, writing critically about pendulum motion in the late 19th century.

A more detailed criticism derives from the mid–1970s experiments by psychologists Randolph Easton and Ronald Shor. They argue that when a

Dowser Jack Timms and an assistant demonstrate water diving in a paddock in Oxfordshire, England, in 1937 (Mary Evans Picture Library).

person holds a pendulum, *kinesthetic* (body) information is sent from the fingers to the brain indicating there are slight, unavoidable muscle movements — movements that will result in a small pendulum swing. However, these subtle signals are overwhelmed by the visual information derived from actually seeing the pendulum move. The mind immediately forms an image of the motion and this automatically feeds back to the pendulum and sustains it (Easton and Shor 1975). Unfortunately, the dowser remains unaware of the faint, uncontrolled muscle contractions that initiate the circling pendulum's movement, and instead assumes outside forces (or their own psychic powers) are responsible. Easton and Shor use the analogy of a yawn to help their argument. If you see someone yawn, the idea of yawning enters your mind, and you can't help putting the thought into action — a type of psychological "law" — by yawning back (Easton and Shor 1976). It's an automatic thing ... we simply can't help doing it.

Likewise, another explanation for dowsing that's been discussed for over 100 years is that the dowser has an expectation of psychically controlling the pendulum's (or stick's) movement. This increases the likelihood they'll see motion which isn't there. In a separate experiment, Easton and Shor found that when participants in their pendulum studies had to attend to other tasks — and weren't allowed to imagine the pendulum oscillating — the reports of pendulum movement diminished (Easton and Shor 1976).

To convince you of the ideomotor effect, a scientific psychologist might encourage you to hold a pendulum. Before long it is likely that a circular motion will be produced. You might even come to believe you can influence the direction of the motion, either clockwise or counter-clockwise, using "the powers of your mind." Before letting you leave with your newfound discovery, however, the psychologist would want to put you through another test in which you attempt to "psychically" oscillate the pendulum with your hand supported — a technique proposed by the early 19th century French scientist Michel Chevreul. They might even tie the pendulum to the arm of a chair, so that it hangs freely. Not unexpectedly, when the pendulum hangs from the supported hand or chair arm there is significantly less movement (if any) generated by concentrating on it, compared with when the pendulum is held by a free arm.[2] The psychologist might also ask you to hold the pendulum again but not actually look at it, and get you to think of something entirely different. Anyone watching would observe the pendulum oscillates much less than when you're looking at it, willing it to move. The pendulum effect is therefore a product of a demonstrable psychological process — case closed.

A proponent of dowsing might retort that actual physical contact between the dowser and the pendulum is crucial, and movements shouldn't be expected if the pendulum is not actually being held, or concentrated on, for that matter. Nevertheless, from the viewpoint of mainstream psychology, dowsing is just another instance of an *automatism*— actions a performer can't feel themselves doing, and attribute it to a paranormal agency. Other examples of automatisms would include our old favorite, table-turning, as well as automatic writing (spirit communication using a medium as the writer) and the Ouija board (where sitters place a finger on a movable planchette and spell out the words and phrases of a communicating spirit) (Burgess, Kirsch, Shane, Niederauer, Graham and Bacon 1998).

Extraordinary Powers

Psychokinesis (PK), also known by its older name *telekinesis,* is an extraordinary ability that allows practitioners to (allegedly) influence objects and events in unconventional ways — most obviously in the absence of physical contact. Occasionally PK is labeled a form of ESP. However, PK is not strictly a type of perception at all, since it doesn't actually involve perceiving anything. Instead, it is more correctly defined as an *extraordinary human power*, and both ESP and PK are popularly considered to be different expressions of a more general psychic concept termed *psi* (von Lucadou 1984).

Demonstrations of PK include anything from moving a plate on a table without touching it to bending spoons or influencing the digital output of a computerized random number generator. It can also involve affecting changes in the behavior or physiological responses of another person, a technique known as *direct mental interaction with living systems* (DMILS). In a typical session, a participant acting as an agent is required to influence the *electrodermal activity* (EDA) of another person, the subject. EDA is best thought of as the amount people sweat, and is measured as a component of the lie detector test that we're all familiar with. The parapsychologist can then measure changes in the subject's skin conductance compared to normal, or if they have the appropriate equipment, they could even measure more subtle alterations such as hemolysis in their red blood cells (Delanoy 2001).

While it is generally accepted that PK is different from (and is perhaps rarer than) ESP, it has been suggested that the two concepts are strongly related, and that the obvious differences between them are a product of the various ways the two abilities are measured (Roe, Davey and Stevens 2003).

This rather famous 1908 photograph captured Polish medium Stanislawa Tomczyk levitating scissors using psychokinesis. Like any photograph of a paranormal event or activity it is controversial; it is claimed to show nothing more than trickery, with Tomczyk using fine thread to perform the feat. Investigator Julien Ochorowicz (sitting next to Tomczyk) agreed there truly was a "thread" involved in the demonstration, but it was of a more etheric nature and psychically derived, rather than physical material (Mary Evans Picture Library).

Powers of healing can also be categorized as an extraordinary power, and might be related to the phenomenon of PK (e.g., see Palmer, Simmonds-Moore and Baumann 2006 for an interesting review). On the other hand, many healers claim their abilities are derived not from themselves but from discarnate beings such as deities or spirits (Krippner and Achterberg 2000), which brings us back to the omnipresent concept of LAD and mediumistic ability. The same might be said for the phenomena of *poltergeists*. The translation from German is roughly that of a "noisy spirit," which by its very name suggests the agent is a dead person, haunting a building (or more rarely, an outside area[3]). The noisiness of the poltergeist frequently comes from the mysterious "rapping" sounds made on walls or bed heads, and which on occasions have been tape recorded (Colvin 2010).

However, the poltergeist is by nature invisible, and its presence is only inferred from changes occurring inside a room, such as crockery flying, furniture moving around, or a pictures falling off walls. For this reason, the event might equally be attributed to *recurrent spontaneous psychokinesis* (RSPK). This label implies a human, rather than spirit, cause — the most popular being that someone in the house (usually a pubescent female) — is expressing their emotions through the release of psychic energy.[4] Yet despite the impressive title, RSPK is still only a descriptive label of what happens in an episode. The psychokinetic behavior — which itself is not understood — occurs anytime (it's spontaneous) and frequently (it's recurrent). As an explanation, it's not necessarily any better than attributing poltergeists to an invisible, supernatural ghost.

Altered States of Consciousness

The spiritualism craze lasted some decades into the 20th century, and it was during this later period that psychical researchers recognized an alternative phenomenon suggestive of LAD: the *near-death experience* (NDE). Typically, the NDE involves an individual journeying to some otherworldly place while in an unconscious, critically ill state. A set of core experiences are associated with the NDE, including a feeling of calm and peace, travel through or up a tunnel to a distant light, meeting a being in the light with the possibility of some form of instruction or imparting of knowledge, a "life review" (that is, reliving your live in an instant), a feeling of unconditional love, and a reluctance to return to the living body (Bonenfant 2000).

People reporting NDEs usually classify the event as a *peak experience*, meaning it has profoundly affected them. They might now have no fear of death, or have gained greater personal empathy.[5] A typical statement from an NDE experient is that they "become one with the universe," which appears to mean that their sense of themselves as an independent being is no longer relevant. This view is expressed in the experient's apparent lack of concern as they float above their lifeless, corporeal body on the operating table, or as it lies bleeding on a road following a traffic accident.

Peak experiences are also occasionally reported by individuals who enter an *altered state of consciousness* (ASC). To understand what an ASC entails, it is necessary to tackle the concept of "ordinary" consciousness. Unfortunately, this isn't easy. Consciousness is a very difficult concept, to the point where it is a rarely-used expression even in many university-taught psychology courses. This is despite the fact that consciousness is central to the human experience. Superficial definitions of consciousness are common, and can be useful until you try to understand them more deeply, when you often become stuck!

For the purpose of this introductory book, the definition of consciousness by neuroscientist Gerd Sommerhoff is useful. Sommerhoff neatly defines consciousness as an awareness of three things: your surrounding world, yourself as an autonomous entity and your thoughts and feelings (Sommerhoff 2000). From a scientific point of view, these processes derive from an underlying physical source, so mental events are considered by many psychologists as secondary to tangible reality[6] (Carpenter 2004). The cognitive part of consciousness is termed an *integrated global representation* involving knowledge of internal (body) and external (real-world) situations. Specific information concerning the current states of the external world is also referred to as the *running world model*.

From this definition (which I must add is only one of many), a person in an *altered* state of consciousness would have reduced or altered awareness of the running world model, and of themselves as a distinct and separate entity from this external world, yet would still be processing some kind of perceptual experience through their senses. This is somewhat different from being in a coma, where the individual has no awareness of anything occurring. There are plenty of different varieties of ASC, the most common being the states of sleep and hypnosis.

With this in mind, a scientific psychologist would likely consider a near-death experience to be a variety of altered state of consciousness, albeit rarer than sleeping. They would apply the same reasoning to an "out-of-body experience" (OBE), in which the experient typically perceives themselves to be located at a place other than where they know their physical body to be (Tart 1998) and has a reduced awareness of the running world model. It can happen in a time of life-crisis when the experient is wide-awake, but is just as likely to occur when they're relaxing and drifting off to sleep. Psychologist Charles Tart explains that in an OBE, the out-of-body "traveler" feels no different from their normal self, and is well aware of the concepts of space, time and location, which makes the experience very different from hypnosis. Yet another type of ASC is the *astral projection*— a journey of the "soul" that isn't necessarily associated with death, but shares characteristics with NDEs (for example, contact with extraordinary beings) and OBEs.

The variety of ASCs underlines how difficult it is to form a single, comprehensive model that defines all manifestations of the condition. For this reason, a distinction could be made between *mundane* altered states, such as sleep and hypnosis, and *extraordinary* (paranormal) altered states encompassing OBEs, NDEs and astral travel. These extraordinary altered states necessarily involve consciousness functioning at a level that has no grounding in physical reality, and allows access to hidden information unobtainable through more mundane altered states that are tied to the physical body.

Quite obviously, most psychologists would have difficulty accepting the view that extraordinary altered states of consciousness are intrinsically different from ordinary states. Firstly, they are unlikely to possess a belief in dualism — the proposition that the mind and the body are fundamentally separate entities. Recall Sommerhoff's standard psychological definition of consciousness. In this model, "mind" is a derivative of physical brain function (Bensley 2007), so the claim that the mind can operate independently of the brain is considered logically absurd.

There's also no sensible way for the psychologist to experimentally distinguish between an imagined OBE or NDE and one that is truly paranormal. Much of what is reported by the experient happens on some other "plane of existence," so it's virtually impossible for them to prove their claim of visiting other places or other worlds (not that most experients care if they can't prove what they've witnessed, since to them it was such a genuine occurrence that justifying it to other people seems unimportant and unreasonable). This attitude is in contrast to the demands of the scientific psychologist, who expects hard evidence of this other world before they would even begin to consider the experience as legitimate — while full-well assuming that such evidence is impossible to gather, so they never really have any intention of acknowledging the event as anything but imagined.

For many years, supporters of extraordinary altered states have proposed that any anomalous knowledge gained by the OBE or NDE experient would constitute strong evidence for the legitimacy of the phenomenon. One such task might employ the parapsychological technique of *remote viewing*, which was developed in the early 1970s by Harold Puthoff and Russell Targ (e.g., see Puthoff and Targ 1978). Typically, the method involves a participant, acting as "receiver," positioned in a parapsychological laboratory. Their role is to gather information about an object or event at a distant place — anywhere from the next room to another country (Schlitz and Gruber 1980).

The expression *remote viewing* implies that the receiver travels "out of body" to get this information. However, the actual procedure perhaps has as much in common with ESP as an OBE because a parapsychologist might attribute successful results in a remote viewing task to telepathic communication between the receiver and "transmitter" positioned at the distant location. Therefore, as a descriptive term referring to a specific practice, no necessary explanation of why or what is happening is fixed onto the remote viewing label. Does a person in an allegedly out-of-body state bring back with them information about a distant place or event, or do they stay where they are and receive telepathic information from the transmitter?

A stronger demonstration for the reality of an OBE might be for the traveler to actually cause some real and measurable change in a place different from where their physical bodies are, as opposed to just asserting knowledge of that place. In one famous example, the OBE practitioner Robert Monroe claimed to have pinched a friend while he was traveling out of his body, and the friend apparently had a bruise to show for it (Inglis 1986). Unfortunately, such examples are extremely rare and anecdotal and aren't accepted by the scientific psychologist, although this lack of concrete evidence doesn't trouble a handful of theorists who remain interested in the reality of extraordinary altered states.

One such theorist is Ilja Maso. Writing in the *European Journal of Parapsychology*, Maso acknowledges the difficulty of adopting dualism when trying to account for all paranormal phenomena, because dualism entails there can be no interaction between mind and matter. This might still allow astral travel, or an OBE or NDE, but rules out the possibility of phenomena such as PK, where mind is said to influence matter (Maso 2006). Instead Maso suggests a *panpsychic* approach, whereby all matter is infused with some level of consciousness, and mind and matter exist along a continuum — with "pure" mind up one end, and "pure" matter down the other. In its extreme manifestation, mind can operate in a non-spatial and non-temporal way, but could also manifest itself in spatio-temporal reality. This handy approach means that the "liberated" mind can wander in a state of astral travel, OBE or NDE, and communicate with other minds in a manner free of the constraints of space and time. It can even survive after death. Yet the same mind, when it adjusts its functioning, could potentially influence matter in a PK experiment. Suffice to say that mainstream psychologists grounded in materialism (not dualism) would not be terribly receptive to Maso's panpsychism.

Crisis Apparitions and Apparitions of the Living

While on the topic of extraordinary altered states, it's worthwhile considering living apparitions. *Crisis apparitions* and *apparitions of the living* typically involve the witness seeing someone they know (the *apparent*) materialize briefly, ghost-like, in front of their eyes. This is in spite of the fact that this person might be quite alive and residing thousands of miles away. Sometimes the apparition may seem hazy or part-formed, or look as solid as a real human being. Nevertheless, however they manifest, the apparent will not communicate with the witness or seem to notice their presence. Their image then simply fades away.

As expected from the label, the defining aspect of this variety of apparition is that the person is not dead or dying (that's a different type of ghost[7]). In fact, they don't end up dying at all. According to some parapsychologists, the apparent is likely to be suffering a crisis a long, long way away, or is simply feeling homesick. While the apparitional nature of a crisis apparition has structurally much in common with that of the traditional ghost sighting, and has been associated with the notion of LAD (particularly if the apparent ends up dying after all, following their crisis), most psychical researchers have tended to view these appearances as a purely psychic event, with elements common to an extraordinary altered states such as an OBE.

Other Paranormal Topics

Flying Saucers

Some topics widely accepted as paranormal, when examined more carefully, might not be truly paranormal after all. Perhaps the most popular of these topics is the study of unidentified flying objects (UFOs). Typically, UFOs are objects seen in the sky from a distance, usually at night, and are popularly assumed to be extraterrestrial (ET) spacecraft.[8] If this is the case, there is nothing necessarily paranormal about UFOs. Presuming such objects are physically real and are extraterrestrial in origin, then perhaps the scientific field of astrobiology might be more appropriate to classify the content of these objects. It's unlikely a professional astrobiologist would agree, however. Astrobiology is academically respectable and tries to avoid association with anything related to flying saucers and aliens — the discipline's *International Journal of Astrobiology* instead discusses topics such as "cosmic prebiotic chemistry," "extremophile biology" and the reputable search for extraterrestrial intelligence. It is also commonplace for people to believe in aliens, but as astrobiological extraterrestrials rather than UFO pilots (Swami, Chamorro-Premuzic and Shafi 2010). This has nothing to do with the paranormal.

Alternately, there has been considerable anecdotal "weirdness" associated with the UFO phenomenon over the last 60 years, when it truly became the

A UFO of the cigar-shaped variety, said to have been photographed by Domingo Troncoso, a Peruvian customs official, in 1952 as it flew over the Madre de Dios River. It is alleged that there were multiple witnesses of this object at different South American locations. Flying cigars were a popular form of UFO in the 1950s (Mary Evans Picture Library).

focus of public attention. This has led some researchers to believe that UFOs share more in common with ghosts than visitors from outer space. For example, there are reports of UFOs apporting in a similar manner to a disembodied hand or face at a séance. They can also behave in very personal, almost ghostly ways. A celebrated case from Papua New Guinea in 1953 involves a film (which has since "mysteriously disappeared" following government involvement) shot by an Australian official called Tom Drury. Drury was filming a boy spear-fishing at Port Moresby when his attention (and the camera) was drawn to a small cloud materializing above him. Drury watched as the cloud grew into a thick white mass in an otherwise cloudless sky.

Very soon a metallic, bullet-like shape shot out from the cloud in silence and sped rapidly away (Chalker 1996). Such "cloud-cigars" are quite commonly reported throughout the history of UFOlogy, and supporters who believe UFOs to be spacecraft from other planets might argue that this is clear evidence of advanced alien technology in action. Alternatively, proponents of the paraphysical nature of UFO dispute the materialistic nature of the alleged spacecraft and suggest a more paranormal — even supernatural — explanation. The skeptic, of course, sees wishful thinking in both sides and offers straightforward physical and psychological explanations to account for these sightings.

"Aliens"

Claims of human contact with the alleged occupants of UFOs also may, or may not, be paranormal. Many different alien entities have been classified, and again these are commonly assumed to be exobiological, although the *paraphysical* researchers refer to the fantastic and dreamlike nature of many contact cases. For example, people who claim to have encountered these aliens often include NDE and OBE-type experiences in their tales. There are also reports of "aliens" displaying ESP and apparitional behavior — much like the UFOs they embark from. Just one of many famously "weird" UFO encounters occurred in Saskatchewan in 1963. While playing behind their school, four children were approached by an airborne oval shape. The object detached a box that lowered to earth and hovered nearby. From the vicinity of the box, a 10-foot tall entity in a white monk's robe appeared and floated towards them, moaning in a clichéd, ghost-like way. Understandably the children were terrified, and one had to be hospitalized (Keel 1976).

With cases of high weirdness common to the UFO phenomenon, I'll regard sightings of UFOs, and kidnappings by their alleged occupants, as paranormal. As a result, these experiences are open to critical examination using the various psychological explanations applied to other, more traditional paranormal topics.

"Monsters" and Other Strange Creatures

A similar debate can be had about the paranormality of encounters between humans and creatures not necessarily disgorged from a UFO. These might involve sightings of shambling hairy human-like beings in dense forests (called *hominids*, to use the technical term). Alternately, the entity might be a large cat seen in a place where it doesn't belong (the ubiquitous "alien big cat"), or a dinosaur-like animal in a river, lake or the open sea. Such sightings might be evidence for as-yet undiscovered, but perfectly real, animals. The study of these types of creatures is known as cryptozoology, and strictly it is not a paranormal pastime since someone could potentially capture one of these creatures and send it to the zoo for everyone to see and study. The beast would eat, breathe and defecate like any other natural animal.

However, stories of these beasts often refer to paranormal characteristics. On occasion they behave like a ghostly apparition, or display extraordinary powers. There are even stories that UFOs release these creatures. The paranormal researcher Scott Corrales provides us with the wonderful labels of "para-ape" and "manimal" to refer to bipeds that seem to haunt a location (often with other strange paraphysical creatures and objects), rather than just scratch out a living there like any typical animal. Yet even when they don't alight from a pulsating UFO, vanish before the startled eyes of a witness, or show an imperviousness to bullets, such "monsters" can still display quite unusual behavior. The elusive nature of out-of-place cats (typically of the "black panther" variety) in the U.K. and Australia is a typical example. Sometimes they appear in quite populated areas for a few weeks, observed widely but never caught, and then aren't heard of again. Decades later they reappear in the same vicinity, as though they've returned to haunt it.

Some authors also allege that witnesses can enter a strange, dreamy dissociative state when encountering entities such as the Loch Ness Monster (e.g., Craft 1996) or hairy hominids such as Bigfoot. I've been told of a man, living rough in mountainous bushland on the outskirts of Sydney, Australia, who encountered a Yowie (Australia's equivalent to a Bigfoot). This huge, smelly and hairy hominid came out of the scrub and right up to the witness's shack, yet for three days following the event the witness forgot that it had ever happened. Only later did he remember what he'd seen, and told a neighbor with some bemusement. Such delayed recall is often a feature in UFO encounters, and in the case of the Yowie the witness believed he experienced as much a spiritual encounter as a physical one.[9] Under these circumstances, monsters can also be categorized as paranormal.

Other creatures alleged to roam the earth are even more fanciful than hairy hominids, black panthers and lake monsters. Examples would be winged fairies or swamp-dwelling humanoids (with names like "Lizard Man" and the "Bunyip"), or creatures that don't look anything like humans — for example a disgusting 10-foot caterpillar-slug a witness claimed to have seen crossing the road in front of them one night in New South Wales, Australia (a story told to me by that very witness!).

Re-examining a Definition of "Paranormal"

Having briefly examined the most popular paranormal topics, it is worth constructing a definition of "the paranormal" that suits the psychological focus of this book. Many would unreservedly accept the reality of any one these topics, from psychic powers to fantastic monsters. The scientific psychologist, however, is likely to brand the events as explainable, and refer to a witness's psychological characteristics as a prime contributing factor to the encounter. Still, both believers and skeptics would concur that the extraordinary events are ultimately solvable and as a consequence, understandable.

Alternately, *fringe* psychological theories exist that also explain paranormal events in terms of psychological characteristics, yet attach a degree of "unsolvable mystery" to any case. In this light, the paranormal might be considered explicable by some, but ultimately inexplicable by others (Cherry 2003). To be explicable means that the events popularly defined as paranormal operate within the realms of currently formulated theories and laws. These laws philosopher Chris Cherry terms *basic limiting principles*, and scientific psychology follows these principles. Allowance is made for the possibility that current theories and laws might require future modification. For example, an advanced meteorological explanation could be proposed to account for a mysterious glowing ball of orange light you witness floating gently across the night sky. Nevertheless, the basic limiting principles are the obligatory tool when understanding the "hows" and "whys" of events that occur in the world. Speaking of events occurring beyond the limits of this envelope of scientific reality is meaningless.

However, Cherry also acknowledges the paranormal may involve something inexplicable, in which case we will not know where to begin to look for an explanation, and if one arose it might neither be scientific nor imbued with any common sense at all.

Therefore, viewing (psychological) explanations of paranormal events as explicable or inexplicable is perhaps more useful than long-winded attempts at distinguishing between paranormal things and supernatural things. The example of a ghost-sighting might help to illuminate how the many different explanations proffered can be sorted into explicable and inexplicable categories. If the scientific psychologist proposes the ghost is nothing more than a shadow in a dark bedroom, the paranormal event is easily explicable though standard theories of perception and cognition. Alternately, a parapsychologist might argue the witness has actually perceived a form of natural energy, normally invisible to the naked eye, which is the residual of a deceased person somehow impressed into the walls of a haunted house. In this case, the paranormal is at least partly explicable (e.g., the notion of "energy"), and psychological theories of perception and cognition can account for some aspects of the encounter. Nevertheless, additional knowledge of the natural world must be obtained using the principles of physics and chemistry before a complete theory can be derived to account for the ghost sighting. Standard principles of reality might have to be improved upon, but not necessarily overturned.

On the other hand, an *analytical psychologist* might suggest that the ghost is a symbolic representation from an unknowable, unspeakable order of existence transgressing the boundaries of reality. In such a theory, the ghost's appearance to the witness cannot be accounted for by the *basic limiting principles* that the science psychologist assumes will determine all that can ever be known or experienced. This variety of psychological theory therefore acknowledges the possibility of fundamental unknowns, and although they attempt in part to explain the reasons why the encounter occurred, they can't present a step-by-step account of how it occurred, or easily predict when it might occur again.[10]

In summary, psychological theories of the paranormal will be categorized in this book as either explicable or inexplicable. Let's begin with the explicable, and assume that there is a straightforward, even mundane explanation for any paranormal event that is claimed. In later chapters we'll dabble with the possibility that the paranormal is fundamentally inexplicable.

PART 1: THE PARANORMAL AS EXPLICABLE

CHAPTER 1

Parapsychology

Extraordinary Powers

A scientific psychologist is of the opinion that paranormal events are inherently explicable. However, before rationalizing an event using the many theories at their disposal, the psychologist first might want to distinguish between so-called paranormal events that are personally experienced through the conventional senses of seeing or hearing, and those that are experienced without the use of these pathways, or acted-out in ways other than through normal behavior.

Phenomena such as ghosts that are seen, heard, perhaps felt and even smelled are the subject matter of the first type of event, while ESP and psychokinesis are the subject matter of the second type of event. Mainstream psychology has much to offer when explaining both types of phenomenon. As we've learned, the formal investigation of unusual phenomena associated with life after death (e.g., séance phenomena) historically preceded ESP research; however, it's probably best to critique ESP first since this is a more orderly field of study, hence a good place to start.

ESP and Laboratory Parapsychology

Although the extraordinary manifestations associated with mediumistic abilities in the mid to late 19th century were, at the time, attributed to the influence of spirits, clever investigators such as the astronomer Camille Flammarion suggested the events occurring in a séance room could be fully understood within the parameters of scientific investigation. Subsequently, a formal organization called The Society for Psychical Research was founded in London in 1882 to scientifically examine the events associated with the Spiritualism movement. However, by the early 1900s some members of were questioning whether a medium's powers were necessarily caused by the actions of transcendental spirits at all.

Following Flammarion's lead, these members recognized the possibility that extraordinary *human* powers may be responsible for miraculous paranormal cases. Therefore, while the majority of the membership maintained the traditional search for evidence of life after death, a small but growing number sought evidence for abilities (such as telepathy) that were conceptually independent of life after death. At the society's congress in 1923, the words *metapsychics* and *parapsychology* were discussed as potential labels for the study of extraordinary abilities. While the former term was accepted formally by the congress, the latter name stuck publicly despite its actual translation as "erroneous psychology" (Inglis 1986). Later, the expression *psi* was derived to describe the abilities allegedly demonstrated in both the parapsychological laboratory and the "real world."

Imagine you are a member of the society in the early part of the 20th century and you are puzzled by the wealth of cases investigated. You're also clever enough to realize that these cases, assuming they are not hoaxes, could be explained in terms of either life after death or psi.[1] For example, you know a medium who consistently tells visitors to her drawing room (known as "sitters") personal information that only the visitors are privy to. The medium claims her spirit guide is responsible for the information, but you suspect instead that a mysterious and unconscious transference of "thought information" is occurring between the parties in the séance. You're quite convinced the medium is not discovering this information through fraudulent means, so what is actually happening?

The Chaffin Will case might convince you that satisfactory evidence of life after death exists. As the story goes, James Chaffin was a farmer from North Carolina who died in 1921, and a will dated from 1905 was found shortly after his death. The farm went to Chaffin's third son, who subsequently died in 1922. In 1925 the second son began having dreams of his dead father. In one dream, the father told him, "You will find my will in my overcoat pocket." The coat was found in the oldest son's house, and in a pocket was a note asking the second son to "read the 27th chapter of Genesis in my daddy's old Bible." The two brothers subsequently found the Bible and, where expected, came across a new will sharing the estate between all Chaffin's sons (Holroyd 1980). Putting aside the long-winded complexity of the case, which involves a note conveniently found in a pocket leading to a Bible and another will, the argument of the life after death supporters is that "thought transference" cannot be a factor in the discovery of the will, because no one alive knew anything about it. On the other hand, you could favor a psi explanation and suggest the brother's subconscious clairvoyant ability somehow "found" the hidden note. After all this back-and-forth quarrelling, you've returned to where you started; is the Chaffin Will case an example of life after death or psi? Ultimately your decision will be determined by personal taste.[2]

Apparitions as Psi

Some champions of *extraordinary human powers* further assert that ghosts can be psi events, rather than expressions of life after death — an issue we've touched on previously when discussing the crisis apparition. The early psychical investigator George Tyrrell theorized that many ghost cases involve telepathic transmissions from living people rather than having to be the spirit of someone long dead. He suggested that if a person could be "dissolved" in some way, leaving only the sensory information that others utilize to perceive him, then the result would be no different from a traditional ghost (Tyrrell

The ghost of long-dead Fanny visits her husband in William Thakeray's poem "The Cane-Bottom'd Chair" (1894, artist unknown). In this conventional representation of a haunting ghost, that apparition is transparent, in period clothes and with lots of fine details. However, contemporary ghost experiences are rarely so consistent, with apparitions displaying a vast range of features. From the point of view of mainstream psychology, this variation is derived from the characteristics of the witness, which includes their unique cognitive and personality profiles (Mary Evans Picture Library).

1963). With this in mind, Tyrrell described four varieties of apparitions. There are *experimental apparitions*, meaning the agent for the ghost was alive and well and deliberately trying to appear to someone else in this form. We're already familiar with the *crisis apparition*— a ghost of someone not necessarily dead (yet), but in deep trouble nonetheless. The *post-mortem apparition* is the ghost of someone who is recently and definitely dead — but whose temporal appearance is similar to a crisis apparition, and finally, there is the *haunting apparition*, which stays around and haunts locations — presumably for a very long time.

How could sensory information remain if the material substance from which it's derived no longer exists? Tyrrell would argue from a dualistic perspective, which allows separation of mental states from materialistic states. Furthermore, such an apparition does not necessarily consist of physical energy perceived through regular senses such as vision, which require the presence of light rays bouncing off an object to be collected by the retina of each eye. Instead, this psychic apparition is an "idea" that is formed with the help of deeper biological processes in the witness's brain that mimics the "sense-data" used in normal visual perception.

In other words, the psychic apparition is a mental state perceived "telepathically" through channels distinct from the eyes, ears, nose, mouth or skin, and is reconstituted by the brain, having bypassed the normal senses. The ghost looks real, but might be derived from a mental representation generated by an external (and living) human transmitter, who directly induces the specter in the perceiver's mind. Such a ghost isn't purely subjective (and imaginary) because it has a legitimate origin, and this is what makes the experience paranormal. Is it explicable? Very likely, Tyrrell might argue, since there might come a time when science understands how the transmitter telepathically transmits an image for others to perceive. Tyrrell's views on the telepathic variety of ghost are still popular, and widely quoted, today.

Early Parapsychological Research

Scientific research methods were utilized from the very earliest days of the Society for Psychical Research to test ESP. One early study in the late 1880s by members Malcolm Guthrie and James Birchall required a participant to draw simple figures on paper while another blindfolded participant acting as the receiver sat some distance away. The transmitter then stared fixedly at their drawing, stopping only when the receiver felt they were ready to write down the impressions they'd telepathically received on paper (Heywood 1974).

Excellent agreement was found between the transmitter's drawings and their "telepathically-inspired" replications. Since publication over 100 years ago, these results have been criticized for all sorts of reasons, yet from a technical perspective the design and controls in the study appear quite good for the era, acknowledging that the experimental process was in its infancy.

Rhine's Research

The techniques used by early parapsychological researchers such as Guthrie and Birchall were later refined by a founder of parapsychology, Joseph Rhine, and his colleagues. Initially interested in Spiritualism, Rhine would become the foremost researcher of extraordinary talents in the first half of the 20th century. By the middle of the 1920s, he had established the discipline of laboratory parapsychology at Duke University, and he became convinced that ESP (a term he derived) was a learned ability, not an inherited one. For this reason, he employed ordinary members of the public as his test subjects in preference to the practicing mediums favored by researchers in the preceding century. To intellectuals and academics, this was considered far more acceptable than studying the mediumistic phenomenon, with its association with fraud and the unscientific supernatural.

Rhine is perhaps most famous for developing, in conjunction with colleague Carl Zener, the Zener card method of ESP testing. Before Rhine's influence, normal playing cards were used in parapsychological experiments with somewhat indifferent results. To test "extraordinary powers" using a standard card pack, participants were required to guess the number or suit of the cards hidden from them by the

The five types of Zener cards. There are five of each card in the pack, giving a total of 25 cards. Zener cards would surely be the most famous tools in parapsychology, although they are rarely used in the modern laboratory where a wider variety of more sophisticated techniques are preferred (Mary Evans Picture Library).

experimenter. A problem with these regular cards, however, is that they hold certain biases. For example, a subject might have an unconscious preference for spades over clubs that had arisen from many years of recreational card playing. This preference might affect their performance on the psychic card task, even if they perform the test very studiously.

In contrast, Zener cards differ from ordinary cards in that the pack is smaller and has less variation, consisting of only 25 cards comprising 5 circles, 5 squares, 5 stars, 5 wavy lines and 5 crosses. Rhine and his team then spent many years in the laboratory presenting shuffled arrays of the cards to their participants, each presentation known as a run. Typically, the participants were required to perform tasks such as correctly naming the shapes of each of the 25 hidden cards (a test of clairvoyance), or "reading the mind" of the experimenter as the experimenter examined the range of cards (a test of telepathy) or even guess the order of the cards before they were randomized and dealt (a test of precognition).

According to Rhine, the advantage of Zener cards over normal playing cards is that there is less chance of inherent bias towards any particular card type. Controlling for personal preference, when using normal playing cards participants still consistently favor some famous cards (e.g., the ace of spades) over others — a problem not encountered with the Zener pack. And being a structurally simpler pack, it's also easier to calculate probability levels in a Zener card task. That is, on any trial there's a 20 percent chance that a random guess will turn out to be correct. Clarifying this concept of probability as it applies to a Zener card session, imagine you agree to participate in a run of Zener cards even though you are completely disinterested in doing the task. You offhandedly choose "star" for the first card and are surprised when you get it right. However, if you're not displaying any hidden psychic talent, this initial success should be cancelled out by all the mistakes you make by the time you finish the run. In fact, you should have guessed correctly 5 out of 25 cards (which is 20 percent). Anything substantially above this success rate would be considered better than chance, and potential evidence for psi.

General ESP

Although Rhine and his colleagues conducted an array of distinctly different experiments testing for telepathy and clairvoyance over many years and presented positive findings for each phenomenon, a match between any specific extraordinary power and a supporting result remains tenuous. That is, putting aside the possibility of fraud, or what might be expected by chance alone, a participant who scores highly on a run of Zener cards in a trial testing for telepathy might have actually demonstrated clairvoyance instead. So, are clairvoyance and telepathy distinctly different abilities? Or are they different labels for the same ability? We've already encountered this type of conundrum when attempting to distinguish between life after death or psi events, or out of body experiences and clairvoyant events.

Consequently, in order to describe successful performances on psychic tasks parapsychologists have since introduced the term *general extrasensory perception* (GESP) to avoid using specific labels such as telepathy and clairvoyance. Another more recent "mechanism-neutral" expression is *anomalous cognition* (May 2001, May and Lantz 2010). The necessity of creating these broader titles simply reinforces the fact that the closer one studies psi, the harder it is to get a handle on the putative mechanisms underlying the phenomenon.

The use of Zener cards, and the dozens if not hundreds of "runs" the technique requires, also lost fashion from the 1960s onward. This was because a new generation of researchers felt this style of testing was too boring and laborious for participants, as well as being open to fraud. Computers subsequently became the instrument of choice for testing GESP, and with their greater power and flexibility came a more interesting array of targets for participants to choose and interact with. This also helps the parapsychologist avoid accusations of cheating (although skeptics allege that they can still cheat in the programming of the computer). A computer-generated target can be something as simple as a number, a shape or a basic picture. Computers also have the advantage of being able to automatically analyze the subject's results to see if there is evidence of psi ability (Wiseman and Greening 2002).

The Fragility of the Psi Effect

Whether parapsychologists use Zener cards or computer devices as their test instruments, the popular assumption by mainstream psychologists is that the results derived from parapsychological laboratories remain inconclusive. Parapsychologists argue in return that the phenomenon is elusive and fragile, and it is difficult to predict the appearance of psi in a laboratory setting — a proposition veteran psi-critic and psychologist Ray Hyman applies to other, failed pseudoscientific ideas that have ended up on "science's discard pile" — examples of which include N-rays, polywater, mitogenetic radiation, and Martian canals (Hyman 1985).

The fragility of psi findings are particularly notable in the long-term findings of Zener card experiments, where participants can initially do very well, but eventually perform at a level no different from chance. The argument made by Rhine and others when they found such an effect is that the powers of the human mind are strongest when the will is "aroused" at the beginning of an experiment, yet poor when it is bored by repetitive tasks. Skeptics are very suspicious of such a claim, seeing it as a poor excuse for inconsistent findings.

Nevertheless, modern parapsychologists such as J.E. Kennedy remain committed to the notion that experimental data from laboratory-based psi studies are messy because the results are influenced by psychological variables, or states of consciousness, that are "precarious" (Kennedy 2001). For example, personality traits such as extroversion, neuroticism and defensiveness correlate with psi ability (Irwin 1986). Gregarious, outgoing extroverts seem to be more "psychic" than introverts, perhaps because they have a lower level of cortical arousal. The logic behind this reasoning is intriguing. Cortical arousal is the overall amount of neural activity in the cerebral cortex — the "smart" surface area of the brain that is broken by all the wrinkles or "sulci." Extroverts are considered to be more open to external sensory stimuli, whereas introverts are more receptive to internally generated (perhaps imaginative) stimuli. This internal stimulation is arguably "noisy" enough (hence the expression "cortical arousal") to interfere with the telepathically transmitted signals sent by another person — if they do exist. The fragile manifestation of psi on any particular day could therefore depend on the participant's level of introversion or extroversion. Likewise, it might be influenced by their emotional state when they arrive to do the test session, as much as any intrinsic psychic ability they might possess. We'll return to explore these psychological variables, and their interactions with a broader range of paranormal beliefs and experiences, later in the book.

Psi as a Superseded Ability

Although appearing contradictory, proponents of psi occasionally champion the phenomenon's elusiveness when explaining what the phenomenon actually is. They argue that the high cortical activity demonstrated by introverts suppresses psi because psi is an ancient method of receiving information that has been superseded by rational thinking in later human beings (Bem and Honorton 1994). In a similar way, the popular 1970s author Colin Wilson contends that advancement of the intellect is necessary for the evolution of human civilization, however, it is incompatible with deep instinctual powers such as telepathy (Wilson 1971). To regain these instinctual powers is to lose faculty of concentration, and Wilson quotes the example of the Dutch psychic Peter Hurkos, who complained of difficulties he experienced attending to everyday chores — a side effect of his psychic ability. Therefore, if you're a proponent of psi then it's worth pondering whether it is a sporadic, emergent property of the developing of mind, or a fractured and superseded ability overcome by later, more efficient communication techniques. Either possibility might underlie the psi fragility effect.

Alternative Psi Research Techniques

Acknowledging psi's elusiveness, contemporary parapsychologists prefer to use target objects that are meaningful to the participant (thus more likely to be robust and observable) than old-fashioned materials such as Zener cards. In these studies, which resemble the remote viewing paradigm we discussed earlier, a participant who assumes the role of the transmitter might be required to relay information about interesting things they're observing, such as the content of photographs or films, or physical locations. And rather than simply sit in a room waiting for this information to arrive, the receiver might instead rely on more esoteric methods to maximize reception, such as entering an ordinary altered state of consciousness such as sleep or hypnosis (Bem and Honorton 1994).

More recent parapsychological studies have occasionally hypnotized participants in the hope of strengthening psi findings. From a practitioner's point of view, hypnosis is a "state of inertia" where the participant's attention is drawn away from the outside world to focus inwards on an array of mental experiences (Rogo 1980). This change of mental state isn't that much different from extreme relaxation or daydreaming, and is considered by parapsychologists to be *psi-conducive*.

A popular method assumed to induce such a psi-conducive, hypnotic-like state in the parapsychological laboratory is known as the *ganzfeld*. Ganzfeld means "total field" in German, and the technique typically involves recruiting a participant as a receiver and placing them in a prone, comfortable position alone in a darkened room. Their eyes might be covered — half-ping-pong balls are popular — so if they open them all they see is a hazy white light instead of distracting visual stimuli. To prevent voices or other meaningful sounds from disturbing them, low volume "white" or "pink" noise might be played in the background. As a result, a homogenous perceptual environment is created (Bem and Honorton 2002).[3]

The rationale behind this methodology is that when all the mundane "real world" external sensory stimuli are minimized, the mind is free to introspect and obtain subtle signals otherwise lost. During a ganzfeld session (a flexible adaptation of the "remote viewing" paradigm), a participant stationed in another room might attempt to psychically transmit the image of a skyscraper. Meanwhile the receiver gathers, and relays to the experimenter, any impressions that enter their consciousness. This information then helps them to decide, once the session is terminated, the correct image the transmitter

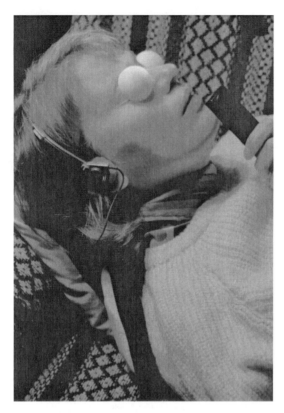

During a ganzfeld test, participants seek to obtain information originating from a distant location. In this example, any impressions the receiver acquires are relayed verbally to the experimenter using the microphone. External stimulation is minimized in the procedure, allowing the participant to concentrate on hidden signals unhindered by any "noise" entering though the conventional senses (Fortean Picture Library).

was sending. To generate experimental data that is quantitative (numerically-based), the receiver might be shown four pictures, one of which is a skyscraper. This corresponds to a 1 in 4 (25 percent) probability of guessing the correct image, so if a participant performs ganzfeld 100 trials, and gets only 25 percent of them correct, then the parapsychologist shouldn't get too excited because this hit-rate is no more than should be expected by chance alone.

What "Score" Is Needed to Show Evidence of Psi?

The next question is, how it can be determined whether a participant is performing better than chance on a psi task? Put another way, if you were participating in a ganzfeld study, how well would you have to do to consider yourself psychic? Obviously, you'd need to score over 25 percent correct, but would the magic number be 28 percent, 63 percent or 99 percent? The same issue arises with interpreting a Zener card test. Recall that five out of 25 is chance for a run of Zener cards. Would six correct guesses be better than chance, or would you have to score as high as 12 out of 25 to be considered something special?

Mathematically-based statistical analyses are extremely helpful in determining whether your score is out of the ordinary, or just what you'd expect if you were simply guessing. The type of analysis parapsychologists use depends on the design of the study they've created. Selecting the appropriate statistical analysis is just like selecting a recipe from a cookbook — you've got certain ingredients in the kitchen (the study you've done) so you can only cook certain types of dishes (the types of analyses available).

Regardless of what statistical procedure used, the calculations will show whether your result is significant (different from chance) or not significant (the same as chance). Computer programs and mathematical tables in textbooks help the parapsychologist decide whether a research finding is significant or not, and it might turn out that the 34 percent success rate you displayed over three weeks of performing a ganzfeld task is statistically significant. Conversely, it might transpire that your average score of six out of 25 after a month spent doing Zener card runs is not significant.

Criticisms of Laboratory Parapsychology

The simplest explanation for significant results is cheating, and the most famous case of this involves a former British critic of psi, Samuel Soal. In the 1940s and 1950s, Soal published statistically significant parapsychological findings he'd discovered in his laboratory at the University of London. Unfortunately for Soal, later scrutiny of his raw data suggested that the results gathered from participants had been altered, although whether this was deliberate, or inadvertent, is not certain (e.g., Mundle 1974, Markwick 1978). The tampering was minor, but just large enough to produce supportive findings for a psi effect. And with this one example, all other significant claims of laboratory parapsychology are open to questioning, perhaps unfairly.

And even where obvious fraud hasn't been found, problems with the processes used in parapsychological laboratories have been identified. For instance, psychologists Julie Milton and Richard Wiseman criticize aspects of the ganzfeld methodology which might inadvertently lead to statistically significant results (Milton and Wiseman 1999). One issue involves sensory leakage, which occurs when receivers acquire information about the transmitted signal from environmental, rather than psychical, cues. This might be as simple as overhearing the muffled voices of the experimenter and transmitter in another room as they discuss what type of visual targets they have chosen. Conceivably, such knowledge would give the receiver enough information to guess the target at a rate better than chance. Later, when it comes time to select the most appropriate images from a choice of four, the receiver picks correctly about 50 percent of the time, having recalled the vague conversation and used it to their advantage. This performance still doesn't sound that great, but in fact it is a statistically excellent achievement. It might emerge that there's only a one in 10000 chance of them demonstrating this result by guesswork — which of course it wasn't. Nevertheless, officially they are performing significantly better than chance, and might be labeled a psychic.

Over the years, techniques have been introduced in an attempt control sensory leakage. For example, as long ago as 1939 the psi-demonstrating Pratt-Woodruff screened touch matching experiments made use of two experimenters to reduce the possibility of fraud committed by the receiver, and used duplicate records, locked boxes, and answer sheets that were numbered and stamped — although allegations of fraud have been directed at this study (Hansel 1989). By the 1980s, an improved ganzfeld methodology was developed to combat accusations of sensory leakage in remote viewing tasks. The *autoganzfeld* (short for automated ganzfeld) uses a computer to control stimulus presentation. This substitutes for a human experimenter, who might be prone to inadvertently disclosing stimulus information to the receiver. However, claims of sensory leakage during autoganzfeld tasks have nevertheless persisted due to inadequate auditory shielding between sender and receiver, despite the use of a computer as an intermediate. So the receiver might still overhear what the sender is telling the experimenter about their mental projection.

To make things even harder for the parapsychologist, sensory leakage doesn't have to involve something as simple as the receiver accidentally overhearing the conversation of the experimenters. Early parapsychological studies had problems with the actual apparatus they used. One example is the natural bias inherent in playing cards, mentioned previously. Nor did the switch to Zener cards remove sensory leakage; skeptical psychologist James Alcock accuses early Zener cards of being partly transparent. Without this crucial shielding, receivers had the opportunity to distinguish the pattern on the reverse side when cards were held by an experimenter sitting opposite them (Alcock 1981). Nevertheless such an assertion is discounted by parapsychologists, who maintain that mass-produced, poorly printed cards were never used by Rhine in his experiments (McClenon, Roig, Smith and Ferrier 2003).

Another example of sensory leakage during a Zener card test involves body-language. If the transmitter and receiver are sitting opposite one another, the receiver might gather useful information from the expression of the transmitter, who's face contorts as they try to telepathically communicate the illustrated shape of the card's face. Perhaps the transmitter unconsciously purses their lips when broadcasting a triangle, but squints a little when they attempted to send information about a star. If the receiver can somehow work out this pattern, either deliberately or unconsciously, better-than-chance results might be expected (Hines 1988).

The skeptic Terrence Hines also suggests that the Zener card test occasionally requires the transmitter, on any one trial in a run of 25 cards, to draw the card's shape on a sheet of paper before they asked the receiver what they think the shape is. The experimenter might be seated opposite the receiver, with an upright wooden panel on the table between them. However, if the panel isn't high enough there is the chance that the receiver can see the movement of pen as a card's shape was drawn. Again, such subtle information might (consciously or unconsciously) increase the chance of getting better than five out of 25 for the trial. Similarly, the sound of the pen as it moves might allow basic differentiation of the five different shapes.

Less familiarity with confounding variables in experimental designs in the first half of the 20th century, coupled with the more primitive standard of experimental records, convinced skeptics that confounding variables contributed to all significant experimental findings in early parapsychology. Once controls were sufficiently tightened in the parapsychologist's laboratories, less spectacular results were achieved. Findings as elegant as those found by Guthrie and Birchall in the 1880s are rarely seen in modern times.

Psi-present and Psi-missing

Sensory leakage isn't the only methodological problem leveled at psi research data. A more subtle issue that critics allude to is the widespread acceptance of psi-present and psi-missing. Using Zener cards as an example, pretend you agree to perform a day of psychic trials in a laboratory and achieve an average of five out of 25 correct. In this case, you can be confident that you aren't demonstrating any psi abilities. Alternatively, you might achieve an average of nine out of 25 correct, and are excited to think you possess an unusual power. That is, you've demonstrated *psi-present*.

Now, what would you conclude if you averaged only one out of 25 throughout the day? This is way below chance, yet is also indicative of psi ability and is termed *psi-missing*. The theory goes that for some reason, perhaps because you're actually psychic but in some kind of deep denial about your abilities, you're inhibiting your psychic powers. In fact, you unconsciously give the wrong answers for some deeply hidden purpose. This notion is perhaps linked to the *experimenter effect*, whereby experimenters who are skeptical about the reality of psi (and therefore might be considered psi-inhibitors) are less likely to find psi results in their studies, whereas experimenters who have a positive attitude are far more likely to find supporting evidence. Naturally, the skeptic will argue that the experimenter effect is easy to explain. An experimenter with a positive attitude can't help but leak a few choice details of the target to the receiver, whether they realize it or not.

When assessing psi-missing, skeptics refer to the way individual or group findings in psi tests are frequently presented as *averages* (means). Thus a participant might perform 1000 runs on Zener cards, and achieve on average eight out of 25. On the other hand, a group of people might average seven out of 25. From a mathematical point of view, however, a mean has to be understood in its context. That is, if you were to perform 1000 runs of Zener cards and achieve an average of 5 after all the time and effort you put in, this still wouldn't necessarily mean that in each of the 1000 trials you scored five out of 25 — that's obvious. Rather, some of your trials will be seven out of 25, some would be four out of 25, some could be as high as nine out of 25, and a few could be as low as zero out of 25. Overall, the high trial scores and low trial scores cancel themselves out, and in combination with the chance scores, your average will be five.

The point a skeptic would make is that psi-missing is to be expected on occasions by chance alone, just as psi-present results are also to be expected. It's the same principle as rolling the number six on a dice six times in a row; it will happen eventually, and in fact is as likely as predicting any other combination before it happens; for example two, five, four, three, one and six in that order. In the grand scheme of things, psi-missing and psi-present should cancel out over a lengthy set of runs, leaving no evidence whatsoever of anything resembling psychic powers.

The question that arises is, how many trials are needed to show a psi effect? If you had performed those 1000 card trials and your average was two correct out of 25, can you still argue that this is to be expected?— that the next 1000 trials might show eight correct from 25 on average, and the grand mean for the combined 2000 trials blends back to five correct? What about 10,000 trials showing a mean of two out of 25? Will a similar blending occur when another 10,000 trials are performed? Strong results have been demonstrated for certain psychic individuals, but does it mean that when combined with results from all participants ever tested, things will even back out to five?

Supporters of psi argue that certain naturally talented people demonstrate ESP better than others, and it is merely an unfortunate coincidence that their successful results can be mistakenly interpreted as a statistical anomaly across a population. There's also the belief that gifted individuals run "hot and cold." They can perform wonderfully well over a couple of weeks, then (as Rhine writes in his landmark 1934 book *Extra-Sensory Perception*) get bored or become upset in their personal lives and provide results no different from chance, perhaps for the rest of their lives. In a psi study incorporating a small number of successive test sessions, this *decline effect* might be due to mental fatigue (Tressoldi and Del Prete 2007). Over the longer term, it could be related to the personality, mood and belief of the subject, which perhaps isn't surprising because the whole concept of psi ability is meaningless without reference to the individual who is demonstrating it.

Realistically, unconsciously motivated performance marking a participant as psi-missing, or a run of "hot streaks," could be an intrinsic characteristic of psi related to the fragility effect. One hypothesis is that a person who naturally integrates their normal sensory experiences (such as vision or hearing) in a very defined, focused way might be prone to ignore any elements that do not fit well with the context of that experience (e.g., psi information). This is known as *disassimilation*, which is the antithesis of psi-receptiveness. Psi-missing is a practical outcome of such a state of mind. On the contrary, a person with an unfocused mind might legitimize information that normally wouldn't fit well into context. This receptiveness to a wider source of stimuli results in psi-present (Carpenter 2008). However, despite detailed models that try to account for the vagrancies of experimental psi results, most mainstream psychologists prefer to view psi-present and psi-missing as no more than a natural demonstration of the laws of probability.

Displacement

Psi-present and psi-missing aren't the only controversial aspects of parapsychological design, analysis and interpretation. For many years, parapsychologists have reported an effect called *displacement*, which in its simplest form is the appearance of a psi effect consistently out of step with the corresponding trial (Crandall 1985). Using Zener cards to help demonstrate this concept, imagine you've participated in a parapsychological study and have completed a single run. The results you display are unexciting; just five cards guessed correctly out of 25. However, the parapsychologist running the experiment has faith in your abilities and looks a bit more closely at each of your 25 attempts. Interestingly, they discover that while you might have guessed 20 of the card shapes incorrectly, these guesses match up surprisingly well with the card on the next trial.

In other words, the card you had to guess was "star-shaped" and you said "squiggly lines," but this answer just happens to match the next card in the pack. To this subsequent "squiggly-line" card you say "square," which is the next one in the pack, and so on. Displacement refers to the situation where your guesses are correct but displaced one away from the target card (one-ahead, or one behind if you're not given feedback on your answers). When your results are re-analyzed by the experimenter and the possibility of displacement is recognized, you might end up getting 13 out of 25 cards correct — a very impressive result indeed.

So why might displacement arise? And does it occur frequently enough to acknowledge as something more than just rare luck? James Crandall and Donald Hite, writing in the *Journal of the American Society for Psychical Research*, suggest the displacement effect arises when the receiver is talented at psi but not focused on the correct target (Crandall and Hite 1983). Specifically, they are not tuned in to the specific Zener card the psychic is transmitting during any particular trial. Instead, the receiver is randomly, and unconsciously, focusing on the card after that, or the one four cards ahead. Naturally, critics argue that the displacement effect can easily be found if you look hard enough for it.[4] That is, trawling through the results to search for a relationship anywhere that looks interesting. In reality, there's nothing stopping displacement from being one-ahead, or two ahead, or three-ahead — the more you look, the more chance you'll find something. Combine all this rummaging with the psi-missing effect and the chances are even better that psi will be demonstrated in some form or another. Over time, the critic argues, this is how significant results emerge. According to other researchers, the evidence just isn't there in the first place (Milton 1988).

In response to the skeptics, parapsychologist Richard Broughton argues that the displacement effect is statistically meaningful. He suggests that similar displacement effects can't be found when randomly searching other types of non-parapsychological data (Broughton 1992). And from a theoretical perspective, the psychoanalyst Jule Eisenbud, writing in the 1950s, argued for the reality of displacement using the simple analogy that if a marksman, shooting a rifle, "repeatedly and consistently" hits a spot a foot to the right of the target, then this wouldn't be a case or random and poor aim. Rather, the aim must be considered excellent, but on account of interference from a poorly zeroed weapon, or perhaps even the mischievousness of the marksman, they have not been able to score a hit (Eisenbud 1954). Eisenbud also refers to an individual who, over 11,000 trials in the early 1940s, was "one-ahead" (+1) in a card guessing task to a significance level of one in 10^{35}, or one in 100000000000000000000000000000000000.

Further Methodological Problems Associated with Psi Testing

Psi studies that don't require participants to match from memory their target with a restricted range of response options are troubled by additional methodological problems. Cast your mind back to the remote viewing technique and imagine you are a psi-receiver in such an experiment. Your task in this experiment is to sketch whatever transmitted image appears in your mind as you relax in the laboratory with your eyes closed. The sketch is then judged by an independent analyst, who ranks your impressions, from best-match to worst-match, with target pictures — only one of which is correct (May and Lantz 2010).

This procedure arguably provides more open and meaningful results than memory matching tasks. However, it is exceedingly difficult for the analyst to determine how good the match is between a transmitted pictorial scene (for instance a stone bridge spanning a meandering stream) and the subsequent drawing by you, the receiver. It might even transpire that you don't even recognize what you have drawn — instead you simply transfer onto paper impressions that pop into your mind — and the picture doesn't really look like anything real at all.

Scientific research is based on numbers — known as quantitative data — and this process of turning pictorial similarities and differences into a numerical "success" score is not a well established procedure, even in mainstream psychology. Researchers at the now-defunct Princeton Engineering Anomalies Research Laboratory acknowledged the problems of generating quantitative data from drawings made in remote viewing (or as they termed it, remote perception) experiments, and applied a complicated quantitative methodology to the measurement of perceptual similarities among pictures. As might be expected, participant performance declined in accuracy as the scoring procedures for picture-matching were tightened, although the psi effect was apparently still replicable (Dunne and Jahn 2003).

Richard Wiseman and Emma Greening mention two further practices that potentially affect the interpretation of parapsychological findings (Wiseman and Greening 2002). One is *optional stopping*, which refers to participants who don't do so well initially in the study and terminate their participation early. Conversely, they might do so well that they leave the test out of boredom, or fright at their new-found abilities! Ignoring the first type of data, or including just the second (incomplete) set of data can result in research findings unfairly favorable to the existence of psi.

Optional stopping also arises when bias is created by an experimenter terminating a study when they believe they have enough data confirming their expectations. They never collect the disconfirming data that might follow had they "seen the study through."

The second methodological problem is called the *stacking effect*, whereby participants share a common response predisposition in a psi-experiment (Wilson, Morris, and Tiliopoulos 2004). For example, a group of participants in a Zener card-reading task might, for whatever reason, choose the "square" shape more than the other four shapes — an ironic outcome because Zener cards were developed in order to avoid the stacking affect associated with ordinary playing cards. Now, if the task is performed with replacement — meaning after each trial the target card is returned to the pack — then following a run of 25 trials it is likely that not all five shapes will be represented equally. For example, there might be as many as 10 trials where square is the target card. Should this occur by chance alone, and participants have an inherent preference of bias for the square shape, then the overall result for the run will likely to be above chance. Nevertheless, the result is an artifact of the procedure, and has nothing to do with psychic ability.

Effect Size in Parapsychology

Having discussed some of the methodological difficulties associated with psi research, it's timely to ask, just what evidence is there for true psychic ability? To answer this question it's first important to understand that significant psi results possess different levels of strength. Imagine you've participated in a Zener card experiment and achieve an average score of eight out of 25, which is statistically very significant — meaning that, to a very high percentage of certainty,[5] your performance is different from the chance score of five you should attain if you're truly guessing.

But before you get too carried away that you're psychic, just look at the result and ask yourself how convincing it really is. Eight out of 25 is only three cards better than chance, and doesn't seem very strong despite the fact that it's statistically significant. In this case, you've only demonstrated a small effect. Had you achieved 12 correct out of 25, you might be showing a medium effect, and 20 out of 25 a large effect. The smaller the effect size, the less "potent" the variable we're studying. It also means that only mild sensory leakage is required for an experiment to prove statistically significant (e.g., Milton and Wiseman 1999). Perhaps a participant might have exploited the sound of the scratching pen in the Zener card trial to get one extra card correct per trial. Across many runs, that's enough to make their results just significant, but it's still not strong or meaningful evidence for something called psi that's consistent and replicable. With too many confounding variables interfering with data collection, and such a small effect size, skeptics argue that it's hard to ever be certain whether psi is a true phenomenon.

Since psi exhibits such a small effect size — a function of its "fragility," parapsychologists require large numbers of participants and repeat experiments to demonstrate it. An example will help explain how participant numbers influence statistical outcomes. Imagine a parapsychologist conducting a Zener card study using a group of friends to test the legitimacy of psi in the general community. Each participant performs only a single run, and the average result found across the group of 13 out of 25 is determined to be statistically non-significant.

The parapsychologist then decides to complete the experiment again, this time using a different sample of participants. After spending years testing this new group (each performing a single run) they achieve a result, on average, of only seven out of 25. Again the experimenter calculates the necessary statistics, and now it turns out to be mathematically significant. In other words, getting seven out of 25 on average for this experiment is better than chance.

How can this second result be better than the first result? The reason is that in the first study the experimenter used only three friends. Getting 13 correct out of 25 sounds fantastic, but there simply weren't enough participants to show significant results because psi has such a small effect size. Should the experimenter employ three different friends and do the test again, a week later, they're just as likely to achieve a disappointing average result of four out of 25.

In the second study, the experimenter collected data from 10,000 people and found significance. Now, this is not necessarily a bad thing — it simply proves that you need plenty of data to demonstrate significance when manipulating variables associated with small effect sizes.

A number between 0 and 1, called *power*, can help the experimenter make sense of these findings. If we think about the first study conducted with the experimenter's three friends, the raw result looked good, but wasn't statistically significant and the power was low (that is, nowhere near 1). This would tell them that with an increase in power, the result might reach significance after all. There are a variety of ways to improve power, but practically this is accomplished by increasing the number of participants. In all, power is useful in letting a parapsychologist know whether a non-significant result could be salvaged by a repeat of the study, but with more participants included.

Meta-analysis and Psi

The proposition that psi is an elusive talent with a small effect size has led parapsychologists and other interested psychological researchers to dabble with a range of advanced statistical techniques that can compare the results of many parapsychological laboratories simultaneously. This is difficult, since variations may exist not only in the number or types of participants, but also the setting of the studies, or even the instruments used to test psi ability in these participants.

Fortunately, a statistical technique called *meta-analysis* can combine all these different results and come to a conclusion about what they all have in common. A typical use for meta-analysis in parapsychology would be to combine all the different ganzfeld findings collected over many decades to see whether the procedure as a whole is *psi-conducive*, acknowledging the difficulties surrounding the interpretation of any one set of positive findings.

To conduct a meta-analysis, the data from as many similar studies as possible have to be collected. The results of these data then have to be normalized, or turned into something that is comparable. Happily, this shared unit or metric is the *effect size* of the study, something we're already familiar with. In very simple terms, the analysis allows trends in statistical outcomes for these combined effect sizes to be determined. Namely, does the collection of studies used in the analysis demonstrate an overall successful ganzfeld effect, or is there no trend at all?

This seems a relatively simple rationale, yet both parapsychological and skeptical camps still argue heatedly over the fundamental purpose of performing meta-analysis on psi data. There's also disagreement over the way the meta-analyses are calculated using the databank of historical psi studies. For example, skeptics often claim that the findings from just a handful of parapsychological laboratories contribute most of the significance, and this could arise because "successful" laboratories are not as good at controlling confounding variables.

Another issue is the *file-drawer effect*, whereby parapsychologists allegedly conduct many more studies than they ever formally report, and the ones they don't report are the ones that are not significant and uninteresting. These insignificant findings are filed away and forgotten about. Therefore, a laboratory might have performed 40 psi studies over five years, but publish only 15 of them (12 of which show significance). Of the 25 studies they don't report (and noone will ever know about), all are non-significant. The allegation is that the 15 published studies are the only ones entered into the meta-analysis, so it's not surprising if meta-analysis shows overall trends in favor of psi. An additional concern is the possibility that *pilot* studies, which are practice studies that should only be used to sort out methodological issues, are reported as though they are proper studies once they are found by the experimenter to be significant. Richard Wiseman, writing recently in the journal *Skeptical Enquirer*, mentions this "cherry picking" of results as an explanation for the significant parapychological findings that are quoted in the literature (Wiseman 2010).

Yet in spite of the ongoing arguments, the meta-analyses that have been performed every few years on the growing database of ganzfeld research tends to favor the existence of a psi effect. For example, one early meta-analysis of ganzfeld results by parapsychologist Charles Honorton found an overall participant success rate of 38 percent (Honorton 1985).[6] Remember that these participants have a one in four (or 25 percent) chance of correctly picking the transmitted material as they sit quietly in the receiving room. When analyzed, the difference between 38 percent and 25 percent is highly significant, although critics would still argue that sensory leakage and other control problems have contributed to this inflated percentage. Alternately, some parapsychologists argue that non-significant results from unsuccessful laboratories included in the meta-analysis might not be enacting the special conditions which facilitate psi — for example, they haven't removed variables that create "noise" and interfere with the psychic signal (Pérez-Navarro, Lawrence and Hume 2009), or have used participants without the apparent psychic ability, confidence or motivation to do the study (Storm, Tressoldi and Di Risio 2010a). In this case, inclusion of this data could actually degrade the outcome of the meta-analysis.

In the 1990s, further meta-analyses of various psi techniques, including autoganzfeld results, also supported overall significance (e.g., Bem and Honorton 1994), although Julie Milton and Richard Wiseman claim a *non-significant* result for a ganzfeld meta-analysis they conducted using data collected across a 10 year period (Milton and Wiseman 1999). However, as is typical of the "to-ing and fro-ing" over the reality of psi, Milton and Wiseman's finding have in turn been criticized by Dean Radin, who says these researchers ignored the sample size of each study included in the meta-analysis and didn't give enough credit to bigger studies, with larger numbers of participants, that did find significance. These studies, Radin claims, should have been allowed to contribute a greater share to the overall results. Had this been allowed, Milton and Wiseman's meta-analysis would have been significant after all (Carter 2010).

A recent meta-analysis across a database of psi studies has once more confirmed an "anomalous" communication effect (Storm, Tressoldi and Di Risi 2010), yet this still doesn't convince skeptical psychologist Ray Hyman. Hyman believes that the process of meta-analysis detaches the original data from the parapsychologist, who then manipulates what's been created by the statistics (e.g., effect sizes and so forth) without reference to the original studies, which might be poorly conducted and full of inconsistencies. Hyman is only interested in considering psi a communications anomaly when it allows the development of hypotheses that predict outcomes that are "consistent, lawful, and independently replicable." Something that meta-analysis can't do.

The arguments don't end here. Even assuming a legitimate psi effect exists, critics still complain about the practical value of such a finding, taking into account the small associated effect size. The likelihood of achieving a noticeable result for any one psi trial is very rare. The small effect size means that many, many trials need to be conducted to even get a hint of the true underlying phenomenon. So, irrespective of skeptical arguments about sensory leakage, fraud and carelessness, there remains the issue of usefulness ... is psi really of any practical value, even if it exists? This takes us back to the earlier discussion of psi as a superseded ability. Perhaps it's of little value because it's no more than a fragile leftover of development, or an archaic communication device.

The Lack of a Theoretical "Framework"

Perhaps surpassing criticisms relating to the presence of interfering variables, the complications of meta-analyses and the inherent practicability of psi are claims that psi research lacks a consistent theoretical framework. In other words, it's all very well for a parapsychologist to present statistically significant results in a card-reading or remote viewing experiment, but what is the explanation for this ability? Without an underlying theory it's easy to fall into a circular argument when trying to explain psi events, as shown in this imaginary conversation (e.g., see also Alcock 1981):

> EXPERIMENTER: This participant has been shown to be psychic when I tested them in my laboratory.
> CRITIC: How do you know?
> EXPERIMENTER: Because they did very well on my psychic test.
> CRITIC: What is a "psychic test"?
> EXPERIMENTER: It is a test that demonstrates whether you have psychic power or not.
> CRITIC: But how do you know such a test can demonstrate psychic ability?
> EXPERIMENTER: Because this subject has been shown to be psychic....

The argument goes around in circles, and this is because one statement is defined by another, which in turn is defined by the original statement again. Psychic ability is defined using a psychic test, and a psychic test is defined in terms of its capacity to determine psychic ability....

This ability is frequently used as a label not for what it actually is, but how it's publicly demonstrated — an issue we covered in the Introduction when discussing the importance of "explanation" in science. Psi cannot be explained by simply distinguishing between concepts such as ESP and psychokinesis. In response, parapsychologists propose theories of information thought-transference, or some kind of connectedness among human minds that are supported by the elusive results of a psi research paradigm. Yet skeptics counter this by claiming that if the theory behind psi as a communication method is so vague, and the predictive power of the model so weak, then significant laboratory results could be due to anything happening — and this opens to the door to all the criticisms we've previously examined, from fraud to sensory leakage to annoying statistical anomalies.

Without strong theory, significant results that emerge from a psychic test can be interpreted with a lot more flexibility than is acceptable to mainstream psychology. For example, if a participant undertakes 10,000 Zener card runs and not one trial proves superior (or inferior) to chance, this does not necessarily refute the existence of psi because the theoretical foundation is liberal. The parapsychologist might simply argue that their participant wasn't "psychic" enough during the study because of the unhappy mood they were in.

A skeptic would prefer to be shown a theory of psi that espouses a testable hypothesis before the experiments are ever performed. For example, telepathy as a form of thought-transference between two parties might be caused by an incredibly small and brief pulse of energy passing between them through the atmosphere. From a careful consideration of the theory, a new, whiz-bang piece of ultra-sensitive equipment might be constructed to detect this energy. If nothing can be found empirically then the hypothesis is incorrect.[7]

Of course, an alternative theory to test psi might then be publicized, and if that fails another one proposed, and so on ... forever. However, the methodological problems said to plague supportive laboratory results means that the phenomenon is unlikely to ever be accepted in wider academic circles. That's where we're at, as of this moment.

The Frustration for Parapsychological Researchers

In summary, the complicated "for-and-against" case for psi has been around for decades and frustrates both skeptics and parapsychologists. Therefore, it's not surprising that by the late 1970s parapsychologists showed less enthusiasm in proving the repeatability[8] of psi findings to skeptics. Not only was this due to their heightened sensitivity to criticism, but also their inherent annoyance at the lack of acknowledgement by critics of any significant result show over the decades. Even the supportive meta-analyses of ganzfeld have generally been ignored by the wider scientific community. For this reason, a greater separation of parapsychology from mainstream science occurred by the end of the 20th century. Duke University parapsychologist Joseph Pratt summed up the feelings of his colleagues by stating psi is a spontaneous natural event and there's as much chance of predicting when it occurs in the laboratory as there is in everyday life (Pratt 1978). The logical conclusion to this argument is, why expend so much energy trying to convince mainstream psychology of its legitimacy using these laboratory techniques?

Philosopher Hoyt Edge also makes the interesting point that parapsychologists accept dualism, yet confusingly attempt to investigate their "non-spatial, free, purposeful and value-laden" subject matter using a scientific approach developed specifically to explain "spatial, determined, mechanistic and a-valuable" events in the physical world (Edge 1985). He asks how psi can be understood using a method designed to test something entirely different.

Perhaps as a consequence of this mismatch, parapsychological research in recent decades has become far more eclectic. To a certain extent the optimistic days of the mid 20th century, where psi was overwhelmingly tested using a limited range of strictly scientific procedures, has passed. Yet from a research standpoint this isn't necessarily a bad thing, since it counteracts the limitations of a restricted set of procedures and encourages the creation of new methods of study. An example of the new research paradigm would be the experiments conducted by Robin Wooffitt of the Anomalous Experiences Research Unit at the University of York in England (Wooffitt 2007). Wooffitt collected actual recordings of a variety of mediumistic sittings and demonstrations and analyzed the data using a method called *conversation analysis* which, as you might suspect, involved analyzing the recordings' conversations in a stringent, structural manner devoid of subjective interpretation.

Wooffitt didn't simply study what words are used by the medium, but they way they're spoken. An analogy to describe the procedure is the way a scientist might examine a plant or animal (in a medium's case, the conversation) to identify properties of the respective fauna or flora species (in the medium's case, what they communicate). Results suggests that psychics do not necessarily frame a conversation in such a way as to strategically draw hidden information out of a sitter — a technique skeptics call *cold-reading*. Rather, the conversation between the medium and sitter seems quite normal, and what would be expected in a regular conversation. Now, this doesn't prove mediums are receiving information from the "Spirit-World," but it perhaps counteracts some of the claims that psychic sittings are predominantly fraudulent.

Nevertheless, developing new laboratory-based research paradigms can be complicated, risky (in the sense of gaining peer acceptance) and expensive. It's not surprising that many parapsychologists have left the parapsychological laboratory and returned to the approach their forebears took in the 19th century … the study of spontaneous cases.

Spontaneous Cases

Poor methodology and statistical vagaries aren't the only criticism leveled at psi research. Even during the heyday of laboratory parapsychology, skeptics were aghast that the existence of psi would mean the current, fundamental limiting principles of the scientific process are not actually limitations after all (Price 1955), and this a dangerous area of speculation. George Price[9] therefore preferred the historical arguments of Lucian, David Hume and Tom Paine, who warn of the trickery and mass deception associated with claims of the paranormal. To Price, it was more acceptable to conclude that human error (and fraud) contributes to significant findings, rather than undermine the foundations of science on the basis of a few — apparently dubious — results.

This tends to be the approach skeptics take when examining alleged psi events occurring outside the controlled laboratory environment — for example a ghost sighting, hunch or precognitive dream — that can't be formally measured or recorded (Ebon 1966). Although frequently brought to public attention through the media, these cases have often occurred months or years previously, therefore are of little value in confirming the reality of anything paranormal. And yet the vast majority of paranormal experiences are of this nature, intrinsically spontaneous and difficult to examine scientifically. It's hard to imagine studying ghosts in a university laboratory.[10]

On occasions, a spontaneous paranormal case is investigated by skeptics, and like any parapsychological finding human error or fraud is considered the most obvious solution. One more recent example involves the claims made in the European media in the mid-1990s that an English Yorkshire terrier named Jaytee displayed psychic behavior. It was alleged that the dog could predict when his owner was returning home, since he'd consistently rise from his resting place on the front veranda of his owner's house just before she'd arrive. Experimental tests of the dog's ability by Richard Wiseman and Matthew Smith were conducted in 1998 and according to Wiseman, the dog had no special ability when taking into account how accurate Jaytee was at arriving on the porch just before his owner came home (not very accurate), and how often he journeyed to the porch throughout the day while his owner was absent (quite often, for no apparent reason).

Wiseman and Smith came to the conclusion that straightforward explanations other than animal psi could account for the dog's behavior. For example, the people at Jaytee's home only remembered the times the dog arrived on the porch at the correct time (called "hits"). They forgot all the "misses," or times when he didn't arrive on time (an oversight known as *selective memory*). Apparently they were also somewhat liberal in their identification of what actually constituted a hit (a mistake known as *multiple guesses*). Finally, it was alleged that the observers paid more attention to the animal's supposedly psychic behavior around the time they expected the owner to return (an error known as *selective matching*). In combination, these cognitive mistakes contributed to the dog's undeserved psychic reputation.

Wiseman and Smith's resolution of the Jaytee case surprised other researchers, including the famous biologist Rupert Sheldrake, who had previously tested Jaytee's behavior. Apparently Sheldrake had demonstrated to his own satisfaction that the dog's ability to predict the arrival of his owner was anomalous, and not what you'd expect from random chance. Chris Carter, writing in the *Journal for the Society of Psychical Research*, also argued that Wiseman himself "cherry-picked" Jaytee data, ironically from a skeptical point of view. He complains that Wiseman and Smith's findings actually replicated

Sheldrake's however, the different criteria Wiseman used to interpret the dog's results allowed him to ignore "most of the data he gathered" (Carter 2010).

Nonetheless, the lack of a theoretical framework for the findings from a psi laboratory apply equally strongly to spontaneous cases, and without this framework mainstream psychology views cases such as "Jaytee the psychic dog" as caused by human cognitive error, rather than invent a complicated model that destabilizes the credibility of current scientific thinking.

Explaining Spontaneous Psi Events
Using a Theoretical Framework

Interestingly, and in spite of the accusation that psi lacks a theoretical basis, some studies have examined spontaneous psi cases from a theoretical perspective. Specifically, they link the psychic performance of practitioners with specific patterns of brain activity. In one set of experiments, psychologists William Roll, Michael Persinger and colleagues (Roll, Persinger, Webster, Tiller and Cook 2002) carried out tests on a male psychic who was allegedly able to garner hidden information from a variety of sources, such as the content of a book he had never read. The psychic was tested on various cognitive and neurophysiological tasks, including intelligence and memory. In addition, electroencephalography (EEG) was used to measure the sum of all the electrical activity in his brain through electrodes attached to the scalp. This allowed the researchers to get a rough idea of what psychological events might be occurring while the psychic was using his "powers." The experimenters also conducted positron emission tomography (PET) on the psychic. This is a brain-imaging technique that injects a type of radioactive sugar into a blood vessel traveling to the brain. Once in the brain, the sugar is absorbed by active nerve cells but can't be broken down and eaten-up by the cells as energy, so takes up residence inside them and glows. Recording the location of the strongest glows gives a measure of what part of the brain is most active — for example during a live psychic reading.

While hooked up to the equipment, the psychic performed a number of anomalous cognition tasks successfully. Later analysis of his data showed a positive relationship between his psi ability and a type of brain activity called *alpha waves* in the occipital lobes — a part of the brain important in vision. To Roll and colleagues, the presence of alpha waves indicated that the psychic was not processing actual external visual information, but rather internal visual imagery from his imagination. The PET imaging also showed less activity from left hemispheric prefrontal regions during successful psi readings. The prefrontal cortex, located the top-front of the brain, plays an important role in attending changes in the external world (Knight, Grabowecky and

Scabini 1995). Simultaneously, increased metabolism occurred in the right parieto-occipital cortices, a cortex region located towards the rear of the brain. Activity in this area is associated with reasoning ability and making visuospatial associations (Fangmeier, Knauff, Ruff and Sloutsky 2006). Combined, such brain anomalies suggest to Roll and his team that the psychic was displaying a more internally-focused, introspective state during psi experiences that might allow detection of subtle information arriving from deeper brain areas such as the hippocampus, and not directly from the standard senses such as vision and hearing.

The hippocampus plays an important role in processing everyday memories, but the investigators suggest it might also act as a receiver of information acquired through nonclassical means. This input is speculated to be imperceptible but real stimuli in the form of very low intensity magnetic fields that the brain detects through channels other than vision, hearing, touch, taste or smell. Simply put, the field passes directly through the skull to the brain for detection (Koren and Persinger 2002).[11] These fields contain millions of bytes of information and are converted in some ill-defined way to the electrochemical signal that characterizes normal sensory information. Often a psychic is unable to interpret this imperceptible information due to the overwhelming "noise" of their dominant visual and auditory systems, but if they have superior introspective abilities (in this psychic's case, apparently due to a brain injury suffered at an early age) they will display above-average psychic ability.

Another theory for psi proposes that information is transferred between individuals during a psychic episode using another scientifically acceptable medium, electromagnetic radiation. We'll examine in a little more detail the concept of electromagnetic radiation in a later chapter, but for now just think of it over-simplistically as some kind of invisible ray that isn't necessarily consciously sensed, but might have subtle characteristics that we can detect in other ways. For many years researchers have been trying, without much luck, to detect electromagnetic radiation emanating from people performing psychic tasks. For instance, the skeptical mathematicians Balanovski and Taylor, in an article published in the journal *Nature* in 1978, explain how they weren't able to distinguish any rays coming from participants attempting PK tasks such as psychokinetic metal bending (PKMB),[12] psychic healing and dowsing. Nor were these participants especially sensitive to detecting electromagnetic radiation, and Balanovski and Taylor claim the dowsers weren't even able to detect strong magnetic fields, let alone fields of the low intensity emitted by the earth (Balanovski and Taylor 1978).

On the other hand, parapsychologist Gordon Rhead studied Polaroid photographs of a psychic healer called Matthew Manning and was adamant that bright and dark "rings" emanated from the man's body corresponding to electromagnetic radiation in the frequency range of infrared to microwave. According to Rhead, the reason for such a pattern is that the energy Manning emitted was of a wavelength that is not refracted by the camera's lens. Rather, the energy simply passed through the camera's small aperture and diffracted in a typical light/dark fashion on the film.[13] The rings are therefore representations of a well-understood form of energy that is normally invisible to the naked eye. How it was produced is the unusual thing, and to Rhead this could very well be labeled as paranormal (Rhead 2001).

Other parapsychologists, however, have produced results that contradict this electromagnetic theory of psychic transmission.[14] For example, Puthoff and Targ shielded a psychic named Pat Price from electromagnetic radiation during remote viewing tasks using a Faraday cage, which "earths" a surrounding electromagnetic field. The success of the tasks was apparently unaffected by the absence of the fields, suggesting that transmission of electromagnetic energy wasn't responsible for their successful psi results (Targ 1996). To Targ and his parapsychological co-workers it appears something else mediated Pat Price's psi transmissions.

One potential explanation for psi that doesn't consider the anomalous transmission to be electromagnetic energy is intriguing. James Carpenter of the Rhine Research Center suggests that, on a tiny scale, the boundaries between physical objects is very blurry and there's a "transactional zone" where one thing (such as your hand) blurs into another (the mug of coffee that you're holding). Applied to mental processes, Carpenter argues that there's a point where a person loses their individual identity and blends with their surroundings (Carpenter 2004). From the perspective of human perception, this "blurry bit" precedes the act of consciously identifying an object or event in the surrounding world — for example a motor car speeding towards you and swerving dangerously. It even precedes the earlier perceptual sensation that will allow identification of this car as life threatening. Carpenter alleged that the "blurry bit" corresponds to the point where an extrasensory anticipation of the car takes place and this helps initiate the subsequent perceptual process of recognition. Carpenter calls this psi process "first sight," as opposed to the label "second sight" that's often given to psychic perception. It's first sight because psi is the initial stage of any perceptual process (Carpenter 2008).

Perceiving and recognizing the car, through normal sensory channels, comes from the part of you that is an individual. Psi anticipation, however, is part of you as blended with the infinite surrounding environment. Carpenter argues that these psi processes are always operating, so you shouldn't think of psychic information as some kind of energy being sent and received rarely and intermittently during psi testing. However, we remain unaware of this constant stream of blended knowledge because it's swamped by the "louder" processes of conscious perception. An analogy is the way you can't see stars in bright daylight — even though the stars are still there.

A tangible example of first sight might be when you gaze at a line of square windows in a building as you walk through the city, and the mental image of a "checkerboard" springs immediately to mind. Now, a mainstream psychologist would have their own straightforward interpretation of what's happening in the brain to allow this obvious association between windows and checkerboards. However, Carpenter instead sees this imaginative link between a physical reality and a disconnected idea as the mind interpreting psi impressions of the windows before it has received more tangible sensory information that would allow formal recognition.

This process is strongest when you aren't thinking too deeply, and as a consequence you're more receptive at a subconscious level to psychic apprehensions. From a practical perspective, if you're sitting in an exam, and have studied the topic well, you can rely on memory to answer the questions. This "cognitive closure" will shut out any psi sensations. Alternately, if you haven't studied at all for the test, then you might be better off relaxing and hope that the delicate psi impressions — some of which might involve the answers to the questions "floating around" in the blended environment — will emerge as though a distant memory from your subconscious (which they're not). Experiments performed over the last 40 years apparently demonstrate this relaxation effect (Carpenter 2008), so if you're ever in an exam situation and you're stuck, perhaps this technique is worth a try?

Mistaken Belief

Although most mainstream psychologists have little or no interest in parapsychology, some are still interested in researching psychic powers, but for very different reasons. In their opinion psi does not exist, and yet psychics and their supporters (including parapsychologists) still believe that it does. Consequently, these psychologists would maintain that the believers in psychic powers are either perpetuating a fraud or are deluding themselves — as we've seen with Wiseman and Smith's explanation of the Jaytee case. When it comes to psychics, it may be that they are acting slyly at the beginning of their career and are well aware of their fraud, but later begin to believe they possess imaginary powers. On the other hand, perhaps certain psychics never realize they are misguided, and have always believed in their imagined abilities.

In a similar way, a laboratory parapsychologist might be so obsessed with their desire to prove psi is true that they can't think critically about the research they conduct, leaving their results open to bias and false interpretations. The scientific psychologists who hold these opinions don't actually study practical or theoretical psi (or other spontaneous paranormal events) in the fashion of parapsychologists, but rather explore the reasons why humans believe in psi, or ghosts, or superstitions. They tend to regard humans as somewhat irrational creatures, more mechanical in their behavior than is commonly assumed. Let's make this psychological approach to the paranormal the subject of the next chapter.

CHAPTER 2

Superstition and Belief in the Paranormal

Forget alien abductions. The most common paranormal experiences that everyday people report are nothing more than an assortment of psychical events best labeled as hunches and intuitions. Even more common than these are everyday practices people carry out that aren't necessarily related to the paranormal at all, and which we term superstitions. Examples include the wearing of a lucky pair of socks to an exam, or the avoidance of a crack in the pavement. Scientific psychology can explain hunches and intuitions, as well as more simple superstitious behavior, using comprehensive theories that have been around for decades. Fundamental understanding of how humans learn and think is a crucial part of these theories.

Superstitions are a set of behaviors usually, but not always, accompanied by a range of beliefs. Early psychologists felt that superstitions were a method people used to lower their anxiety when an adequate explanations for the uncontrollable events that affected their lives was lacking (Vyse 1997). For example, in a pre-scientific society the role of bacteria in causing disease is unknown. Irrelevant practices based on incorrect beliefs are therefore performed—one archaic example being the way a peasant might seek the touch of the reigning monarch in an effort to cure an illness they might have, such as scrofula. Behaving this way helps the peasant to reduce the fear of becoming infected and dying.

The problem is, superstitions persist even when modern science allows people to understand the causes of disease, so the anxiety-reduction theory has flaws. Perhaps a better definition for a superstition is as a behavior and/or belief, not necessarily anxiety-reducing, which does not conform to the current scientific standard of the culture. In this way, a belief or practice in a non-scientific culture that would be superstitious in modern Western society is not necessarily defined as superstitious relative to that culture. Another defining aspect of superstitions is that they are commonly associated with personal luck. That is, people behave (and believe) in a certain way to avoid bad luck, and in other ways to achieve good luck.

Conditioned Superstitious Behavior and Superstitious Belief

Previously, the point was made that the word *superstition* relates to a person's behavior, and this behavior is potentially linked to an underlying belief. The word "potentially" is important here, since a person's superstitious behavior might not be accompanied by any consciously held belief at all. In other words, a person might act in a way that's identified as superstitious, but they might not even be aware of the reason for their actions — or that they even acted in the first place!

To understand superstitious behaviors in more detail it's a good idea to examine the basic theories of learning that were developed in the early 20th century and which help explain a person's behavior that seems automatic and unintelligent (classical or Pavlovian conditioning) or appears to be voluntary and intelligent (operant or instrumental conditioning).

A Simple Overview of Classical and Operant Conditioning

The Russian physiologist Ivan Pavlov is famous for developing a model of automatic learning in animals that was later used to explain human behavior.[1] It is a truism to say that *organisms* (a psychological term for anything living) show any number of necessary behaviors to environmental stimuli. These include blinking the eyes to a puff of wind (for protection), or flicking a tail when a fly lands (for protection), or salivating when smelling food (preparing the digestion system for the food's imminent arrival).

Pavlov's model, as it is conventionally represented, proposes that an organism's brain is flexible to environmental changes. Sticking with the famous example of salivating dogs, should a stimulus that isn't normally associated with salivation be consistently presented alongside food, then this stimulus may eventually elicit salivation in the food's absence. Such as stimulus is called the *conditioned stimulus*, and could be anything, a noise like a bell or a flash of red light. The effect is most potent, however, when the conditioned stimuli is matched to the species. An animal with poor vision but excellent hearing is likely to be conditioned better to a sound than a light, and vice versa.

This inherent flexibility in environmental learning allows an organism to adapt to change. If a novel stimulus, for whatever reason, allows prediction of what will soon happen, then the organism will be able to change their behavior accordingly. In humans, such learning is considered to be beneath conscious awareness. At the simplest level, given enough time and a lot of patience, a human participant in a psychological laboratory might be conditioned to blink their eyes to the smell of strawberries (an unnatural association) simply because the smell had been consistently paired with a puff of air.[2] Outside the laboratory such conditioning is commonplace, and can even include the conditioning of emotional reactions. For instance, your phone might ring every day for a week with consistently bad news. The following Monday it rings again and you feel a lurch of the stomach before you pick it up. The phone ring is not naturally associated with bad feelings. Rather, the emotion has been conditioned in you because of a unique association you have learned the previous week. It will not apply to anyone else.

Operant conditioning is the term for a set of rules governing more complex types of behaviors in animals and humans that appear to be volitional, or of free-will, but are assumed to be just as automatic as simpler classical conditioning. For the first half of the 20th century, a dominant school of psychology called *behaviorism* saw human lives as governed primarily by conditioning, with thoughts and feelings merely epiphenomenal (or a non-causal side effect) to our behaviors. We might kick a rock and blame the behavior on our current state of anger, or attribute a visit to the cinema as a spur-of-the-moment act. However, the strict behaviorist would say that we have incorrectly attributed the behaviors to our free will because we are unaware of the deeper conditioning responsible for these actions. Strict (radical) behaviorism no longer has many followers because modern psychology has accepted the importance of cognition and affect (emotion) in determining human behavior. Nonetheless, this does not imply operant and classical conditioning are no longer relevant. The processes certainly do play an important part in human life. It's just that they can't explain absolutely everything we do.

In the operant conditioning model, organisms may respond randomly to their surrounding environment, and sometimes this response is followed by something good happening (known as positive reinforcement) or something bad happening (known as punishment). A reinforcer will increase the likelihood that the behavior immediately preceding it will be repeated, and a punisher will lower that chance. There are countless examples of conditioned behavior change in the laboratory and in everyday life. For instance, a rat will learn to press a metal bar for food (the reinforcer) when nothing instinctive in its nature will ever predispose it to such an action. A child will learn to avoid patting a cranky cat if they receive a scratch or bite every time they do so. And again, the association between a response and its outcome is accepted as having been created beneath conscious awareness.

Operant conditioning mechanisms are of particular importance when explaining superstitious behavior. Moreover, because these rules apply to everyone, then anyone might be prone to operantly-conditioned behavior. The psychologist who coined the term operant conditioning (because organisms *operate* to receive an outcome) and pioneered the discovery of operant conditioning processes was B.F. Skinner. His conditioning box (the *Skinner box*) was designed to hold a rat or a pigeon, and in its simplest form possessed such features as a pressing bar (rats) or pecking key (pigeons) the animal could manipulate (their behavior), a tray where food could be dispelled (reinforcement) and even metal bars on the floor that could be electrified (punishment). In a typical conditioning routine, a pigeon might be trained over time to peck at the key to receive a single pellet of grain. The more the pigeon pecks, the more grain it will receive.

Superstitious Conditioning

In 1948, Skinner performed a fascinating modification to the standard conditioning box routine in which hungry pigeons were allowed five-second access to food pellets at regular intervals without having to perform any specific behavior to receive them. One might expect the pigeons would just wait patiently to receive the automatic reinforcement, but a certain bizarre pattern emerged instead. The pigeons began to behave in strangely consistent ways during the periods between presentation of food. One pigeon might turn in circles; another might bob up and down. Skinner termed these outcomes *superstitious* (Skinner 1948). His explanation was that all pigeons behave in a random fashion once they're placed the box at the beginning of the trial. Perhaps it simply bobs up and down, as pigeons commonly do. The first delivery of food is made, and as a consequence of the laws of operant conditioning the pigeon is more likely to repeat the behavior that immediately preceded the food (bobbing) in spite of the fact that such an action didn't cause the arrival of food.

The term used to describe the causal relationship between a behavior and an outcome is *contingency*. In superstitious conditioning, there is no contingency between the pigeon's behavior and a reward, yet the animal's "nervous system"[3] assumes such contingencies frequently exist in the surrounding environment. After all, scratching in the dirt is likely to reveal a worm or a bug, so reinforcement is contingent on scratching — a worthwhile behavior. When placed in the unnatural situation of a laboratory and a constant reinforcement schedule, the pigeon's "nervous system" still looks for a preceding circumstance for that reward ... and chooses the most recent behavior it made.

Extrapolating these results to humans, psychologists have identified behaviors in people that are superstitiously conditioned, in the sense that a person's responses are accidentally correlated with reinforcement (Rudski 2001). For example, children can be conditioned to make faces at a mechanical clown that automatically dispensed marbles as a reward (Wagner and Morris 1980). Outside the psychology laboratory, an adult might consistently scratch their ear before they hit a golf ball on the course. Perhaps they scratched once before and hit a great shot, and this increased the chance of scratching before the next shot. This next shot was also pretty good, the behavior was reinforced to an even greater degree, and so on. Unthinkingly pulling on a pair of lucky socks is also a behavior, perhaps superstitiously conditioned. The list is endless. While it happens to all of us, this habitual associationism is nevertheless considered a primitive trait by many psychologists, and their contempt for a population that practices it is summed up by skeptic Michael Shermer's frequently quoted statement, "The dumb human, like the dumb rat, only needs an occasional payoff to keep pulling the handle" (Shermer 1997).

Magical Thinking and Superstitious Belief

Few, if any, psychologists today would deny the role of cognition in human experience. In fact, as long ago as the 1950s the sociologist Melford Spiro was questioning the view that superstitions are solely learned behaviors, at a time when conditioning theory was predominant in university psychology departments (Spiro 1953). Examining the overwhelming role that the evil, ghostly *alus* plays in the lives of a Micronesia tribe called the Ifaluk, Spiro pondered how such a superstitious belief is reinforced when it is by its very nature punishing. It is a belief, not strictly a behavior, so it makes sense that cognitive processes must allow its progression from one generation to the next. And even if superstitious behaviors are conditioned, humans still have the ability to consciously reflect on their actions and come to certain conclusions about why they are doing what they are doing. Perhaps some of these people will interpret their superstitious behavior as conscious and volitional. This might then lead to other, more sophisticated superstitious behaviors that aren't derived from conditioning.

For many years researchers have studied how people reflect on their behavior and justify it in all sorts of different ways. Most famously, the psychologists Leon Festinger coined the term *cognitive dissonance* to describe how people use personal judgment strategies to make inconsistent psychological events more consistent (Festinger 1962). For example, individuals who are required to perform a routine, boring task might justify their reasons for doing it in a way that is optimistic but untruthful. This helps them to lower the level of anxiety (or dissonance) they experience when they seek to understand their seemingly inconsequential behavior. For example, a participant in a psychological study might be required to build a house out of playing cards, destroy it, then build another house, then destroy it, then build another one and destroy it, and so on. The person might be doing this task for very little money, or no money at all if it's an experiment, and after a while ask themselves, "Why am I doing this at all?" They could resolve this anxiety by coming to a decision that fits their behavior, such as "I'm doing it because I'm enjoying it!"

Carrying this desire for seeking purpose in behavior to the superstitious realm, imagine yourself in a situation where you observe yourself behaving in a strange or uncharacteristic manner. Naturally, you're not aware that you've accidentally "superstitiously conditioned" yourself sometime in your past, which has given rise to this current behavior. Nevertheless, you begin to see rational, meaningful patterns in your actions because you'd shudder to think the behavior has been accidently conditioned. In this case, your superstitious behavior has given rise a superstitious belief. Now you possess this belief, your subsequent, "conscious" behavior might change accordingly.

The psychologist interested in human superstition might argue that this trait is typically human, and is not limited to any one individual. This doesn't negate the fact that it is still irrational. That is, while a great many behaviors and outcomes in our lives are contingent on each other, a great many aren't. Humans are nevertheless fixated with the importance of contingency, perhaps due to some archaic "evolutionary process" which is advantageous for survival. Consequently, people won't give much consideration to the possibility of random noncontingency — they can't help but see meaningful connections among objects and events in the world, ignorant of the multitude of meaningless connections that really exist.

Magical Ideation

The misidentification of causation has been named *magical ideation* (Brugger and Graves 1997), and examples include peoples' belief in psi powers and "spirit influences" in their everyday lives (Einstein and Menzies 2004).

The analogy of a small, furry animal hiding in a forest is a good way to represent magical ideation. Imagine you're that furry animal and you're surrounded by dense scrub, with no inkling what predator might be lurking nearby. You see and hear a rustle beyond the nearest trees, and your (assumedly) primitive brain must decide whether the noise is due to wind — or something alive trying to eat you. Those small, furry creatures that associate the noise with a predator (but without any evidence) will run, and probably survive. Other small, furry creatures might decide that an innocuous breeze is responsible, or rationally assess the whole episode, carefully weighing up the probabilities of various events occurring. While these decisions are processed, a real predator might be approaching, and these little creatures will be eaten for their troubles.

Irrational associations of cause-and-effect therefore appear to be encouraged by natural selection. Charles Tart suggests it is quite normal to think irrationally, and people need to carefully interpret the things happening around them (such as a rustling in the scrub) to assist with the control of outcomes — most importantly survival (Tart 1998). In the extreme, an organism's ability to control outcomes might mean the difference between life and death. And yet even the presence of mild uncertainty can prompt the appearance of irrational thinking. For example, a person might believe themselves to be psychically gifted, but secretly lack confidence in their ability to succeed in a card-reading task. Instead, they prefer to trust the card choices of an alleged psychic over their own choices, even though this psychic is an experimental "plant" and is simply guessing the cards (Case, Fitness, Cairns, Stevenson 2004). Put simply, the person doesn't believe they can control the outcome of the task and consequently indulge in superstitious thinking — preferring another person's card choices over their own despite the fact that the psychic's choices will be no more successful than their own.

Therefore, "thinking magically" acts in an opposite fashion to beliefs attached to superstitious conditioning. Rather than reflect on a preceding behavior and form a belief about why that action occurred, people build irrational associations between causes and their effects, and from this superstitious belief develops consciously-generated superstitious behaviors. It might arise that a superstitious belief leads to the (incorrect) assumption that acting out the belief will cause or prevent some outcome. This could involve someone carrying a broken cigarette lighter (the behavior) as a lucky charm to prevent mischief (the belief).

To the scientific psychologist, the annoying thing about superstitious beliefs and behaviors, whether they're conditioned or derived through magical ideation, is that they are strongly held and resistant to extinction. This means that once they've been conditioned, it's very difficult to remove them without psychological intervention. This is in spite of the fact that the beliefs and behaviors usually aren't complicated. For example, when questioned about why a broken cigarette lighter works as a charm a believer might reply, "Because it just is." If it were possible to examine the believer's personal history closely, a researcher might find that the charm figured strongly in a passage of extinction-resistant conditioning many years previously. Having been identified as "lucky," the owner now "behaves" with it as a foil to newly formed superstitious beliefs. No more complicated theory is necessary to explain the belief and the persistence of any other associated behavior.

Are Some People More Superstitious Than Others?

Psychologists generally accept that everyone can at times behave superstitiously, and that it's natural to think superstitiously too. However, a category of people has been identified who are prone to "over-associate" their behaviors with suspected outcomes. Sometimes people showing these extreme levels of magical ideation have been labeled *psychopathological*. As far back as the 1930s, psychotic individuals were identified as more superstitious than "normals" (Page 1935), and the superstitious behaviors associated with disorders such as schizophrenia have been documented over many decades.

However, people don't need to be schizophrenic to show above-average levels of superstitious belief or magical ideation. A distinction exists between the superstition shown by psychopathological people and that shown by "normal" people (Vyse 1997). In "normals," relationships exist between their level of superstitious belief and the psychological variables of anxiety, depression and low self-esteem, although the effect is only mildly significant (e.g., Epstein 1991). Put simply, someone who is depressed, anxious and doesn't think highly of themselves might show more superstitious ideation than normal. Superstitious belief has also been linked to emotionality (Plug 1975), meaning the more emotional you are, the greater the number of superstitions you possess. Likewise, superstition has also been associated, albeit to a small degree, with pessimism (Rudski 2004).

Paranormal Belief

While there are no actual numbers to quote, it's likely that most psychologists would consider superstitious beliefs and behaviors to be quite common compared to reports of actual paranormal experiences. However, the same psychologists would acknowledge that paranormal beliefs are quite common in the population. Consequently, there are as many contemporary psychological research papers focusing on paranormal belief as there are superstitious belief.[4]

Perhaps this is because the topics of paranormal belief are stranger and more fascinating than superstitious belief. Understanding why people believe in paranormal things like UFOs seems far more interesting than understanding why people believe their red socks will bring them luck.

Paranormal belief is also different from superstitious belief in that the former implies a reasonably sophisticated set of ideas underpinning the beliefs. To believe in ghosts, widely viewed as a "spirit of the dead," would surely require acceptance of life after death. Believing that your faded red socks give you good luck requires no such foundation.

Naturally, mainstream psychologists are scandalized by the amount of paranormal belief that exists in the broader community. Polls that come out every few years show that belief in psychic and paranormal phenomena remains strong, although there might be variations in specific types beliefs over time (such as a decline in belief in demonic possession, which nevertheless might rise again sometime in the future).

Why, then, do so many people believe in precognitive dreams, ghosts and UFOs? It's not necessarily because they've experienced (or seen) one. Believers in UFOs far outnumber those who actually encounter them (Paltry and Pelletier 2001), leading to the conclusion that some deep psychological need must be satisfied by holding the belief (Grimmer and White 1990). From a psychological perspective, personality variables are most likely responsible for the unshakable adherence to paranormal topics, such as psychic powers (Irwin and Green 1999). For this reason, interested psychologists busy themselves with identifying inherent characteristics that predisposes people to believing in paranormal things.

Probably the most benign characteristic contributing to paranormal belief is the believer's sex. In one study, a group of men from New Zealand showed higher levels of belief in extraterrestrial life-forms and UFOs compared with women, while the women tended to believe in psychic ability and life after death more than the men (Clarke 1991). However, it might not be simply the sex of the believer that determines the type and level of paranormal beliefs. Recently, the broader concept of gender roles and paranormal belief has been studied. It seems women who think in a psychologically feminine way, and women who show psychological androgeny—that is, thinking styles that have a masculine component — score higher on belief than women who are undifferentiated and neither traditionally masculine or feminine. The proposal is that femininity involves intuitiveness and androgeny involves complementary thinking — that is, a combination of intuition and "male" rationality. Both styles are apparently conducive to paranormal beliefs, whereas undifferentiated women are resistant to unusual beliefs (Simmonds-Moore and Moore 2009). Women who were masculine thinkers, however, scored no different from the feminine or androgenous thinkers, which was somewhat unexpected — surely "male-thinking" women should be less believing? This goes to show that the deeper you study the paranormal, the more confusing it can get.

Other individual differences contributing to paranormal belief involve general personality traits possessed by both men and women of any age. Over the years, many of these traits have been identified more strongly in believers (labeled "sheep" in the psychological literature) than non-believers (labeled "goats"[5]) (e.g., see Thalbourne 2001). Some common ones are listed below, although inter-relationships do exist so these traits aren't necessarily independent of one another. When reading about these traits also keep in mind the thoughtful words of Harvey Irwin, who informs us that much of the psychological research into paranormal belief has the "implicit objective of demonstrating that believers ... are grossly deficient in intelligence, personality, education and social standing" (Irwin 1993).

Traits Associated with Paranormal Belief

Actual paranormal experience— A relationship between paranormal belief and personal experience is obvious, and has been discussed extensively in the psychological literature (e.g., Irwin 1991, Persinger 2001). Of course, this just shifts the need for explanation onto why the person had a paranormal experience in the first place, which is a separate issue entirely and might be related to their personality or cognitive ability (we'll begin to examine this further in the next chapter).

Reasoning ability— Deficits in the ability to reason have been found in paranormal believers compared to non-believers (e.g., Wiersbicki 1985, Roig, Bridges, Renner, and Jackson 1998, Merla-Ramos 1999). This irrationality manifests as behaviors that could include worrying excessively, avoiding personal problems, demanding approval from other people and showing emotional irresponsibility. Believers in ESP also avoid responding to stimuli in ways that are repetitious compared with (rational) non-believers (Brugger and Baumann 1994). That is, if ESP believers are required to choose either the letter "a" or the letter "b" eighty times in a row, they will be more likely to avoid giving two "a" letters, or two "b" letters in a row, compared to non-believers. This is in spite of the fact that it is very likely clusters of either letter will appear by chance alone if the task is performed by a random letter generator.

To Brugger and Baumann, this hesitancy to choose strings of the same letter implies that ESP believers prefer non-verbal mental processing styles over analytical (rational) processing styles. This is not to suggest that believers are less intelligent than non-believers. Rather, their methods of thinking might differ slightly and this predisposes them to accept the truth of seemingly irrational events without evidence.

Deficits in working memory— Working memory can be loosely defined as a mental storehouse of information of limited capacity that is capable of holding and manipulating the material a person perceives through their senses. This processing could involve comprehending what that material actually is, and what it can be used for (Youse and Coelho 2005). To demonstrate the role of working memory as it related to paranormal belief, the psychologist Thomas Dudley performed an elegant study in which participants had to rehearse a 5-digit number to themselves at the same time as filling out a questionnaire about their own paranormal beliefs. A matched group of participants just filled in the questionnaire. Participants who verbalized the number actually scored higher in paranormal belief than those not performing the task. Dudley concluded that if a person's working memory is kept busy, they become less critical, and this shows up as an increase in their belief of the paranormal (Dudley 1999). Taking this to its logical conclusion, a person with naturally poorer working memory would be expected to show stronger belief in paranormal topics too.

Suggestibility—Suggestibility is the notion that some people display uncritical and involuntary acceptance of a proposition made by other people, which potentially leads to the formation of paranormal beliefs. This might entail them trusting, more than they should, the legitimacy of a spooky story told by an unreliable friend, or being overly impressed by a display of psychic power (Hergovich 2003)—even if the psychic is only a magician pretending to possess paranormal ability. Furthermore, what the suggestible individual has seen or been told will help reinforce an already-strong belief system, making it difficult to change their opinions through reason and logic.

Context-dependency—Some psychologists argue certain individuals are also more reliant on a paranormal context to interpret the stimuli they gather through their senses. Context is like a framework with which incoming information can be sorted and made sense of. If the information is unclear, then a belief that "it must be paranormal" helps reassure these individuals that a solution has been found (Snel, van der Sijde and Wiegant 1995). Even a scary paranormal belief is better than having no belief at all.

Personality (based on Carl Jung's typology)—Personality has many facets, and some psychologists like to measure its various attributes using the ideas developed by early theorists. One example is the personality typology Carl Jung created in the 1920s. Jung's typology of personality has four measures; introversion/extraversion, thinking/feeling, intuition/sensation and perception/judgment. Each measure is a separate continuum, so someone could fill in a typology questionnaire such as the Myers-Briggs Type Indicator[6] and be labeled as (for example) highly introverted, a thinker, strongly intuitive and reliant on judgment. Conversely, another person might be extraverted, highly respondent to feelings and sensations and influenced by external perceptions. It has been shown that high feeling (less thinking) and high intuition (less sensation) types are moderately more likely to be paranormal believers (Fox and Williams 2000). A suggestion has also been made that paranormal beliefs are held not because there's a deficit in the believer's ability to reason correctly, but rather arise from a personality type that's intuitive. In this model, the paranormal believer inteprets events that happen to them in terms of meaningfulness and purposefulness, and something that can't be explained through logical argument (King, Burton, Hicks and Drigotas 2007). Since this attitude is independent of the rational system, trying to reason with the believer to relinquish their paranormal beliefs is a futile exercise. Consequently, some psychologists take an interest in studying the role paranormal beliefs play in the intuitive believer's wellbeing — an approach adopted by some of the therapeutic models we'll explore in later chapters.

External locus of control— External locus of control is the tendency of certain people to shift responsibility for their actions from themselves onto outside forces beyond their control (Scheidt 1973). With regard to paranormal belief, a person possessing this trait might attribute their behavior to a guiding spirit rather than their own volition. Complementing what we've discussed previously, a person demonstrating external locus of control might also display more superstitious behaviors than they should, coupled with a sense of pessimism when they become convinced they're not in control of their own lives (Rudski 2004).

Field dependency— A trait similar to locus of control that contributes to paranormal belief is field dependency. This implies that some people do not have the same sense of separate identity from the world as other people. In fact, they seem to be dependent on cues from their surrounding environment to make sense of their own behavior. They also show a greater level of social orientation (Hergovich 2003). As a consequence, "field dependents" tend to view the world in more animistic (living) terms, where the concept of scientific materialism is less relevant. Studies have also shown that these "field dependents" possess heightened belief in the paranormal, because these beliefs often assume the machinations of outside forces at play in the believer's life.

An implication of the theory is that field independent individuals perform better on tasks requiring higher cognitive abilities — subtle way of saying they're more intelligent. Furthermore, since they have enhanced self-concept these "independents" can process information irrespective of the opinion of other people. For example, they are not dependent on social cues to behave in the appropriate manner. The argument implicit in such research seems to be that it's better to be a field independent individual than a field dependent individual. The notion that field dependent people are paranormal believers, and therefore less intelligent, supports the skeptic's viewpoint that paranormal belief (and by association, anything to do with the paranormal) is dumb.

Death anxiety—Some psychologists speculate that belief in paranormal topics, such as life after death, might serve the purpose of reducing death anxiety (Tobacyk 1983, Lange and Houran 1997, Thalbourne 1996). This is known as the *psycho-anthropological* view of both superstition and paranormal belief, since the theory considers the origins of these beliefs as rooted in antiquity and the fundamental development of human culture (Houran, Thalbourne and Ashe 2000). Nevertheless, the relationship between paranormal belief and a reduced fear of death does not appear to be statistically strong, although a mild age factor might be implicated whereby psychologists consider paranormal beliefs to be invoked by older people to ease the fear of death, much in the fashion of a religious belief. Furthermore, it's been argued that if a person is already religious and they are reminded of their own mortality, they might even be open to accept the existence of supernatural beings that are unfamiliar to their own particular religion, such as ancestral spirits even if they are Christian (Norenzayan and Hansen 2006).

Schizotypy— Schizophrenia is a disease characterized by symptoms including hallucinations, delusions, disorganized speech and behavior, and attenuated emotion and volition (Walker, Kestler, Bollini and Hochman 2004). Interestingly, the primary schizophrenic indicators, such as delusions and hallucinations, can be present in people without the disease (Pizzagalli, Lehmann, Gianotti, Koenig, Tanaka, Wackermann and Brugger 2000). Psychologists therefore propose that a continuum of schizophrenic symptoms exists. In other words, an individual's propensity to show these symptoms can be represented by a mark on a scale, with one end anchor being "no symptoms" and the other being "true schizophrenic."

The term *schizotypy* is used to characterize the non-psychotic symptoms that resemble schizophrenia. A person who expresses schizotypy might show elevated levels of magical ideation, greater interpersonal problems (for instance, social anxiety and a lack of close friends), and mental disorganization which might include anything from odd mannerisms to strange speech (Irwin and Green 1998). For this reason, many psychologists associate paranormal belief with the schizotypy trait (Windholz and Diamant 1974, Brugger, Gamma, Muri, Schafer, and Taylor 1993, Thalbourne, Dunbar, and Delin 1995, Brugger and Graves 1997, Pizzagalli 2000).

In this context paranormal belief refers to global belief. That is, belief in a wide range of paranormal events and abilities. Relationships have also been identified linking schizotypy to more specific types of paranormal beliefs such psi and spiritualism (Thalbourne et al. 1995). Researchers from the psychology department of the University of Essex, using the Multidimensional Schizotypal Traits Questionnaire (measuring perceptual aberration, magical ideation, cognitive disorganization, paranoid ideation, physical and social anhedonia[7] and impulsive nonconformity) have even uncovered a relationship between schizotypy and belief in UFOs (Chequers, Joseph and Diduca 1997).

Measuring Paranormal Belief

The University of Essex study is typical of research into paranormal belief, whereby the relationships among beliefs and personality factors are quantified (or turned into numbers) with the help of questionnaires.[8] At least two questionnaires need to be completed by participants in such a study, one measuring the amount of paranormal belief they hold, and one measuring the personality factors that are purportedly related to this belief level. A correlation coefficient can then be calculated which gives the psychologists a description of the strength of the relationship.

The answers a participant provides on any questionnaire can be scored, and these scores are added up across all participants in the study to give an overall score. When there are just two overall scores measured from two tests, for example paranormal belief and fear of death, then a *bivariate* correlation coefficient is calculated. Simply put, the bivariate correlation coefficient is a number between -1 and +1 and expresses the relationship between the two overall scores.

If participants who consistently score high for paranormal belief also score high for fear of death, and those who score low on paranormal belief score low on fear of death, then the relationship is strong and positive (close to (1). This suggests a strong relationship between the two variables exists.

Alternately, if participants who consistently score high for paranormal belief also score low on fear of death, and those who score low on paranormal belief score high on fear of death, then the relationship is strong and negative (close to -1). This suggests a strong relationship between the two variables also exists, but in the opposite direction. Finally, if a participant's score on paranormal belief has no apparent relationship to another score, such as their shoe size, then the relationship is weak and likely to be close to zero.

It's crucial to appreciate that causation is not implied by correlation. That is, just because a relationship exists statistically doesn't mean a person's high score on one variable necessarily causes them to get a high score on another. If a psychologist demonstrates that paranormal belief is strongly related to anxiety, it doesn't have to mean that naturally anxious people are necessarily driven to paranormal belief. Perhaps the belief causes the anxiety, or a third "hidden" variable causes both belief and anxiety to be elevated. For example, someone who has actually been frightened by a ghost might start believing in the paranormal, and at the same time show an increase in anxiety after the event. In this example, belief and anxiety are only related — one doesn't cause the other.

It's also worth noting that when many questionnaires are administered to participants, the statistical analyses and interpretation of findings become more difficult. Furthermore, participants often attempt to guess the purpose of the questionnaires they're required to complete, and this can influence the answers they give. It's commonplace that when the same questionnaires are given over the space of a few weeks to the same people, different results are sometimes achieved (Roig et al. 1998), confirming the fragile nature of questionnaires as a means of uncovering hidden relationships between paranormal belief and personality traits. A fascinating example of such a dilemma involves the nebulous relationship between paranormal belief and religious belief. In 1999, Michael Thalbourne and Rebecca O'Brien published a study in which they demonstrated a weak, negative correlation between paranormal belief and religious belief using religious-based questions from the Wilson-Patterson Attitude Scale, but a zero correlation between paranormal belief and religious belief when the "traditional religiosity" section of the paranormal belief scale was administered instead. More perplexing, they then found a strong significant correlation between paranormal belief and religious belief when applying the religiosity scale developed by the Icelandic psychologist Erlendur Harroldsson (Hergovich, Schott and Arendasy 2005).

Frequently, more than two questionnaires are given to participants in a session. For example, paranormal belief (and occasionally paranormal experience) might be measured in a sample of participants using the Paranormal Belief Scale–Revised (PBS–R), the Anomalous Experiences Inventory and the Magical Ideation Scale. The contributing traits psychologists might suspect underlie such belief and experience could simultaneously be assessed using instruments including the Death Anxiety Scale and Attitude Towards Death Scale and the Rational Behavior Inventory (measuring reasoning ability). Many small relationships will likely arise when such batteries of tests are given, and these can be analyzed and discussed in a thick scientific paper published in a psychological journal.

Creating a Paranormal Questionnaire

Very simply, questionnaires used to explore psychological and paranormal variables usually start as a rough version containing many more questions (or items) than are needed. A statistical technique called *factor analysis* then correlates all these items and bunches them into ones that go well together, meaning the people who fill out the questionnaire tend to answer these questions in the same way. For example, if the questionnaire covers a variety of paranormal topics, someone who believes strongly in the reality of telepathy is probably going to believe strongly in the reality of clairvoyance too, since these concepts are related.

Likewise, someone neutral to the existence of telepathy is probably going to be neutral to clairvoyance, and someone who rates telepathy as unlikely is almost certainly going to rate clairvoyance as unlikely too. All together, data from all these different people will show that a question about telepathy will strongly match a question about clairvoyance. These questions are then said to reside in the same *factor* (also known as a *component*, or *dimension*). Sometimes groupings occur because the items are asking exactly the same thing. In such circumstances, the unnecessary questions can be identified and removed from the list. A final questionnaire is then prepared[9] and can be administered in conjunction with other questionnaires.

The Paranormal Belief Scale

One of the most widely used questionnaires measuring paranormal belief is the PBS–R, a revision of the original PBS developed by Jerome Tobacyk and Gary Milford in 1983. The revised PBS (Tobacyk 1988) has 26 items covering a range of paranormal topics chosen to conform to an early definition given by C. D. Broad in 1949 that something paranormal violated the "basic limiting principles" of science (Dagnall, Munley, Parker and Drinkwater 2010)—reminding us of Chris Cherry's characterization given earlier in this book. Understandably, people who complete this questionnaire answer the items in many different ways; however, Tobacyk argued that if enough people are tested, and factor analysis is performed on the data, then seven dimensions of belief emerge. These are (1) traditional religious belief, (2) psi belief, (3) witchcraft, (4) superstition, (5) spiritualism, (6) extraordinary life-forms[10] and (7) precognition.

This finding implies that there is not simply one type of paranormal belief but seven, therefore it is simplistic to assume that people either believe in the paranormal or they don't. Rather, people can be strong and consistent believers in some paranormal topics — like psi — but not in others, like aliens. From these results, it would also appear that belief in psi might not involve a uniform acceptance of all extraordinary powers — telepathy, clairvoyance, PK and precognition. The results of the PBS–R instead suggest that if people believe in precognition (dimension 7), they don't necessarily have to accept that a person can be telepathic (dimension 2). The PBS–R also confirms that superstitious belief is separate from paranormal belief (Rudski 2003), a point identified in the previous chapter.

Most psychologists researching this field accept the multi-dimensional nature of paranormal belief, although the actual number of dimensions has been strongly debated over the last 20 years (e.g., Johnston, DeGroot, and Spanos 1994, Lawrence 1995, Hartman 1999). One of the reasons for this debate is the way items are selected for inclusion in a paranormal belief questionnaire. Test items are derived from such variable sources as personal experience (Grimmer and White 1990), paranormal books, movies and television shows, or are modified from earlier questionnaires (e.g., Tobacyk and Milford 1983).

Topics therefore range from logical inclusions such as psi and spiritualism, to those with arguably little association with the paranormal. Examples of allegedly non–paranormal items are those which cover alternative health techniques such as feng shui, iridology and homeopathy, and those related to mysterious phenomena including the Bermuda Triangle, the Loch Ness monster and UFOs. There is also some criticism that standard paranormal belief questionnaires possess a cultural bias (e.g., an item about Bigfoot) that might lead to misleading conclusions about the nature of paranormal belief in the population (Díaz-Vilela and Álvarez-González 2004).

Some Issues with Survey Questions

Less discussed, but equally as important, are potential problems with the items themselves. Close examination of a paranormal belief questionnaire reveals the existence of two distinct question types. The first type involves paranormal or anomalous concepts, whereas the second type concerns concrete paranormal events, entities or personalities. Such a distinction is important because the two types of items may not be equivalent in their ability to identify genuine paranormal or anomalous belief structures.

To give an example, imagine you have a friend who claims they believe in the concept of PK. Can they be considered a stronger believer in the paranormal than another friend, who says they believe in the Loch Ness monster? You might argue that belief in something like the Loch Ness monster is more superficial than belief in psi, and held in isolation from similar beliefs or the broader implications of that belief. It might transpire that your Loch Ness–believing friend has read quite a few books about the monster and seen television shows about it. Furthermore, he likes the idea of such a creature existing. Yet when you question him further, he might ridicule the possibility of similar creatures living in other parts of the world, or the prehistoric (or even otherworldly) origins of such a monster.[11]

Alternately, it could be argued that your other friend, who believes in PK, has considered more deeply the implications of the topic, since there are few famous examples that quite match the caliber of the Loch Ness monster. Therefore, an item which taps into a person's opinions of PK is potentially a better indicator of their deeply-held paranormal belief system than a more superficial item concerning a famous lake monster.

Likewise, an item determining a participant's belief in something like acupuncture bears little relationship to belief in the Bermuda Triangle. Most people who believe in the effectiveness of acupuncture do so because they've tried it themselves and are convinced it worked for them — a belief based on experience. On the other hand, a person might believe in the Bermuda Triangle simply because it sounds exciting, not because they've flown into it an disappeared! To date, the presence of unrepresentative items in paranormal questionnaires remains a potential problem when interpreting the findings of psychological studies.

And despite the complicated processes leading to the creation of a paranormal questionnaire, they still lack an adequate number of items to satisfactorily encompass the breadth and complexity of the various topics they purport to cover. For example, the "witchcraft" subscale of the popular PBS–R consists of four questions; (1) Through the use of formulas and incantations, it is possible to cast spells on persons; (2) Black magic really does exist; (3) There are actual cases of witchcraft and (4) Witches do exist.

Looking closely, you'll notice these questions only touch on the many different facets of belief in witches. Notwithstanding the fact that even skeptics could answer in the positive to some of them — since people calling themselves witches undoubtedly exist (Lawrence 1995), the items are unable to establish whether a temporal aspect is relevant to witchcraft belief, or even a moral one. That is, people might be prepared to accept witches once existed a long time ago (the same way that werewolves or vampires once might have roamed the earth) but no longer exist. Alternately, they might believe that good witches exist (with real magical powers) but not bad witches.

Including items about extraterrestrial belief, often simplistically equated with belief in flying saucers, also make some psychologists uneasy about accepting the findings of studies that have used paranormal questionnaires. This is because it's quite plausible for someone to believe in life on other planets but be completely adamant that such life-forms will never visit earth (Lawrence 1995). After all, there are plenty of paranormal skeptics who are passionate about the scientifically respectable Search for Extraterrestrial Intelligence (SETI) program. It's also quite plausible that a person might not believe in life on other planets but presume that flying saucers are the vehicles of demonic forces sent to torment humankind, which is perhaps a manifestation of the much stronger relationship that seems to exist between UFO belief and more general paranormal belief (Dagnall et al. 2010). The way people respond to items in the more commonly used paranormal belief questionnaires may therefore reveal only fragmentary and distorted information about their actual belief systems — an issue we need to appreciate before fully accepting the findings of a published study claiming to have uncovered the personality traits underlying paranormal belief.

The Problem Identifying Individual
Differences in Survey Participants

By the same token, it's also worthwhile casting a critical eye over these personality traits themselves. We've already touched on the problem of causality, whereby it's not possible to say a person's traits cause them to believe in the paranormal. The person might experience a UFO event, start to believe in UFOs, and become personally affected by the experience to the point that it ruins their life. There are plenty of examples of this type of thing happening. If this witness was then tested using a battery of questionnaires, would it be possible to claim that their personality was responsible for their earlier experience, or was the experience responsible for their current state of personality?

We also have to be careful with referring to personality traits as though they are "things." Here's an example using an imaginary conversation similar to that used when trying to "explain" psychic events in Chapter 1;

QUESTION: "What is field dependency?"
ANSWER: "Field dependency is a personality trait that refers to an individual's dependency on the context around them."
QUESTION: "But what is it?"
ANSWER: "Field dependency means people are dependent on context."
QUESTION: "But what *is* it ... where is it found, what causes it?"
ANSWER: "Oh, it's got something to do with the brain ... it's found in the brain and different people have it to different extents."

This frivolous discussion indicates clearly that labels such as field dependency or death anxiety simply describe a hidden trait that presumably generates a type of behavior. This is not to say that these labels don't define an important behavioral determinant. It's just that they can be very difficult to study. For example, if a person scores highly in a death anxiety questionnaire it means they've written many "yes" answers to items such as "I am afraid of dying." A significant correlation might then be uncovered between the answers on this death anxiety questionnaire and a score for psi belief on the PBS–R (that is, lots of "yes" answers to "I believe ESP exists" also).

The experimental psychologist conducting the research might then publish this superficially straightforward relationship. However, the results alone still don't really touch on the deeper issues of death, or why people fear death, or whether psi actually exists. For the finding to be worth writing about, the psychologist needs to include additional theoretical discussion alongside these basic results.

Therefore, while it seems alluring (and scientific) to consider paranormal belief as caused by the way people's brains are "wired up" — and that believers' brains are wired up differently from non-believers — the tools for testing this hypothesis (and the very descriptive psychological traits that are assumed) are not without fault. It is intriguing that discussion of personality traits is quite acceptable in mainstream psychology because the subject matter is not controversial. After all, everyone has a personality. Yet similar descriptive terms in parapsychology are completely rejected by mainstream psychology. Let's look once more at the previous conversation, changing a few words;

QUESTION: "What is clairvoyance?"
ANSWER: "Clairvoyance is a trait that refers to an individual's ability to gain information from other places without use of the senses."
QUESTION: "But what is it?"
ANSWER: "Clairvoyance means people are clairvoyant."
QUESTION: "But what is it ... where is it found, what causes it?"
ANSWER: "Oh, it's got something to do with the brain ... it's found in the brain and different people have it to different extents."

"Simple" Paranormal Experience

Having touched on paranormal beliefs, it's pertinent to go the next step and explore the concept of a paranormal experience. From the definitions given in at the start of the book, a paranormal experience could be anything from a ghost sighting to a person finding themselves levitating off the floor during a moment of high excitement or spiritual ecstasy. It could involve visiting another time and place while in an out-of-body state, or choosing the correct target picture when participating in a remote viewing task. It might even involve being abducted by aliens. Such claims aren't unusual either, despite what a mainstream psychologists might think. Surveys such as the 1991 Gallup Poll indicate that up to 25 percent of a U.S. sample has had an actual psi experience, and one in six claim to have contacted the dead.

Now you might suppose that researchers would overwhelmingly prefer to study the exciting paranormal content ... ghosts and aliens, rather than the dustier findings from psi research. However, many psychologists avoid studying incidents of a more startling nature, preferring to stick to the simpler types of paranormal experience that are attributable to straightforward cognitive mistakes. These are primarily psychic events such as precognitive hunches or dreams, although mild "poltergeist" infestations where household objects seem to go missing or have moved could be included in this category. By sticking to explanations for these quite ordinary experiences only, psychologists maintain close theoretical contact with the research findings of studies of paranormal belief. It also helps them to avoid getting their hands dirty and reputations damaged by touching the "weird stuff" like alien abductions.

The most important psychological explanations for simple paranormal experiences are presented below in terms of the individual differences people possess. In common with those determining paranormal belief, the traits are not necessarily independent of one another, and a witness's paranormal experience might be shaped by these traits acting in concert.

Misjudgments of randomness and probability— We've seen how the rationality of the general public is not held in high regard by many skeptical psychologists, and this includes people's understanding of probability and its relationship to their everyday experiences. Recall the findings of Brugger and Baumann, who demonstrated that the significant deficits in reasoning ability in paranormal believers is a function of their lack of understanding of how randomness in nature operates (Brugger and Baumann 1994). For instance, imagine you are participating in a simple card game that requires you to guess the color of the next playing card to be drawn from a standard pack (black or red). After every draw, the card is returned to the pack and the pack is shuffled before the next draw. It just happens that five black cards have been drawn in a row, and you can't help but think that the next card has to be a red — a guessing behavior characteristic called *repetition avoidance* (Houtkooper 2003). Yet if you think about it closely, on any one draw it is equally as likely to be another black card as a red card. We think we are "due" a win, but in this task there's really no such thing as being "due" at all. It is unlikely, but still possible, that 15 black cards could be drawn in a row, or 20. In this way, even if there's only a 1 in 100,000 chance of an event occurring, it is still likely to occur sometime, particularly when the event has been carried out 100,000 times already (which is why people actually win lotteries).

With this in mind, psychologists frequently assume that the simplest types of paranormal experiences — precognitive dreams or hunches — are simply caused by misjudgment of probability and the inability of people to deal with really large numbers. Billions of dreams are dreamed every night. That's a huge amount, so why shouldn't a few "come true" by chance alone? Most people promptly forget the many they've dreamed in a night which don't come true (if they even remember them in the first place). James Alcock discovered that when required to keep a record of their dreams, people who have dreams which they personally believe "always come true" actually show no particular prophetic ability when their records are methodically examined (Alcock 1981). It appears these people overwhelmingly concentrate on the rare "hit" of a dream that is loosely followed by something resembling the dream event. Dreaming of an old friend who unexpectedly visits the next day is one example of this. The dreamer then conveniently ignores the many misses that also occur, for instance dreaming of old friend who then doesn't visit the next day, or next week, or even next month.[12]

There's also the possibility of *multiple outs*, whereby the contents of a person's hunch or dream don't exactly match what ends up happening to them. This little bit of inconvenient reality is quietly ignored by the claimant (Zusne and Jones 1982). We've seen this issue already with the case of Jaytee the psychic dog. Musch and Ehrenberg (2002) sum up this view by stating that psychic experiences are cognitive illusions derived from peoples' inability to determine the probabilities associated with everyday events.

Misjudgments of probability and illusions of memory—Alcock further suggests that people overstate the reliability of their memories, little realizing that memories are a constructive process, and not, in his words, a "literal rendering of past experiences" (Alcock 1981). Consequently, a person's memories are prone to distortion, to the point where they no longer represent an actual, historical truth.

This effect is sometimes labeled an *illusion of memory* (Blackmore and Moore 1994), in that people can be mistaken in their memories of events, in particular events they interpret as paranormal. Just like memories of dreams, they happily recall an experience that's interpreted as meaningful after it's happened, but tend to forget the many random events that occur far more often—and which would place the former event in a more mundane context. We'll revisit people's memory of paranormal events in more detail when we study more intense experiences such as ghost and UFO sightings.

Loose associations—People who claim to have had simple paranormal experiences also create more liberal associations among the objects and events they encounter compared with non-witnesses, a trait linked to schizophrenia and schizotypal thinking. This is *loose associationism* and, forgive the jargon, refers to a "decreased inhibition of the spreading activation within semantic networks" (Pizzagalli, Lehmann and Brugger 2001). *Spreading activation* is a theoretical model of cognition which implies that humans hold ideas or "nodes" in their mind that are part of a semantic (meaningful) network, and these nodes are connected to each other by theoretical lines of a variety of lengths and strengths (e.g., Loftus 1975). Pretend someone mentions the word "red" to you. In the past, you have made associations between the color red and concepts including other colors (e.g., green) and objects (e.g., apples and fire engines). Of course, apples can also be green so there's an association between these two concepts too. Once you've moved on to thinking of fire engines, based on your personal set of nodes you could eventually end up thinking of almost anything. This is why the process is called *spreading* activation. Fire engines are motor vehicles, as are trucks and cars. Once you start pondering about vehicles, you remember car needs a mechanical service, which requires the money that you've already spent on a present for your friend's birthday, who's ... (and so we can go on and on, as you pass from one mental node to another).

It has been suggested that some people are more prone to making wider associations among nodes than others — indeed, they display the "decreased inhibition" mentioned by Pizzagalli and colleagues. For example, someone showing strong schizotypal tendencies might hear the word "red" and very quickly come to the seemingly unrelated concept of "Pluto," whereas in the same period of time a "normal" person concludes with the more logical association of "apple." Put another way, Pizzagalli explains that in extreme schizotypy there isn't any focused spreading along the "ideas" network from one concept to another. Instead, travel is along new links, and the outcome that a person reaches is only loosely connected with the original idea.

By this logic, certain people who display loose associationism might end up believing that the coin they discover on the footpath one morning is meaningfully linked to a dream they had about a donut the previous night. The donut is round, and so is the coin. Consequently, they arrive at the loose conclusion that their dream must have been precognitive. However, this doesn't necessarily suggest there's something mentally wrong with these people. The South American researchers Alejandro Parra and Luis Paul borrow the term "happy schizotype" to describe people reporting ESP-type incidents because they remain socially functional in spite of (or perhaps because of) their strange experiences — which Parra and Paul nonetheless consider to be nothing more than hallucinatory fantasies (Parra and Paul 2010).[13]

Temperament— Traits of personality have been widely used to explain paranormal belief, so it's not surprising that connection has also been made between simple paranormal experience and a person's temperament. Temperament is considered a relatively stable aspect of personality that's been inherited, and it underlies the immediate, uncontrolled reactions people make towards emotional stimuli (Snowden and Gray 2010).[14] Thus people who report frequent psychic experiences show a tendency to worry a lot, be depressed and anxious, have psychosomatic complaints, feel tired and be prone to neurosis — all aspects of temperament. Individuals who also demonstrate high levels of maladjustment, gregariousness and thoughtfulness than "normal" people tend to report more psi experiences too (Sebastian and Mathew 2001).

Cognitive style— Put simply, cognitive style refers to the way people think, and a person's cognitive style has been linked to the frequency of their simple paranormal experiences, as it has to their level of paranormal belief (and their reasoning ability). To appreciate the close connection between belief and experience, psychologists Susan Blackmore and Rachel Moore ask us to imagine two people experiencing the same unusual event. One person is a "sheep" (recall this means they're a paranormal believer) and another person is a "goat" (or an independently-thinking non-believer). The sheep might interpret the event as evidence of extrasensory perception, whereas the goat will interpret the event as the natural operation of chance, or something else that's routine and unexciting (Blackmore and Rachel Moore 1994).

Evidence of the relationship among the variables of paranormal belief, experience, and cognitive style was also found by Uwe Wolfradt and co-workers from the Martin Luther University in Germany. Participants who score high on psychological tests measuring rational thinking styles (covering attributes with technical labels such as "conscious," "intentional," "analytic" and "affect-free") give low scores on tests measuring both paranormal beliefs and experiences. On the other hand, individuals who think intuitively (with personal attributes labeled "automatic," "holistic" and "affective") are more likely to report having had paranormal experiences (Wolfradt, Oubaid, Straube, Bischoff, Mischo 1999). The unavoidable implication from finding such as this is that paranormal experients aren't rational.

"Person-centered" causes— Theories of probability misjudgment and loose associationism are well suited to simple poltergeist cases. For example, I was once told of a painting on the wall of a modern home that was continually being tipped from its level — a very mundane event that didn't involve anything as dramatic as objects being thrown around. The residents attributed this event to a poltergeist or spirit (they used the words interchangeably) who apparently had developed some unknown fascination with the theme of the artwork (a young child sitting on a chair). In the absence of any other anomalous event occurring in the house, or in these people's lives, the poltergeist explanation was rather a distance causal association. A far more logical explanation is that the painting was simply balanced poorly.

Alternately, a more sophisticated "person-centered" psychological explanation for poltergeist phenomena was proposed by sociologists Alexandra Teguis and Charles Flynn. These authors suggest a psychosocial explanation for paranormal experience (Teguis and Flynn 1983). This implies that the experience is psychologically generated by the witness, perhaps to counteract certain social difficulties they are enduring. In these author's opinion, people who claim to have supernatural powers (or perhaps an interaction with a poltergeist) do so to covertly undermine conventional symbolic social and cultural constructs such as time, space and physical laws. This way, the believer avoids confronting the overwhelming and threatening reality that surrounds them in their everyday life.

In such a theory, the percipient's affliction might be caused by interpersonal or family problems, and this results in repressed anger or guilt manifesting as a perceived poltergeist.[15] Interestingly, Teguis and Flynn don't rule out the possibility that real psychic causes contribute to the physical events associated with some poltergeist cases.

A photograph said to show a poltergeist in action, throwing papers around a workplace in Leeds, West Yorkshire, England, in 1970. A teenaged office worker was widely considered the focus of this particular infestation: an example of a human-centered explanation for poltergeists with recurrent spontaneous psychokinesis responsible for the anomalous activity (Mary Evans Picture Library).

Somatization—As a final example of how individual differences might contribute to simple paranormal experiences, people who are—for whatever physiological or psychological reason—hypersensitive to their bodily sensations and body position (known as *proprioception*) may attribute these internal events to an external cause (Houran, Kumar, Thalbourne and Lavertue 2002). For example, if a person prone to somatization starts feeling ill when eating in a cafeteria, they might attribute the sensation to food contaminants, whereas another person might not even notice the symptoms in the first place. Similarly, an office worker overly sensitive to their bodily functions might explained their seemingly unusual feelings as a consequence of poor air quality.

From a paranormal perspective, individuals prone to somatization also report more precognitive dreams than "normal" people, perhaps because their increased sensitivity to internal body states makes it easier to match what they might be feeling inside to previous dreams they've had (Schredl 2009). In a similar way, autonomic (gut) sensations might be interpreted by these individuals as infestation by an evil spirit. Houran and colleagues associate the somatization trait with hypochondria, and term it a *psychogenic illness*.

Educating Against Paranormal Experience

In light of these psychological research findings, one might be prompted to ask how the "problem" of paranormal belief and paranormal experience can be "cured." We're aware that superstitious behavior and belief might be eliminated through education in scientific cause-and-effect relationships. This allows "sufferers" to understand that no simple, superstitious belief or behavior can improve the chance of good luck, or remove bad luck.

Similarly, and notwithstanding the role of a believer's "incurable" temperament or their "incurable" thinking style, many mainstream psychologists would hope that people can still be educated with the view that one day they might realize their simple paranormal experiences are no more than coincidence, or a misjudgment of probability.

CHAPTER 3

Witnessing the Paranormal: Illusions

In this chapter, and for the rest of the book, we'll examine paranormal experiences that are more intricate than simple premonitions. But first let's return to the various categories of paranormal experience presented in the Introduction, only this time reorganizing and expressing them in terms their frequency of occurrence in *real* people, not in some academic, hypothetical individual concocted in a psychologist's imagination. These are individuals who do not necessarily expect to encounter what they encounter. They are very different from witnesses who are strong believers of the paranormal and actively seek out strange experiences. These latter individuals, I believe, are somewhat over-represented in the psychological literature, and yet the former are just as worthy of study.

(1) *Simple psychical experiences*— are the most commonly reported paranormal experience, and we've covered these in the last chapter. A vast majority of these tales are assumed, even by supporters of the paranormal, to be misinterpretation of perfectly normal events (Kennedy 2005).

(2) *"Felt," intuited, or "evidenced" experience of the personal dead*— It's very common for people to feel or intuit (but not actually see) the presence of a dead person they once knew. For instance, just "knowing" the spirit of Great Aunt Gertrude is hovering nearby is typical of this type of experience, and it goes without saying there are countless cases of these across country and era. A cross-section of examples might include smelling grandfather's distinctive aftershave in the lounge when there's no-one else around, or seeing a depression on the couch and believing that it has been caused by his invisible posterior. It could also involve accepting that the constant and mysterious rearrangement of the contents of the drinks cabinet is due to the mischievous spirit of Uncle Bill. The ghostly aftershave example is rather subjective, since olfactory (odor)

experiences are somewhat fleeting and intangible — and as far as I know no researcher has ever tried scientifically recovering potentially anomalous odor molecules from a haunting. The latter two examples, however, are evidenced since they seemingly involve more concrete physical proof of something otherworldly having happened. Although most evidenced cases still fall into the "simple" category because the physical proof is anything but explicit, there are numerous cases that are anything but simple. One dramatic instance of an evidenced spirit is the story told to me by one of two women having a coffee in their family lounge room. Quite suddenly, a cup was seen to rise from the coffee table and hover over the lounge room floor. This event was interpreted by one of the witnesses as a message of comfort from her deceased father. Apparently he was enjoying a cup of coffee too!

(3) *Witnessed personal dead*—Actually seeing the apparition of your deceased Great Aunty Gertrude is less common than feeling she's nearby, and it's an encounter roughly equivalent to Tyrrell's post-mortem apparition. Perhaps you've woken in bed one night to see her floating by the bedroom door, or while having breakfast one morning in broad daylight, you've observed her sitting in her favorite spot at the kitchen table. Generally, these apparitions don't do terribly much. Communication between the ghost and the witness is rare, although there might be an expression on the spirit's face that imparts a personally meaningful message, such as great sadness (causing the witness to question the path their life is taking). Another facial expression is interpreted by the witness as one of comfort, and they feel reassured by the visit of the known apparition. Occasionally the spirit, while recognized as someone known to the witness during life, expresses a rather unpleasant and uncharacteristic demeanor, such as leering. Understandably, the witness can be rather disconcerted by such an apparition. In one case I'm aware of, the witness had enough presence of mind to order the entity to leave immediately (thankfully the entity, whatever is was, obeyed the order!).

Conventional wisdom would suggest that witnessing an apparition of the personal dead is exceedingly rare, although a report compiled by James Houran, Michael Thalbourne and Diane Ashe show that one third of their 60 participants in a study examining the relationship between death-anxiety and paranormal experience claimed that they'd seen such an apparition (Houran, Thalbourne and Ashe 2000). Sixty is a small sample, relatively speaking, but one third is still a large proportion for any study of this type.

Acknowledging the related topic of living apparitions, I should note that I personally have never met someone who has seen a crisis or living apparition — or was the agent themselves. On the other hand, I have met with countless people who have seen relatives who are definitely deceased. Perhaps it's just the nature of the times in which we live?

(4) *Near-death-experiences and out-of-body-experiences*— Reports of NDEs and OBEs seem to occur less frequently than sightings of deceased family or friends, but this might be a function of their highly personal nature. The experient might simply have more difficulty communicating what's happened to them — it's easier to talk about, and "make sense of," an external spirit encounter, compared with explaining the sensation of leaving the body and traveling to a world untroubled by basic physical laws. The same might be said of people who claim to perceive auras emanating from another person. Since these visions are considered a special ability possessed by the seer,[1] such claims might be subject to more personal judgment from those who hear the story than that of an "everyday" ghost sighting. If someone laughs at you when you tell them you saw your dead grandmother, you can at least shrug your shoulders and say, "It was nothing to do with me, I just saw it." Witnessing auras, on the other hand, singles you out as someone different, and it's harder to seem impartial to your claims.[2]

The fear of being labeled as weird or mentally ill makes those who see auras very careful about mentioning their experiences. When I was teaching a subject on paranormal experiences at a university, on more than one occasion after class a student would approach me explaining how they would sit in the room watching the auras bounce off all the other students — and myself. They only did this, however, following a quite open discussion on the aura phenomenon.

(5) *Poltergeist and séance activity*— Recall from the Introduction that the stereotypical poltergeists case involves loud, unexplained noises occurring inside a house, with personal objects shifted or thrown boisterously around (or going missing for no obvious reason). Add to these examples the milder poltergeist reports classified in the previous chapter, and we have a variety of paranormal experiences that are relatively common. With some trepidation I can provide a personal example clarifying how people might come to such an outlandish conclusion.

A few years ago I lost a key to a padlock for an outside gate near my house. I distinctly remember taking it out of the lock and, since all the pockets of my trousers had holes in them, I carried it inside my house. I can't remember what I did with it after that — I presume I must have put it on a table or a bench. A few days later I needed the key, but couldn't find it anywhere. I even tore the house apart looking for it. In the end, I had to hacksaw through a chain to open the gate. I commented out loud how annoying it was that things were going missing around the house (the key being just one of a number of frustrating disappearances) and I wished it would stop. The very next day I was working in a paddock on the property that no one had entered for over a month. For some reason, I decided to shift a pile of rotten firewood that had been there for many years, and under the very bottom log, where the grass was brown and dead, sat a shiny silver padlock key. I knew instinctively it was my missing key, so I wasn't surprised when it opened the padlock perfectly. Of course, it couldn't have been a mischievous poltergeist, could it? Perhaps one night in my sleep I ambled down into the paddock and hid the key somehow under the woodpile ... that's certainly the most rational explanation, but not necessarily the most satisfying.

The popular explanation for general poltergeist infestations is a mixture of psychosocial theory and RSPK. That is, someone living in the house is unknowingly using psychokinesis as a way of calling attention to themselves (dubious in the case of my "poltergeist"). Another fashionable view is that a discarnate is behind the event, either a deceased human or something not human at all — and the story of the floating coffee cup discussed earlier could just as easily be classed as a poltergeist infestation as the expression of a family ghost (or a psychological error, as we shall see).

I'll also include various séance experiences into this category of my paranormal hierarchy, because they frequently contain poltergeist-like behavior. Think of a séance and you either imagine a levitating medium in Victorian London (with ectoplasm streaming out her nostrils), or a B-grade horror movie that ends up with lots of blood and gore. Strangely enough, while the séance isn't practiced as much as it was before the 1960s — when Ouija boards were still a parlor game and any strange things that occurred didn't seem quite so sinister — there are still plenty of contemporary séance stories with a paranormal twist.

Some of these read like a scene from a horror film, which I find strangely disturbing because it's in stark contrast to the vast majority of paranormal experiences that are completely benign. Plenty of seemingly normal people have spoken to me at length, and independently, about the séances they've organized or attended. In these sessions dark eerie figures appear, lights go out and unpleasant smells erupt from every corner of the room where it's held. These séances are amateur events, implying that a group of friends perform them rather than it being lead by a "professional" medium. This tends to rule out the possibility of sophisticated fraud, but not necessarily unsophisticated fraud, or the operation of the ideomotor effect innocently causing the planchette on a Ouija board to move around, seemingly under intelligent control (Easton and Shor 1976). A multitude of other psychological variables, including suggestibility, would be expected to account for all the terrifying side-effects — at least, I hope they do!

Sometimes, the supernatural events arising from the séance persist to the point where the practitioners have to move away from the house where it occurred. Luckily, most appear to be tenants, although the new people who move in might suffer the consequences. In some stories recounted to me, the vehicle of the séance, such as the Ouija board, can't be destroyed. Alternately, if it is destroyed it keeps reappearing in perfect condition at the bottom of a cupboard or a clothes trunk. However, before jumping to the conclusion that evil spirits are at work it would be necessary to first confirm the details of the events, rather than taking for granted the stories as they are told.[3]

(6) *Witnessed impersonal dead*—Witnessing the impersonal dead as a *haunting apparition* (to use Tyrrell's phrase) comes fifth on my list of paranormal experiences. To be considered in this category, the witness has assumed that the apparition they encounter, whether it be inside a building or somewhere else (perhaps beside a stretch of dark, eerie road), is of a person who has died and is yet to "cross-over," haunting the location for some veiled reason. I've labeled these apparitions *impersonal* because the witness claims not to know who they are. These ghosts reportedly take a variety of forms, more likely to be real-as-real in appearance than hazy or transparent. Back in 1919 the psychical investigator Ernesto Bozzano wrote how these types of ghosts tend to dress in the clothes of their time and not the "spectral robes" and chains of the stereotypical ghost. They appear as real as living people, but their transparent nature may range from solidity, to opaque, to vague shadows of a human form (Alvarado and Zingrone 1995).

Michaeleen Maher is long-time researcher of apparitions and similarly relates how these types of ghosts aren't obliged to linger in spooky attics or basements, or to be threatening in any way. Nor do they need to glow, or float, or dress in white hooded garments. They don't point out where treasures are hidden or notify the experient of a coming family disaster. In fact, encounters with ghosts are trivial and lackluster, and anything but harrowing (Maher 1999).

Nevertheless, certain types of impersonal ghosts do seem more frequent than others. In modern Australia, these include an elderly man in a dark suit and a little girl "dressed in Edwardian (1900s)-era clothes."[4] However, the assumption that these are haunting ghosts is just that — an assumption. When questioned closely, the witness often admits that the "ghost" follows them around from place to place. They are sometimes seen in more than one location, and often by other people who are with the witness at the time.

Here's a typical example from a witness called Tom. When he was about ten years old and washing dishes in the family kitchen, Tom looked out the nearby window to see a figure of a man, about 20 or so years old, "dressed in swimming shorts," staring back at him from the garden. Tom claims he didn't recognize the man, and briefly looked away from the window to tell his mother. When he looked back moments later, the figure was gone — an example of an impersonal ghost sighting. Eight years later, Tom was skiing with a friend when both unexpectedly fell down on the slope. Both men looked up to see the same figure (according to Tom's recollection) standing under a nearby tree, complete with swimming shorts! The witnesses looked at each other briefly, as you would do, but when they turned back to the tree the man had disappeared. This case has a number of important elements: (1) the same apparition was seen by the same individual in two different locations, (2) the apparition's materialization was separated by a substantial period of time, and (3) the apparition was not purely subjective, since another person (allegedly) witnessed it and described it in a similar fashion. Such encounters are often termed "ghostly" by the experient, yet the appearance of the entity suggests something a little more complicated than a haunting ghost (if that's not complicated enough!). Since they types of encounters are so interesting, they will be the subject of a later chapter.

(7) *Witnessed aerial events (distant)*—Truly anomalous UFO sightings are certainly not as common as ghost encounters, or even an annoying poltergeist plague. Naturally, plenty of people see lights hovering or moving strangely in the sky at night, and in spite what many skeptics would believe, most interpret these objects as perfectly normal airplanes, satellites or planets. Nevertheless, there's always been an undercurrent of reports of unusual aerial activity up until the present time, suggesting the flying saucer era wasn't just restricted to the heyday period between the mid–1940s and the 1970s. Recently, nocturnal UFOs have returned to prominence, and online news-media and You Tube frequently show video footage of the latest lights in the sky from around the world. Fewer people still report seeing strange and indistinct aerial objects in the daytime, such as a silver disc or flying triangle. And yet, in common with night-time sightings, there is still a constant trickle of daylight UFO reports that indicate the phenomena just won't go away.

So while reports remain rare compared to the myriad of other paranormal experiences, UFO sightings are still the focus of psychological attention because they link elegantly to theories of memory and perception.

(8) *Detailed witnessed aerial events*—Even less common than distant UFO reports are close-up sightings of strange aerial craft. In these encounters the witness not only sees a shape in the sky they don't recognize, but also distinct features which suggest the object has a meaning or purpose that is far from mundane. Most extreme would be the presence of, for example, port-holes through which small alien heads are seen staring back at the witness. Despite the comparative rarity of these experiences they are of great interest to the psychologist because they verge on a category of encounter known as, for want of better term, *intense*. This differentiates them from simpler paranormal events (precognitions, etc.), and also from sightings viewed from a distance

that are completely impersonal, such as witnessing a ghostly light through the window of the old deserted house on the hill, or a small point of light in the night sky that zips back and forth in impossible ways before shooting off to be lost in the myriad of stars above.

(9) *Contact with weird entities that aren't ghosts or spirits* — Recall that an *entity* is the label given to something that isn't human or an animal, and we've met creatures such as para-apes and my giant Australian slug in the Introduction. The expression also covers extraterrestrials — although some researchers would be aghast at my temerity in lumping perfectly respectable aliens in with bizarre

Cardinal Crescentius attended the Council of Trent in 1552, and one night while writing a letter to the pope a black dog entered his chamber. Using clergyman Nathanial Wanley's description of the incident in the later 17th century, the dog was of "vast bigness," with flaming eyes and "ears that hung almost to the ground." It proceeded to lie under his table, at which point the cardinal called out to his servants to search for it. They found nothing, and Crescentius fell ill and soon died. The black dog has a long reputation as a harbinger of death, and is used metaphorically in many historical sources. Encounters with these entities are actually reported — and not as ordinary dogs but something supernatural, with glowing red eyes and of a form that vanishes into thin air. By its very definition the dog brings with it an ominous portent of doom, although I'm not aware of any contemporary deaths arising directly from these sightings (Fortean Picture Library).

creatures such as a para-ape. Nevertheless, that's my decision for the following reason: despite the wonderfully wide range of entities available, human contact with entities — a truly intense encounter — is rare relative to other paranormal experiences.

The rareness of such experiences is reflected in the parapsychological literature. Ralph Noyes points out that the most common type of entity discussed in expert publications such as the *Journal of Psychical Research* are, in order, (1) those that appear as séance materializations, (2) classical (haunting) apparitions, and (3) classical poltergeist (Noyes 1989). To Noyes this is reasonable since — in common with my hierarchy — it's highly unusual for people to bump into weird entities that aren't ghosts or spirits. Yet Noyes is disappointed that these more extraordinary entities — which include conventional UFO aliens as well as more unconventional ghouls, black dogs,[5] alien big cats and anthropoid entities — tend to be ignored in the literature. Noyes is also dissatisfied with the lack of attention paid to "the gentry" (fairies), demons and nature spirits, and monstrous apparitions. This indifference is apparently because early members of the Society for Psychical Research wanted proof of LAD in the same way that proponents of the "extraterrestrial hypothesis" (the idea that flying saucers contain beings from other planets) look solely for proof of extraterrestrial, physical aliens.

Strangely enough, from many years of interacting with paranormal witnesses I've come to the personal conclusion that weird entity encounters are almost as common as seeing a UFO "close up." I've only listed these types of contacts as number nine in the hierarchy, and not earlier, because they seem the strangest of all paranormal experiences. Yet regardless of whether you've seen a "swamp ape" near the local lagoon or meet an alien from a UFO, mainstream psychology explains the experience in the same, rational manner — which we'll examine shortly.

Individual Differences, Illusions and Paranormal Experience

Misinterpreting Reality

Taking ghosts as a starting point, there are plenty of philosophical arguments refuting the proposition that apparitions are "spirits of the dead." For example, the pre-existence theory of classicist Eric Dodds maintains that if a spirit of a human can lurk around after death, then logically it should also be around before they're born (Dodds 1934). Arguably a supporter of life after death could put up a case for reincarnation to counter pre-existence theory, but most psychologists would see no need to indulge in these complicated philosophical arguments because the average ghost encounter can be adequately explained as misinterpretations of a mundane external reality. Such an average sighting happens at night near or during sleep, and there is no communication between the witness and the alleged spirit. The stereotyped ghost that's seen is nondescript in shape (a fleeting shadow or a hazy blur)—or perhaps only sensed in the peripheral vision. These characteristics are shared by other witnessed paranormal encounters, for example a flying saucer sighting, or the brief appearance of a monster's head as it surfaces in a dark and choppy lake.

To a psychologists, the visual stimulus that creates the ghost might simply be the shadow of a chair in a dark room, or if it's a UFO an unusually shaped cloud, or a floating log instead of a sea-monster. However, the witness' brain interprets it as something different and this is leads to an illusion — in this specific case an optical illusion because the misinterpretation has been visualized. Of course this theory doesn't explain some of the other paranormal experiences in the list given at the beginning of the chapter, such as OBE or NDEs which seem to be based on deeper neurological dysfunction. Nevertheless, the illusion theory might still explain a good deal of paranormal reports.

Illusions are a misinterpretation of reality, so what does misinterpretation actually involve? Firstly, a distinction must be made between misinterpretation and misperception. Misperception implies that the very act of perceiving an external stimulus (be it a chair or a cloud) is flawed. If you're spending the night in a creaky old house your basic senses might tell you there's a tall, dark ghostly man at the far end of the corridor and that's what you "see," but in fact there's absolutely nothing there (a concept that has a lot in common with hallucinations, which we'll cover in a later chapter).

Misinterpretation, on the other hand, implies that you perceive the basic elements of the stimulus just like anyone else would. However, while your friend spending the night with you in the creaky old house sees nothing more than a hat rack at the end of the corridor, hidden in a shadow, you construe the shape to be a ghost because your personal and unique higher cognitive processes (for want of a better term) turn it into a ghost. In this example, you and your friend can swap stories about what you think you've seen, then easily walk down the corridor to see if there really is a hat rack at the end of it. However, the witness or witnesses to a paranormal sighting generally don't have this luxury, and we're left with the illusion theory to explain their experience after the fact.

We've already learned that scientific psychologists attribute superstitious behavior, paranormal belief and simple paranormal experiences (such as coincidences) to distinctive features of their personality and thinking processes. The same applies to the creation of paranormal illusions. Here are some of the more important ideas that have been discussed:

Psychological Factors Determining Illusions

Prior belief— The witnessing and reporting of simple illusionary UFO sightings has long been associated with prior UFO belief (Spanos, Cross, Dickson and DuBreuil 1993, Paltry and Pelletier 2001). This belief may not only determine the nature of the interpretation (generating the illusion of a flying saucer), but is also linked with cognitive deficiencies and atypical personality traits such as schizotypy (Chequers et al. 1997). This is in contrast to Eddie Bullard's view that a witness is more likely to make an unusual observation first, and then develop a belief about what they saw. Indeed, they might also not want to believe what they saw is paranormal and subject their experience to rigorous logical analysis which nonetheless doesn't satisfy them (Bullard, 1988). This is simply another expression of the difficulty in determining causation from correlation. Do beliefs cause sightings, or sightings cause belief, or is it a bit of both?

Status inconsistency— In a widely-quoted and rather mean article from the height of the UFO era, Donald Warren claimed that individuals who see flying saucers display status inconsistency (Warren 1970). That is, their social position is at odds with their education or background. They might be highly educated and come from a wealthy family, but for some reason are working in an unskilled job. Warren's argument was that these witnesses report seeing unusual things in the sky order to bring attention to themselves. Such a suggestion was nonetheless strongly disputed not long after it was made (Lee and Lee 1972, Westrum 1977) and is no longer considered a factor in UFO sightings.

Tolerance of ambiguity— More relevant to witnessed paranormal reports is tolerance of ambiguity. The term implies that certain people are intolerant to ambiguity, and do not cope well when they encounter objects and events that are ambiguous (Lange and Houran 1998, Houran 1997). An ambiguous stimulus is one that has many potential interpretations. For instance, the shape at the end of the corridor in the creepy old house could be the shadow of a half-opened door or a hat stand leaning against the wall or the ghost of a man watching you with sinister intent. Ambiguous stimuli don't have to be visual either. They can be sounds or smells that are similarly open to multiple interpretations. We've already discussed how haunting reports often involved odors, be it the lingering aroma of grandma's perfume or grandpa's tobacco smoke. And as ambiguity goes, auditory stimuli can be even more ambiguous than visual ones. For example, strange noises are the most popular haunting symptom reported by tour groups in haunted houses because they are conducive to a form of contagious interpretation. This means if one person breathlessly informs the group they just heard an eerie, whispered voice, suddenly others claim to hear it too (Lange, Houran and Harte 1996).

Rense Lange and James Houran have performed detailed investigations into the prevalence of the tolerance of ambiguity trait in the population. It transpires that many people are quite tolerant of ambiguity in their surroundings. They'll happily interpret a vague shape or soft noise as inherently ambiguous and nothing unusual — and certainly nothing paranormal. Other people might only be moderately tolerant and make the occasional paranormal interpretation. Of most interest, however, are the small sample of people who possess low tolerance of ambiguity. These individuals have atypical difficulty making sense of indistinct stimuli (Lange and Houran 1998, 1999).

Specifically, they seek an interpretation to these stimuli, and if none is readily available they can call up a pre-existing paranormal belief to help them understand the frightening experience, helping to reduce fear and apprehension following the event (Maher 1974). The fear generated by the creaking floorboard upstairs in an old house can therefore be neutralized by labeling it "paranormal." This seems counterintuitive, but makes sense if one accepts that anxiety is generated by the lack of an explanation to a strange event, rather than the nature of the explanation itself— such as "it was a ghost."

From a visual perspective, a strong believer in ghosts, with low tolerance of ambiguity, might transform a shadow outside their bedroom window after midnight into a ghostly face. Alternately, a believer in extraterrestrial aliens, who possesses low tolerance of ambiguity, might see the pear-shaped head of a spindly grey alien staring at them instead.

As you might have guessed by now, the only catch with a concept such as tolerance of ambiguity is that it is purely descriptive. If a witness reports seeing a ghost, and they score highly on a "tolerance of ambiguity" questionnaire (with items perhaps asking them about how frequently they see ghosts), then the participant might be conveniently labeled as possessing low tolerance of ambiguity. Such a label looks as though it explains their encounter scientifically, but in reality it's only a hypothetical psychological trait. Labeling someone as possessing low tolerance of ambiguity doesn't on its own get to the bottom of their apparition sighting, although the trait might be successfully integrated into a wider psychological theory of ghostly encounters.

Transliminality— The same can be said about transliminality (Thalbourne and Houran 2000). Like any trait, transliminality is said to be possessed, to different degrees, by all people along a continuum. This means a person might not express it at all, or show it a little bit, or a bit more, or a lot, and so on. It refers to how easily unconscious material (be it imagery, ideas or anything else stored in our brains below our threshold of awareness) is able to cross over into conscious thought. *Trans* means "across" and *liminal* means "line." Thus, for some transliminal people who are identified using an index called the Transliminal Scale, their forgotten thoughts are more able to cross the line between the unconscious and the conscious, compared with "normal" people.

How might transliminality relate to paranormal experience? In one experiment, people who have been identified as highly transliminal from their performance on the Transliminal Scale strongly believe they perform well in a contrived ESP card-reading task, only to show surprise when the experimenter tells them they were being given subliminal cues regarding the answers to the task before they made their "psychic" decisions. The participants simply didn't realize they were receiving subtle information (Crawley, French and Yesson 2002). From a more supportive perspective, transliminality has been associated with genuine psychic performance (Del Prete and Tressoldi 2005). The highly transliminal participant is said to be able to access material from their "preconscious" that is derived from external but non-sensory sources — an idea that bears a strong connection to James Carpenter's suggestion that psi information is the first level of engagement with the outside world and usually undetectable because it's overwhelmed by later conscious processes. Transliminality has therefore been used to clarify psychic experiences from both a skeptical and supportive perspective.

Applying transliminality to witnessed paranormal events and illusion theory, imagine you happen to see something small and indistinct traveling in the sky to the west of your house at dusk. You are also highly transliminal. Once you see the ambiguous stimulus, ideas of spaceships and aliens rapidly flood into your consciousness thoughts — seemingly from nowhere. You then tell people you've seen a UFO with all the associated paraphernalia attached to it, including antennas, portholes and the aliens themselves.

Transliminality is an intriguing concept that shares similarities with the *boundary deficit hypothesis.*[6] A person displaying the boundary deficit personality trait lacks the ability to distinguish between their own "self" and "non-self" compared with other people. That is, they are deficient in distinguishing the boundary between these two concepts that separate themselves from the world around them. These people are consequently prone to mistaking fantasy for reality. The hypothesis was originally developed to classify people complaining of recurrent nightmares, and it has been noted that people with thinner boundaries and a greater degree of self-absorption are also more likely to report experiences of precognitive dreams (Schredl 2009).

Elsewhere, writer and skeptic Martin Kottmeyer has applied the boundary deficit hypothesis to individuals who report having been abducted by aliens (Appelle 1996). It has also been used by James Houran and colleagues to explain encounters with a wide variety of other strange entity types (Houran, Ashe and Thalbourne 2003). Nevertheless, both transliminality and

boundary deficit display the limitations applied to tolerance of ambiguity —
they are concepts that are descriptive and difficult to measure objectively without assuming it exists in the first place. Here's yet another imaginary
conversation to make this idea bit clearer:

> PSYCHOLOGIST: Do you ever have thoughts that just "pop into your head"?
> PARTICIPANT: Yes.
> PSYCHOLOGIST: That suggests you're prone to transliminality, or perhaps
> "boundary deficit."
> PARTICIPANT: What's that?
> PSYCHOLOGIST: It's a personality trait characterized by thoughts that "pop into
> your head."

Other assorted personality factors— Witnesses claiming to see UFOs provide moderately elevated scores in certain subscales of a personality questionnaire called the Minnesota Multiphasic Personality Inventory (MMPI) (Parnell
1988). Such people overreact to situations and social standards, show increased
social concern, greater interpersonal sensitivity and demonstrate enhanced
sensitivity to criticism. Compared to others, witnesses also display different
thinking styles (creativity), show avant-garde attitudes, possess greater than
usual psychic energy and exhibit greater diversity of thoughts. Results from
the 16PF personality questionnaire (PF standing for "personality factors")
indicates that witnesses also score higher than non-witnesses in traits such as
independent thinking, reservation, intelligence, assertiveness, liberal ideas,
experimentation, self-sufficiency and resourcefulness. Witnesses also prefer
their own decisions to others'.

However, the idea that small personality differences between witnesses
and non-witnesses somehow indicate the former are different — or even dysfunctional — has been criticized. Research by Troy Zimmer indicates that
UFO witnesses generally seem no more alienated, distressed or maladjusted
than non-witnesses (Zimmer 1984). The major relationship Zimmer uncovered is simply that witnesses were more likely to know someone else who had
sighted a UFO compared to non-witnesses.

This doesn't mean that more extreme psychopathology has no role to
play in the reporting of UFO sightings. People who claim to have experienced
intense encounters with UFOs, such as being abducted by aliens, certainly
show more psychopathological traits when completing psychological questionnaires (Parnell 1988). For example, they display a moderate elevation in
traits including interpersonal sensitivity, moral self-righteousness, suspicious-
ness, alienation/remoteness and creativity/schizotypy. We'll look at these types
of cases in more detail in the next chapter. Yet even the differences between
these intense witnesses and ordinary people aren't that large, certainly nothing
to really jump up and down about and say, "Here's the psychological answer

for a paranormal experience!" There's also the recurrent problem of directionality, as acknowledged by Parnell herself— perhaps a real encounter with aliens causes a personality change, rather than personality causing the encounter?

Cognitive deficits— Defining the concept of misinterpretation more rigorously, it might be proposed that paranormal illusions are caused by deficits in the witness's cognitive abilities, particularly the way they recognize stimuli confronting them. For example, witnesses might not be as good as other people in correctly distinguishing familiar objects — a problem with their *autobiographical memory* system. They might also display enhanced creativity when interpreting an ambiguous visual scene, which leads to suggestions of schizotypy. Furthermore, they might have a predisposition to confabulate the memory of what they actually saw following the encounter.

A study conducted at the University of Western Sydney set out to evaluate the cognitive abilities of people who reported frequent visual experiences with paranormal phenomena, particularly ghosts. Witnesses were tested to see how well they could remember pictures shown to them during a memory task and whether they were prone to embellishing the details of these pictures. The participants' results were then compared with the performance of a group of non-witnesses, and no differences existed between either group of people. In fact, witnesses seemed to be slightly (although non-significantly) better at recall on some of the tasks (Dear and Jinks 2005). Extrapolating this finding to real-life events, perhaps witnesses can't be accused of misinterpreting something as paranormal because they suffer from cognitive dysfunction, although there are plenty of other variables that weren't examined in this study which might account for their earlier sightings (presuming they were imaginary in the first place). It is more likely that if cognitive deficits, such as poor memory capacity, contribute to the generation of allegedly imaginary paranormal experiences, then they are problems that anyone can suffer if they're in the right (or wrong) place, at the right (or wrong) time.

"Misinterpretation" in the Normal Population

So, acknowledging the possibility that individual differences might contribute to paranormal illusions, it's more appropriate to accept that misinterpretations are widespread in the population and only a some people will ever give them a paranormal label. Carl Sagan would agree, stating that when people notice something strange in the sky, a minority become excitable, uncritical, and become bad witnesses (Sagan 1996). A sensible person unburdened by hysterical beliefs might see these aerial objects, or any other ambiguous stimulus, for what they are — aircraft, balloons, planets, clouds, lightning, meteors, "luminescent insects," satellites, or rockets — Sagan's list is excessive.

Alternately, the sensible person — perhaps with a high tolerance to ambiguity — might never know what they've seen, yet remain honest to themselves and acknowledge their sighting is unknown but "probably something normal" (Westrum 1977), perhaps using Sagan's list to help them with their assessment. Interestingly, the historical record shows a range eccentric but socially acceptable explanations for anomalous aerial objects. In the late 19th century, a meteorological theme was fashionable with scientifically-minded individuals (Corliss 1983). Back then, anything unusual seen in the sky was attributed to a bolide (meteor or fireball) or some unusual weather event — even when the objects were traveling more slowly than would be expected of a typical meteorological episode. These interpretations seem thoughtful and rational, but in principle it is not much different from someone concluding the object is a flying saucer — the observer in both cases likely makes the decision based only on whatever stock-set of popular explanations is available at the time.

Yet even contemporary, level-headed people can be (almost) misled and turn an ambiguous stimulus into a paranormal illusion. One of the more vocal critics of UFOs was the late Phil Klass. He claimed himself to have seen an indistinct aerial object shortly before he was about to give a lecture on, of all things, UFOs to the Seattle chapter of the Institute of Electrical and Electronics Engineers (Klass 1997). Outside the hall and talking to attendees, someone pointed to the sky and exclaimed "What's that?" Klass looked skywards and spied a small orange object hovering a few thousand feet above. Another witness said it looked like a kite, but Klass shot back that it was too high for a kite, and was more likely a weather balloon, reflecting the setting sun. Someone else suggested it wouldn't be a weather balloon, since it wasn't moving. This type of logical repartee is just what would have satisfied Carl Sagan. Binoculars were fetched, and on closer viewing Klass established the object to be a kite after all. The point of the story, Klass argues, it that had there not been a handy pair of binoculars available, then he might have had to acknowledge the object was a UFO (although knowing Klass' extreme skepticism, he never would have allowed himself the luxury of such a conclusion). By extension, it seems easy to imagine more susceptible people choosing the UFO option, with or without binoculars.

In support of the idea that some people would jump to a paranormal solution before a more rational one, Susan Blackmore and Rachel Moore identified a sample of paranormal believers and discovered they are more likely than non-believers to see images of things like horses, telephones or bicycles when shown an ambiguous picture that was distorted by a computer to make

In November 1995 the town hall in Wem, Shropshire, England, was ablaze. A photograph was taken by Tony O'Rahilly of the burning building, and when developed it appeared to show the ghost of a girl standing in an upper doorway. Typical of a famous ghost photograph, there are supporters who admire the quality of the apparition and sincerity of the photographer, and believe it to show one Jane Churn — a girl who lived in the town in the 17th century. At the time of its publication it was widely believed to be legitimate, although some skeptics considered the image to be a product of *pareidolia,* with burning material from the fire fortuitously resembling a child's face and torso — which seems a bit far-fetched in light of such clear features. In 2010 the story broke that a postcard from the 1920s had been discovered showing a similar-looking girl, and this was taken as evidence that O'Rahilly had cleverly inserted the likeness into his photograph, thereby instigating an infamous hoax. O'Rahilly died in 2005, adamant that the picture was genuine (Fortean Picture Library).

the contents more difficult to recognize. According to Blackmore and Moore, similar uncertain conditions are frequently encountered in real life, and include night-time or dim light (Blackmore and Moore 1994). These are the conditions where ghosts (and other strange things) are typically seen.

Creating Illusions: The Role of Encoding

Appreciating that paranormal beliefs play a role in creating paranormal illusions, it's worthwhile exploring how this might occur. A good place to start is by discussing our penchant for interpreting ambiguous things in terms of *perceptual set*. This is a predisposition towards a specific interpretive response, or a judgment about our present circumstances based on knowledge and beliefs collected throughout our lives (Reed 1972). Psychologist and NASA scientist Richard Haines makes the point that by the time we reach adulthood, we've catalogued in our memories a huge number of simple and complex ideas that we symbolize through words and actions (Haines 1980).

Put more forcefully, people don't necessarily see things for what they are. Rather, what they see is flavored by their unique upbringing. Such interpretations are not only cognitive, but also influenced by physiological needs. As long ago as the 1940s, psychologists discovered that the longer a person went without food, the greater the likelihood that an ambiguous picture they examined would be interpreted by them as an attractive food object (Murphy 1943). Therefore, our internal milieu (environment) also plays a role — as much as our perception of the external world — in generating illusions.

Psychologists often use the words *schema* and *script* to illustrate the properties of perceptual set. Briefly, a schema is the pre-conceived idea of how a situation should appear, whereas a script is a term to describe what should happen in that situation. Scripts and schemas serve a vital function in everyday life — it's very important to have ideas of what bathrooms or elephants should look like when you seen them, or what you should expect to happen when you visit a restaurant. This helps us to understand these objects and events implicitly when we encounter them recurrently through our lives. The problem is that while perceptual set — encompassing schemas and scripts — is a very convenient cognitive tool, it does tend to force individuals to perceive an object or incident as a whole, while causing them to ignore any inconsistent details that would allow more accurate recognition and understanding of that object or event. This leaves the individual prone to making errors of interpretation.

Sticking with the example of seeing a strange object in the sky, we might not be able to recognize it because we can't match it with something already in our memory. This is because the appropriate percepts, or the elements that make up our perceptual set, don't exist. Our brains instead might automatically encourage us to select an "off-the-shelf" schema for our peculiar circumstances — perhaps one that we developed after seeing a television show about flying saucers. Meanwhile, as we interpret the object through the prism of a flying saucer schema, our brains conveniently ignore the small, wing-like detail jutting out the back of the object that might identify it as a conventional airplane viewed at an awkward angle, or affected by some optical distortion arising from the atmosphere.

The Electronic Voice Phenomenon

Not all paranormal illusions are visual, or necessarily involve UFOs. An auditory example might include the *electronic voice phenomenon* (EVP). From the 1920s onwards, a variety of investigators (including Thomas Edison himself) experimented with special measuring equipment in the hope of recording the voices of the dead. In these early days, the record-cutters and wire recorders they used were somewhat primitive (Lampe 1993). However, by the mid–1950s reel-to-reel tape recorders were employed (Enns 2005), and by the late 1950s and early 1960s a Swede by the name of Friedrich Jurgenson had developed a method whereby he would leave a tape recorder with a blank tape running in an empty room. Typically, on play-back it was claimed that among all the crackly noise voices could be heard that would speak his name and answer questions he had put to them during the recording session.

The phenomenon was later investigated and publicized by the Latvian psychologist Konstantin Raudive, who made use of more sophisticated equipment to avoid picking up extraneous radio signals (Sorenson 1990). Although a number of researchers published work on the phenomenon, Raudive's books *The Inaudible becomes Audible* and *Breakthrough* would have to be the most famous in the field. Since these publications, other developments in EVP have been achieved, including a two-way contact device, whereby the alleged spirits can communicate in "real-time" with the investigator.[7]

Making use of the theory of illusions, critics claim that the practitioners of EVP are simply hearing what they expect to hear in random patterns of ambiguous sound. In this way, voices of the dead are no different from perceiving the shape of a UFO in a distant hazy object in the evening sky. Critics also point to the way practitioners freely admit to subjectivity in their judgments of what they hear from the tapes. For example, Raudive claims in *Breakthrough* that the spirit voices are difficult to understand because the language is often rapid, in a variety of languages, in the form of neologisms (new words without fixed meaning) or spoken in short "telegram-style" phrases without a fixed grammatical structure. It's therefore not surprising that practitioners frequently claim that a psychic gift is necessary to perceive the paranormal voices in an EVP recording.

The admission that EVP messages are prone to subjectivity leads to charges of wishful thinking. Like the automaticity of seeing the illusion of a face in a cloud, the EVP practitioner is deceived into hearing imaginary voices — an auditory illusion — because voices, like faces, are so familiar to us. Joe Banks, a sound artist interested in the procedure, describes some of Raudive's EVP voices as no more than short bursts of distorted noise mixed with high amounts of radio interference, coupled with the sound of the actual recording device picked up simultaneously by the microphone (Banks 2001).

Banks further suggests it's the haziness of the voices that gives them a mystique that wouldn't be achieved if they were crystal-clear. They would also be incredibly easy to fake. And even if the intentions of the EVP practitioner are honest, the chance of mistakenly identifying meaningfulness from a small "byte" of monosyllabic information expressed over a short period of time is much greater than from an equivalent stimulus lasting for a long period of time — even if there is plenty of noise in both stimuli. When such a mistake is made, the practitioner has indulged, in Banks' words, in *acoustic projection.*

On the other hand, a theory in support of the paranormality of EVP is that the spirit[8] has to accumulate enough energy before it can communicate as a voice. Apparently, the imparting of this energy comes in a burst — which accounts for the short length of the communication and the way it trails off to something inaudible, as though the energy has been rapidly depleted (Butler 2002).

In the same vein, an article in the *Journal of the Society for Psychical Research* written by Alexander MacRae describes his "Alpha" system — a machine that produces EVP more successfully than traditional tape-recordings of white noise and faint voices (MacRae 2004). Very simply, a person is attached to Alpha by means of electrodes which monitor electrodermal activity (changes in skin conductance). MacRae argues that the person hooked up to the system becomes an antenna, and the electrical signal from their skin is then passed through two voltage-controlled oscillators. These convert the signal into an actual vibration. One of the oscillators mimics the larynx (throat) and the other the vocal tracts. The two sets of vibrations are then combined and channeled through a radio receiver, making them audible. The result is sent through a microphone where it is recorded, with some noise reduction on the way to help make the final sound appear less messy. In other words, the electricity of a person's skin is given the characteristics of a voice.

Of course, you'd have to expect that the "voice" wouldn't actually speak any legitimate words. The noise might have the features of speech, but wouldn't say anything intelligible. MacRae, however, claims that recognizable words can be detected, and the person attached to the system doesn't have to be a medium with psychic powers. Apparently, anyone can act as the antenna for whatever is out there and physiologically (it is alleged) they can convert that energy into audible speech.

In an article published in the same journal in 2005, MacRae recounted how he isolated some of these short EVP utterances of about two seconds in duration and sent them as a sound file, via e-mail, to a group of thirty participants in five different countries. These people were required to listen to the utterances one at a time, and select what each "voice" was saying from a choice of five alternative written statements (four "decoy," one "correct"). He reports that the similarities among the participants' choices was so good that it was very unlikely to have been chance, the odds being billions and billions to one.

Could methodological faults cause this result? For instance, were the five alternative statements so different that it was easy for participants to select the "correct" one because only this statement possessed any resemblance to the jumbled noise on the sound file? MacRae maintained that the decoy statements were well constructed. Each statement had the same number of words (and within these corresponding words, phonemes) as the correct interpretation. Nor were the same phonemes used in the same places for decoy or correct statements, and even the rhythms and stresses of the phrases were as equivalent as possible. This was in order to make the decoy and correct interpretation indistinguishable from one another.

MacRae was also convinced that the people who evaluated the utterances weren't affected by a random auditory illusion. Although the utterances often sounded very silly they were so similar to a real verbal statement that any interpretation was unambiguous. A skeptic might concede that the utterances were voices, but nothing more than snippets of radio sounds, picked up on tape by accident (perhaps through the human antenna of the participant). To test this claim, MacRae prepared tape recordings using the Alpha system in a special Faraday room, where no radio waves could penetrate. Utterances were again isolated from the recordings and sent to seven of the best participants from the earlier study. They were required to analyze the fragments of speech in the usual way, and again were successful in picking the correct statement from the decoy (concurrence of their choice by chance being one in two hundred and seventy seven billion, billion, billion, billion). A subsequent control study, which presented to the same participants random noises passed off as "real utterances," was not successful. That is, no participant claimed to hear coherent spoken words in the random noise.

MacRae's conclusion was that something paranormal is occurring, although he makes no claim as to what actually causes the voices. Since they

Latvian psychologist Konstantin Raudive, pictured here in the early 1970s with equipment used to record the electronic voice phenomenon (EVP). Raudive's books *The Inaudible Becomes Audible* and *Breakthrough* are arguably the most famous in the field on EVP research (Mary Evans Picture Library).

are recordable they're worth studying. Skeptics might nonetheless remain unconvinced of these results and would consider methodological flaws to be at play somewhere in McRae's work (the historically popular claim for laboratory psi studies). Consequently, the voices are either mundane radio signals, or are auditory illusions from meaningless white noise. There's not much in the way of compromise when taking a hard skeptical stance.

Continuing with the theme of paranormal sounds, the rappings from poltergeists in actual haunted locations have also been studied scientifically. In one case, Barrie Colvin compared recordings of rappings from a famous poltergeist case in 1974 — the Andover case[9] — with control rapping sounds such as knuckles tapping on brick walls and plasterboard, teaspoons tapping glass and a rubber hammer striking a wooden desk and other hard objects (Colvin 2010). A control rap displayed a rapid rise in soundwave strength, then a gradual decline to nothing. The frequency of the wave depends on the material that's been rapped, be it wood or glass. It seems the "unexplained" raps from poltergeist cases also come in a range of frequencies, but were much slower to rise to a maximum strength. Ruling out variations in the methods used to record the mysterious raps which may have accounted for the signal delay, Colvin makes the fascinating claim that the unusual acoustic pattern shown by paranormal raps is consistent across samples recorded across a variety of historical poltergeist cases — not just the example from Andover.

Covin's suggestion, which really has nothing to do with psychology but is interesting enough to include here, is that the maximum vibration of the component molecules of a normally rapped object occurs at maximum energy transfer (the point at which one object hits another), and this results in an immediate, maximum sound. Conversely, in a "paranormal rapping" the noises emanate from deep within the material being paranormally rapped, the molecules increasing their vibration rate to the point where the stress is released as an audible sound. Not unexpectedly, the source of such rappings is still unexplained. Perhaps they indicate that not all auditory events of a paranormal nature are illusions?

Convenient Verbal Labels

Returning to visual illusions, it's been determined that people take longer to identify details of an ambiguous object than an easily recognized one (Westrum 1977) and this can been shown in a very simple demonstration. A red ace of spades doesn't exist in a conventional deck of playing cards, but if one is specially created for a psychology experiment and shown to a group of participants, they'll take longer to see it for what it is compared to the true card, a black ace of spades. Given enough time, the audience will collectively say "Hey, it's a red ace of spades ... how weird." However, they need that additional time to discount any *obstructive presuppositions* they might hold (a manifestation of their own, interfering perceptual set) and arrive at the correct judgment. If they're shown the mock card only briefly, they might come to truly believe on some later occasion — quite wrongly — that they'd been shown a black ace of spades to begin with.

This phenomenon adds an additional element to the misinterpretation hypothesis. We've already seen how, if viewing something ambiguous from a distance (like Phil Klass's kite) we frequently interpret it using processes such as our perceptual set. However, if the ambiguous object we're looking at appears only briefly, then we don't even have enough time to leisurely construct an appropriate interpretation. Rather, we grab a readily-available, off-the-shelf label for what we're seeing, based on years and years of experience. You don't even have to rate high in transliminality — everyone is prone to labeling what they see or hear. An example would be the way you might use "elephant-like" as an appropriate term to describe something you fleetingly saw with four legs, a trunk and big ears. All you would be left with, after the animal has disappeared, is a rapidly diminishing image in memory of a shape, a few odd details and perhaps a name for what you think you saw. Combined, these can have a great influence on what you later recall.[10]

If the event you've experienced is highly unusual — paranormal perhaps, then the label "UFO," "ghost," "vampire," or "demon" might pop into your head. These words might consist of very few letters, but they're loaded with all sorts of connotations of how the encounter should pan out, look or behave. There's even a strongly supported psychological assumption that the small number of details you might have remembered about the original event will be distorted by any verbal label you might give it. This will irreversibly affect how you remember the event in the future. Psychologists skeptical of paranormal claims refer to a wealth of scientific findings to support their assumption that the witness has made an encoding error with regards to their experience.

One such study is by the Italian psychologists Lara Pelizzon, Maria Brandimonte and Riccardo Luccio, who found that participants supplying a name to an obscure visual stimuli — one that doesn't actually look like anything — suffer interference with subsequent memory performance for these visual shapes (Pelizzon, Brandimonte and Luccio 2002). This interference is called *verbal overshadowing*, meaning the verbal label that participants "force" onto the picture actually distorts, but doesn't completely remove, an accurate encoding of the picture to memory. The implication for paranormal experience is that if witnesses apply inappropriate but unavoidable verbal labels to their sighting (such as "ghost" or "demon"), it will affect whatever they remember of the event, and mistakenly turn it into something extraordinary when it isn't.

Admittedly, not all studies show verbal interference worsens memory. There is some evidence that applying a label may actually improve memory. For example, when participants in a psychology laboratory are shown ambiguous pictures and then asked to recall the details of the pictures, their memory can be occasionally facilitated if meaningful verbal labels were given alongside the pictures (e.g., Bower, Karlin and Dueck 1975, De Santis and Haude 1993). This is because stimuli given a meaningful interpretation are recognized more easily than nonsense patterns (Wiseman and Neisser 1974). However, these results pertain only to visual stimuli that — while ambiguous — can be provided with correct labels. When labels are inaccurate, recall may suffer (Steinfeld 1967).

Similarly, if the stimulus is truly ambiguous and no correct label is available, then there's no memory improvement. This was demonstrated as long ago as 1906 when a member of the psychological laboratory at Clark University[11] named Frederick Kuhlmann participated in his own experiment. This involved him recalling and re-drawing meaningless pictures he'd previously shown himself. However, to make things more difficult, he made sure these pictures possessed features resembling familiar things. Kuhlmann found he couldn't help but distort his new drawings so they ended up looking like these familiar things, and not the original pictures. These original pictures also had no correct label — they were truly ambiguous — so the interpretation Kuhlmann gave his drawings were by definition incorrect, and recall was made worse by prior knowledge and expectation.

Applying these, albeit early, experimental findings to claims of paranormal experience, psychologists might assert that while a "paranormal" interpretation may act as a label for a mysterious experience, this label is by its very nature incorrect. That is, the experience is not of a ghost, or a vampire, or a fairy at all, and recall of the event by the witness will be poorer than if the label wasn't used — a claim that has been empirically verified over 100 years of research.

This is not to imply that paranormal labels are more likely to result in an illusion compared with mundane labels. When a group of participants are shown a truly ambiguous picture described by the experimenter as a UFO and are required to draw it from memory, they are no worse at remembering the picture's details than participants who were told the same picture was an airplane, or who weren't provided a label for the picture. Nor did they add more details to the drawings they recreated from memory (Steiner and Jinks 2006). Whether this effect applies to real-life sightings, when emotions are running high, is another question. Do real witnesses remember accurately what they see? Do they distort just the peripheral details, or completely mistake the fundamental details of their sighting, leading to an encoded memory that's seriously unrepresentative of what really happened?

It is known that children can fundamentally alter central aspects of events they've experienced (Bruck and Ceci 2007), however the degree to which adults remember paranormal events differently to normal events needs more dedicated research. Nevertheless, Richard Haines remarks that on occasions people misinterpret a weather balloon as a flying saucer, but go on to describe the shape of the weather balloon quite well (Haines 1980). He gives the example of an incident in the U.S. in 1970 when passengers of a commercial airplane reported a flying orange elephant outside their windows. This sounded ridiculous, but later investigations found that an advertising balloon used to promote a circus, of exactly that shape and color, had broken free and was drifting at 36,000 feet. Maybe the results found in the psychological laboratory don't match how people witness unusual events after all?

Factors That Influence Sensory Encoding

Even if there's only minimal sensory input there might still be a desire for the witness to interpret what they think they've seen, or felt, or heard. The stimuli might be barely perceptible, perhaps emanating from the witness themselves, and allows for an illusions of the paranormal to be generated. A curious example would be the way people might attribute subtle but normal body functions such as goose-pimples, or a soft "ringing" in the ears (perhaps caused by tinnitus — internally derived auditory sensations), to the brief touch or voice of a deceased spirit.

In addition to mistakenly interpreting ambiguous stimuli as potentially paranormal, James Houran suggests that *contextual variables* also combine with a witness's state of arousal to determine the nature of this interpretation (Houran 2000). These are variables that exist in the context of the experience, and which interact with the witness's perceptual set to influence the encoding sequence of the memory for the event. For instance, a dark night (the contextual variable) molds with anxiety (the percipient's state of arousal) and their expectations of what should happen on dark nights (perceptual set) to increase the likelihood that something paranormal will be encountered. Another set of variables are the *demand characteristics* of a situation or location. For instance, how would you feel, driving along a lonely road at night, if you were aware of its reputation for roadside apparitions? Perhaps you'd be more likely to misinterpret the moon shining on a fencepost as a shimmering phantom hitchhiker, waiting for another lift? As a consequence, you've conformed to the demands of the situation. Another possibility could be the unnerving thoughts that enter your mind as you stand on an ancient and mysterious earth mound called "Devil's Barrow," or climb the bleak slopes of "Hangman's Hill." You might also encounter *embedded cues,* subtle components of a situation that you don't consciously recognize but nevertheless influence the way you encode and later remember it. For instance, you might not actually be aware of the spooky flickering candles in the dark hallway of a haunted house, but they are subconsciously perceived and processed, and this will influence your interpretation of the shadows around you as ghosts.

Séance environments are wonderful sources of contextual variables, and have the added bonus of *suggestion.* In one of the many studies that Richard Wiseman and colleagues have conducted on paranormal topics, the researchers took paranormal believers to a contrived sitting and found they are more open to suggestion than non-believers. For example, they readily report the movement of an object, such as a handbell, on the séance table in a darkened room. This is in spite of the fact that it never actually moved. The movement was only suggested to the sitters by the experimenters, through statements such as "That's good, the bell is moving now, lift the bell up, that's good" (Wiseman, Greening and Smith 2003).

Wiseman and Greening show a similar impact of suggestion on a participant's belief that a PKMB demonstration is real. Shown a video of a fabricated spoon-bending demonstration, participants who were informed that the spoon was still bending — when it wasn't — later claimed very confidently that they'd seen it bend. From these results, Wiseman and Greening conclude that you simply can't trust the testimony of people claiming to have experienced psychokinetic events.

Creating Illusions: The Role of Recall

We've discussed how our memory of something we see or hear might be altered by cognitive processes such as our perceptual set at the time of encoding. Likewise, when we recall the experience interfering variables (such as verbal label) can affect this process to the extent that the resultant memory is not an original, impartial and completely accurate analysis of what happened.

And like encoding, memory alterations are linked to the witness' belief system. For example, paranormal believers are more susceptible, during a "paranormal event," to notice things around them that conform to their expectations of what they think is happening (Lange, Houran and Harte 1996). Wiseman and Morris go further to suggest that the effect of prior belief on accurate recall of the experience might be even more important (Wiseman and Morris 1995). In one study, "goats" and "sheep" were shown an alleged psychic demonstration on video. However, when asked later about the content of the video the participants recall the event in entirely different ways. The goats, for example, retrieved more relevant information as evidence that sleight-of-hand, or trickery, occurred during the demonstration. The sheep didn't show this degree of accuracy. The insinuation is that even though the two types of participants encode the same information when they see it, they make judgments about the importance of that material in different ways when asked to remember it. As time passes, the information judged less important by the "sheep" (for instance, evidence of fraud) will be more quickly forgotten than by "goats."

The time period between the alleged paranormal event and its recall might also be filled with all sorts of additional, interfering information. As a consequence, later testimony is considered highly unreliable. Debate has raged for many years about whether a memory is completely overwritten by a new one when additional information is processed (so called *storage-based* accounts), or whether the memory is still somewhere "in the brain" but simply harder to access — due perhaps to competition with other, rival memories (termed *retrieval-based* accounts) (Windschitl 1996).

Nevertheless (and whatever the actual process occurring), it's widely accepted that the length of time between an event and its recall has fundamental implications for witnessed paranormal experiences. Imagine that many years ago you were walking in a forest at about midday when you entered a clearing and saw a strange silver object sitting on the grass. You became scared and ran away from it, then forgot all about the incident. As years pass, you learn more about UFOs and spaceship landings and all the extraterrestrial paraphernalia that goes with the topic. You also think back to your strange encounter. The additional knowledge then becomes irreversibly associated with your vague and distant memory, so that each time you try to recall what happened the event becomes more and more typical of a UFO landing.

If you'd been asked, 10 minutes after the original sighting, what the shape of the object was, you might reply, "It was sort of round-ish, and a bit lop-sided." However, you weren't committed you to such a statement at the time, and you never wrote down or drew what you saw. If you had, your statement or picture might have been encoded alongside the memory image to help keep the experience quite close to the original percept. Instead, when asked the same question 10 years later following a decade of exposure to UFO-lore, you now claim the object was "Oval-shaped, like a football on its side. It was perfectly symmetrical.... I think it had little legs attached, like landing gear."

In a set of clever experiments, psychologists Katharine Holden and Christopher French demonstrate how these types of *false memories* can be formed by just about anyone (Holden and French 2002). They showed participants a list of related words, such as *thread, sew* and *pin*. Later, many of these same participants claimed the word *needle* was present in the list, when it wasn't. Their memory has been distorted by later judgment. Similar studies demonstrating this interference of recall have been around since the late 1950s (Roediger and McDermott 1995). By association, paranormal experients would surely be prone to a similar style of cognitive error, especially when many of their stories emerge months, if not years, after the actual event?

Therefore, it's common for psychologists to use research findings from *memory cognition* experiments to explain any complicated anomalous experience that a witness recalls from their past. It is easy to conclude that people are mistaken because their memories of a ordinary object or event are intrinsically unreliable, and worsen as the years pass.

On reflection, there are two awkward points that arise from this assumption. Firstly, cognitive theories apply equally well to potential memories for weird events that might be given a mundane label by the witness. What if you saw the strange silvery object in the woods and ran away, but later assumed (rightly or wrongly) that it was nothing more than a silver car parked among the trees since "you don't believe in the paranormal." The label of *car*, and your hostility towards UFOs, should influence encoding and recall as much as a *UFO* tag and UFO belief (assuming there's no emotional difference attached to these two words, which there well might be). In future years you laughingly recall the flat hood, angular windshield and perhaps the hint of a wheel, then shake your head when describing how you stupidly ran away from it. If that's the case, how can we be sure that the airplane you saw in the sky last week wasn't an ambiguous object forced into a mundane explanation? Was it a real UFO? This argument seems trivial, but it does make the point that theories of memory distortion can be a double-edged sword. Perhaps a witness's report of a flying saucer can't be ridiculed without doubting the veracity of another incident where they were confident that what they saw "must have been an airplane"? That is, unless one is completely certain that truly anomalous UFOs cannot exist. In that case, errors in memory cognition remain a powerful implement in your skeptical toolbox.

Secondly, while people certainly make mistakes encoding and recalling their strange experiences, this doesn't necessarily negate the core experience. Your memory for what you might have seen in the forest all those years ago has most certainly altered a bit over the intervening time — that's clear from the wealth of published psychological research. However, there was still a core experience possessing enough detail for you to notice the object's large size, unusual color and definite shape. Sometimes you'll also notice details (such as protuberances or sections in the body of different color). The sighting was obviously remarkable enough for you to run away — after all, fear of the unknown is perfectly normal. Later, you might come to believe it was a UFO (which really could look like anything, since the term contains the word *unidentified*), or assume it was a car, or a crashed weather balloon, or an elephant spray-painted for an advertising campaign. One of these might be correct, or they might all be horribly wrong. The fact is, unless you've hallucinated the incident the conclusion would have to be that you did see something.[12] Consequently, we have to be careful not to dismiss all reports of strange events or encounters simply on the basis that human memory has been shown to suffer from confabulation over time.

Social Contagion and Collective Visions

Discussion so far has examined how and why individuals are prone to experience illusions of the paranormal. This tends to gloss-over explanations of how groups of people are able to make the same psychological error. For decades, a *social contagion* theory has been proposed by some psychologists to explain waves or flaps of sightings, where lots of people see UFOs or experience other paranormal events such as poltergeist infestations or monster hauntings at a specific location over a short period of time. To the scientific psychologist, there is no legitimate, external cause for the symptoms. Therefore, the experience must have derived from one person, then spread throughout their community like a "psychological virus."

Outbreaks of sickness in schools and workplaces that cannot be traced to any organic source are famous examples of social contagion (e.g., Rockney and Lemke 1992). One famous documented case comes from North Carolina in 1962, where factory workers reported symptoms of pain, nausea and disorientation after suffering insect bites. No trace of an insect was found, and the phenomenon was eventually labeled *psychogenic* following an investigation (Kerckhoff, Back, and Miller 1965). Explanations vary, but one theory is that a country's population sometimes experiences an increase in their "collective" arousal levels. An example could be during a time of national crisis. This arousal, coupled with shared personality factors, such as boredom or an authoritarian group dynamic, or perhaps poor inter-group communication, leads individuals in the population to attribute reasons for their heightened arousal state. Consequently, a widespread delusion of illness might result (Olkinuora 1984). Another famously documented type of social or hysterical contagion are "mad gasser" type attacks, where a mysterious man attacks (but does not seriously hurt) someone in their home by spraying them with a mysterious "gas." Soon reports of the same type of attack spread far and wide (the archetypal example occurred in Illinois in 1944). Again, the attacks seldom have any long term effect, and the "gasser" is never caught.

It is popularly assumed that the Cold War engendered a type of mass hysteria in the U.S., and this manifested as an increase in UFO sightings — although UFO supporters argue that the "waves" occurring during this period were either halfway through, or even over, before the reports received any national publicity (e.g., Vallee and Vallee 1966, Randle 1999). Nevertheless, social contagion remains a popular explanation for multiple sighting cases of all sorts of shapes and sizes over long periods, where the stimulus that generates reports itself is not unusual, but the collective explanation is. It accounts for reports from locals in a small town of a dark ghostly shape that follows travelers on a local road, or from suburban residents visited by strange men and women who don't seem to be quite human, and who ask weird questions before disappearing without a trace.[13]

However, social contagion theory is perhaps less capable of explaining how groups of people give the same detailed description of a paranormal event at the same time and place, although the answer may once again lie with the power of a verbal label. Sociologists have proposed that once such a label, which might be "UFO" or "flying saucer" becomes a pervasive concept in a society, it is possible for people to imagine seeing one in advance of the actual experience (Westrum 1977). Of course, according to these mainstream theorists there's no such thing as a real UFO, so the concept is simply a *social con-*

struction. If people are aware of UFOs they might want to go and look for one, staring at the sky in a way they've never done before. Lo and behold, they start seeing quite normal objects they've never seen before (the planet Venus is a favorite[14]) and these become a real UFO sighting. Pointing at the sky in the company of other people, the episode starts to resemble Phil Klass' story, where multiple witnesses become affected by the contagion and partake in the illusion.

Psychologists apply the tag *collective delusion* to this outcome, created when an initial witness describes something they see in an ambiguous situation, and convinces others around them to see the image too. I've a local case on file from 1997 which involves a 19-year-old man (Steve) who was convinced he saw a Yowie[15] in an Australian bush gully.

Describing with high emotion the shaggy hair, large hands and big feet of the creature to three accompanying friends, two of the three also began to see a Yowie. They even voiced their concern that the creature would run up the hill and attack them all. The third male friend (Jim) could not see anything, and with some contempt climbed down to the tree where the Yowie allegedly stood, looking around to see where it was. Nothing materialized. Needless to say, Steve and the two friends were embarrassed and wouldn't discuss the false sighting further. Jim still remembers the detailed description of the Yowie his friends gave, in a growing state of panic, as their illusionary creature took shape before their eyes.

This mistake occurs because, apart from all the contextual cues present, the suggestive nature of the sensational label "Yowie," and the accompanying description from an eyewitness, can only assist a hesitant bystander make sense of the ambiguous environment that surrounds them. Perhaps when a person's "unconscious" brain has trouble recognizing reality, it is grateful for any outside suggestions to guide it, even if this ultimately means the creation of an illusion. Some psychologists would argue that this process is very individual and unique, and explains why not everyone present during a ghostly manifestation (or any other paranormal event) sees the apparition.[16] Some people are simply more open to suggestion than others.

On a much larger scale, mass sightings throughout history of the Virgin Mary (*Marian* events) are also claimed by some psychologists to be collective delusions. The premier example is the consecutive visions of an entity purported to be Mary at Fatima, in Portugal, in 1917. When thousands turned up to a muddy field one morning expecting to see Mary, and someone in the crowd pointed to an ambiguous light display near a cork tree, psychologists would expect bystanders to claim a shared illusion. The same psychologists would have to find another explanation for the initial, strange luminous stimulus which triggered the vision in the first place (at the worst, they could always claim, a little unfairly perhaps, that the original witness was mentally ill and hallucinating what they saw). Consequently, collective delusion offers a plausible explanation for why the details of a group sighting might be reasonably consistent among witnesses. When the rumor is of a woman, people start seeing a woman (Mary). When the rumor grows that the same woman is holding an infant, people will start to see Jesus, and so on.

I should note that not every psychologist or interested researcher has the same opinion on what happened at Fatima. Apparently the original descriptions of Mary from the main experients, three local peasant children, were somewhat "unMarylike." Their portrayal was simply of a young human lady, and from the cryptic remarks she made the children assumed she was Mary. Witnesses to the later manifestations of Mary at fatima mainly reported watching a spinning, multicolored light. The ambiguity of Marian visions led some theorists to even believe they were anomalous events (such as a UFO landing, or a fairy sighting) given a theological interpretation by an expectant and highly religious crowd.

Is the "Illusion" Hypothesis Enough to Account for Paranormal Experience?

Can the illusion hypothesis account for most, if not all, paranormal sightings? From the perspective of mainstream psychology, there's no doubt that what a witness sees is uncontrollably influenced by pervasive individual differences, and these can affect encoding and later recall of the encounter. The illusion hypothesis is therefore strong when accounting for reports of brief, vague ghostly shapes in houses, or a Bigfoot that's seen slinking into the trees far away across the valley. Nocturnal lights and daylight disc reports are also prone to this illusionary manipulation. The former is the most common UFO sighting — a small to medium light in the sky which really could be anything, but is believed to be a flying saucer. The latter tend to be small, shiny silver aerial shapes that appear and disappear rather quickly. They are more intriguing than mere lights, but again not terribly suggestive of something truly weird.

Many years ago, I personally experienced something that might be considered a type of paranormal illusion — a big black leopard slinking into the trees across a valley, in a country where there shouldn't be leopards at all, except in zoos. From where I stood I saw an animal about the size of my outstretched thumb at arm's length. That's still big enough to pick up considerable detail, and although the sighting only lasted a few seconds, I knew immediately what it was. Like everyone else I've seen leopards on TV, in books, and at the

Doreen Kendall, a nurse at the Cowichan District Hospital on Vancouver Island, opened the curtains in her ward at dawn on New Year's Day 1970 and was struck by a brilliant light emanating from a clear object only 60 feet away and hovering above the children's ward. As the illustration by Brian James shows, there were two male figures in the craft with bodies and heads encased in close-fitting dark material. Operating instruments on the panel to their front, one of the crewmen noticed Doreen and the craft began to wobble and move away. Doreen, who wasn't the least bit frightened during her sighting, seemed to snap out of her fixation and called another nurse to see the object. This nurse saw only a large bright light, without any of the features, before it took off. The degree of detail (and elegance) in the sighting makes it hard to apply the illusion hypothesis to this case. Putting aside the possibility that what she saw was really what she saw, psychologists would need to utilize more sophisticated models of perception and cognition to account for Doreen's otherworldly experience (Mary Evans Picture Library).

zoo. It must have been a big animal, and the most memorable feature was the leopard-like tail that had that kink on the end. There was no question in my mind about ambiguity — it was a completely unambiguous stimulus, to use the psychological phrase.

Now, a panther sighting in the Australian bush isn't necessarily paranormal ... although they're not native to the country, one of them could be captured tomorrow, and there's a degree of acceptance that these animals do exist, for whatever reason (zoo escapees is a popular solution). Nevertheless, these reports elicit almost the same kind of reaction from the skeptic as an alien abduction would, or a vision of an angel. One of the "solutions" I was offered was that the cat was an illusion — nothing more that the shadow of a tree, blowing around on an otherwise windless day. But wait — surely the moving shadow of a tree would have stayed roughly in the same place, to be viewed over and over again? And if I had unconsciously and instantaneously remolded the tree into a panther, then I'm deeply concerned. Are my perceptual systems so prone to error that I can't trust what I know I saw? Can I trust anything I see? Am I actually alive, or it this all a weird dream? You get the drift.

My argument is that if a witness "umms" and "aaaahs" and is prepared to concede the stimulus they encountered might have been ambiguous then misinterpretation is certainly a possibility. If, however, they are adamant about what they saw then apart from them committing an outright lie or being delusional (which is a possibility ... and might still apply to my panther sighting) perhaps their story deserves a closer look?

There's a lovely UFO case from Canada in 1970 showing just how detailed a paranormal sighting can be. To keep the story short, Doreen Kendall, a nurse on a hospital nightshift, drew the blinds of the ward early one morning to see a UFO. It was an exceedingly close-range and detailed image, right down to the steering lever one of the occupants was apparently manipulating on the control panel. Their stool-like seats were also visible through the clear cupola. This sighting is far more comprehensive, and mysterious, than my bush-leopard. Skeptics are unlikely to be impressed with Doreen's report, and dismiss it as complete nonsense. That's easy if you are happy to indulge in *ad hominem* attacks (Doreen was a liar, or tired, or bereaved, etc). However, if you're a more principled psychologist happy to accept she isn't fibbing but didn't really see what she said she saw, then you'll have to concede that an illusion is pretty unlikely. You'll have to delve a little deeper into the storehouse of psychological theories to find your answer.

CHAPTER 4

Witnessing the Paranormal: "Everyday" Hallucinations

Impersonal paranormal sightings refer to things seen from a distance, where there is no apparent interaction between the perceiver and the perceived. Examples would include viewing a distant UFO in the sky, although such cases are often explained away as hoaxes, and illusionary misinterpretations (Hynek 1966). Reports of "monster" or "fairy" sightings also sound so completely ridiculous that most people would have to consider them either fabrications or a product of mental illness. The same applies to more personal (intense) paranormal events where the witness is very close to, or part of, the encounter. So if fabrication is suggested as a potential solution, it's worthwhile paying some attention to the possibility, especially where there's a psychological angle involved.

A Brief Note on Hoaxing

Hoaxing, as you might expect, refers to a witness either making up the story of their encounter for some reason, or who (unknown to them) has been tricked by someone else into believing something extraordinary has happened. There's no doubt that such fabrications and hoodwinking have played a part — perhaps a large part — in reports of the paranormal for over 100 years. In earlier chapters, we've seen examples of cheating in parapsychology, and there are also examples of hoaxing in everything from ghost stories to the claims of seers.

It's more than likely a skeptical book covering paranormal topics has a chapter on UFOs, and there's frequently a hoax or two used as an example. In particular, the "contactee" reports of the 1950s and 1960s make many respectable UFO researchers cringe, and serves as a way of discrediting the

UFO field through humor. Typically, a contactee was a middle aged American male (often with a European background) who reported multiple meetings with beings from a flying saucer. The beings were typically Nordic-looking humans, both male and female, and very beautiful. They'd take the contactee on trips to their home planet, for example Venus or Clarion (allegedly a planet behind the Moon, invisible from Earth) and would lecture the contactee on matters such as the obvious dangers of nuclear war.

Some contactees were discovered to be hoaxers, but not all. Some seemed to be honest visionaries, experiencing a quasi-religious fairy-tale of utopia. Nonetheless, this dreamy justification cuts no favor with the skeptic, who does not distinguish between fabrication by lying and fabrication by delusion. In the modern development of otherworldly contact — alien abductions — evidence of hoaxing can also be found with enough imagination and investigative prowess.

Naturally not every weird monster encounter, ghost story or alien abduction can be forced into the hoaxing mold. And from the perspective of this book there's not too much one can say about the psychology of hoaxing, other than some people might be prone to hoaxing due to their own unique blend of personality factors, or an underlying psychopathology. A fairer and more sophisticated psychological perspective on intense paranormal encounters involves the study of hallucinations — something anyone can experience.

Hallucinations, Mental Illness and Paranormal Experience

Making use of our earlier definition of consciousness, hallucinations occur when "imaginative representations" mistakenly intrude into the *running world model* of a person's *integrated global representation*. Recall that the integrated global representation corresponds to the inner (bodily) environment and the outer world of physical reality. The running world model is the "here and now" of that representation. Practically, this definition is just a fancy way of saying that when people hallucinate, they perceive something as real which is in fact derived from imagination in the absence of an actual physical stimulus. Note there's an important difference between hallucinations and illusions, because we've already learned that the latter involves a real stimulus for the encounter. It's just that the stimulus was misinterpreted by the witness.

An additional feature of hallucinations is that they're not under the witness's control, hence a daydream isn't a hallucination because the daydreamer ostensibly can stage-manage the content of their vision. Nor can those experiences which appear to be authentic, but have an element of unreality about them, be considered hallucinations. For example, a person might find themselves, for whatever reason, deep in conversation with Oliver Cromwell while possessing enough rationality to accept that he died in 1658. This is known as a *quasi-hallucination* or *pseudohallucination,* on account of the fact that the hallucinator appreciates the experience is not real (Kasper, Kasper, Pauli and Stefan 2010). And while extraordinary, it doesn't involve a total departure from reality (Zanarini and Gunderson 1990). Nevertheless, it remains difficult for clinicians to practically distinguish between these states and so-called true hallucinations (Yee, Korner, McSwiggan, Meares and Stevenson 2005).

Most paranormal experiences seem, to the experient, to be *as real-as-real.* This implies a true hallucination, assuming they are hallucinations, and puts the event in league with psychedelic drug use, delirious fever and of course, mental illness.

Psychopathology and Hallucination

Psychopathologies such as schizophrenia possess a hallucinatory element, voices in the head being a widely quoted symptom. Alternately, a *dissociative state*— perhaps derived from an early life trauma — also allows the intrusion into consciousness of hallucinated phenomena that are accepted as real. These visions could include seemingly authentic (but imaginary) human beings. In one case discussed by author Hilary Evans, a 25-year-old woman named Ruth was persistently visited by the real-as-real hallucination of her father. It was alleged that the father had sexually abused Ruth when she was 10, and for obscure psychological reasons Ruth's subconscious hallucinated her father's apparition. The hallucination also acted autonomously. For example, he interacted with the environment around him (sitting on a chair in a room) and with other people — although these people were unaware of his presence. Interestingly, Ruth could also summon her father at will, which gave her psychiatrist, Morton Schatzman, a chance to perform some clever experiments to test whether Ruth was actually seeing something objectively real. On one occasion, Ruth "called up" her father in front of a light placed there by Schatzman. The psychiatrist was able to confirm, from studying the reactivity of Ruth's pupils, that the imaginary father wasn't obscuring the passage of light. That is, physiologically Ruth was responding to an actual light source like anyone else, but her hallucinatory experience was overriding the entry of that world into her consciousness (Evans 1984).

If members of the family can be conjured up as hallucinations, then why can't individuals invoke elves, fairies, witches, angels or aliens? Alien abduction is popular research topic in psychology, so it's not surprising that a mountain of theories have been derived to account for the many abduction stories collected over the last 50 years. Since the syndrome is so complicated, it is commonly held that it must be hallucinatory. Mere illusion could not account for the loss of reality that accompanies the journey into an other-worldly spacecraft. This is because the typical alien abduction scenario is quite complex, and involves elements including the victim being paralyzed by nonhuman beings (sometimes but not always identified as ET aliens), taken to an unfamiliar environment (sometimes but not always identified as a spaceship) and experiencing a physical examination often involving the extraction of bodily samples (e.g., blood or semen). Also regularly reported are a post-examination tour of the ship and a lecture on a variety of topics, such as Earth's imminent ecological collapse.

Now, most psychologists would dismiss the very idea of alien abductions as ridiculous, and would simply use mental illness as the quickest and most convenient explanation before moving on to something more sane. Others, while not necessarily agreeing to the literal reality of the abduction account, are hesitant to suggest that all such stories are the product of a psychopathological state, or are hallucinations. Rather, when a person confesses to having been abducted, a more measured psychological position is that the subject is re-telling some type of pseudomemory which has been created from a combination of personality, cognitive and situational factors. The latter might involve anything from the victim being in a state of hypnosis while being asked leading questions, or their abduction story being supported by the authority figure performing the hypnosis (Newman and Baumeister 1996a, b).

In practice, imagine one early morning you witness an ambiguous shape scooting through the bedroom door as you wake up. Because of your predetermined set of abduction beliefs, you immediately interpret the experience as an alien visitation. Consequently, you seek out an expert with a title in front of his or her name in a hope of drawing out more information about what happened, and they agree to hypnotize you, subsequently encouraging the belief that the abductors were aliens from a Pleiadian[1] scoutship. These expert possesses their own pre-existing beliefs about the topic, known as *interviewer bias*. An example of biased interviewing practice is to structure questions in such a way that only assenting answers can be given to whatever topic the interviewer in seeking to confirm, while avoiding questions which might undermine the legitimacy of those answers (Bruck and Ceci 2007). If the interviewer is a great supporter of extraterrestrial aliens, a question might be "Did the *alien* look small and grey, with big almond eyes?" They would be unlikely to ask whether the shape you saw had ghostly characteristics, or was recognizably human.

Susan Blackmore sums up this position by suggesting that abductees create false memories of an experience though a combination of ambiguous information, "diffuse physical sensations," and "vivid imaginings" (Blackmore 1998). There's no need to resort to an explanation as extreme as hallucination.

Escape-from-self

Another intriguing psychological explanation for alien abductions, which does have a hallucinatory component, was developed by psychologists Len Newman and Roy Baumeister. They propose that abductees are demonstrating *escape-from-self*, a term that describes the periodic denial of their own ego (Newman and Baumeister 1996). In their opinion, abductions are fantasies derived from the stress of constructing a *sense of self* (that is, who we are), which we all experience at some time or another but which in highly unpalatable to certain people. To such people, escaping from the burden of maintaining self-esteem, or the need for social control, creates a sense of relief, and this can be achieved by traveling to an imaginary world where aliens have complete dominance over them.

The periodic escaping from the self has been applied to situations that aren't paranormal, where people really do allow themselves to be restrained, displayed naked to strangers and humiliated at the whim of others. In this view, alien abductions have a lot in common with more standard masochistic fantasies and practices such as bondage. To Newman and Baumeister, the trigger for the escape might involve a recent incident where something humiliating has happened to the abductee. Alternately, the abductee might hold a high-pressure job whereby they are constantly expected to be in control and responsible ... and successful.

In this way, Newman and Baumeister suggest that abductees should often have very successful professional lives, which require a great deal of self-control to maintain. The abduction then becomes an occasional masochistic escape from such a burden, and the strange and frequent gratitude the victims show to their "captors" is suggestive of a purpose served.

Nethertheless, Jamie Arndt and Jeff Greenberg from the University of Arizona criticize the need to complicate alien abduction syndrome with such complex psychological theories, claiming there are simpler ways to escape the concept of self-image than having a "one-off" abduction experience.[2] These include joining an organization which wears a uniform, giving allegiance to a leader or cause, or even going on holiday (Arndt and Greenberg 1996).[3] A further criticism of the escape-from-self proposal, this time made by supporters of the abduction experience, is that "real" abductees often try to do anything but be kidnapped by their aliens so the event isn't serving any purpose — least of all to be something necessary and relief-inducing (McLeod, Corbisier and Mack 1996).

Yet another censure of escape-from-self is that Newman and Baumeister rely too heavily on case histories of abductions that simply cannot be used to bolster the theory. For example, the abduction of Travis Walton in 1975 is taken as evidence for *procedural orientation*— the idea that the masochist (in this case Walton) will concentrate on minute details in the scene they are experiencing to escape understanding the overall, deviant implications of their fantasy. In support of this idea, Newman and Baumeister point to the fact that in describing his experience, Walton could depict the inside of the craft into which he was abducted in great detail. However, the problem with using the Walton case is that he was allegedly kidnapped by UFO occupants in full view of work colleagues, who were logging timber in an Arizona forest. Some, like Phillip Klass, argued that the story was a hoax supported by the workers and Walton's own family for financial reasons. On the other hand, supporters believed that the witnesses were sincere and that something happened. Whatever the truth, the notion that Walton's abduction was a fulfillment of his masochistic fantasies is somewhat far-fetched when considering the wider context of the event.

Dissociation

Less well known explanations for paranormal encounters involve personality factors that aren't necessarily derived from mental illness or trauma, but still contain hallucinatory features. These fall under the heading of *dissociation*. Dissociation is said to occur when a person experiences a discontinuity of awareness (Waller, Putman and Carlson 1996). The trait is believed to exist along a continuum, ranging from a child's pretend play, daydreaming and night-time dreams at one end, through hypnosis, to more pathological states such as borderline personality disorder and the extreme dissociate identity disorder[4] at the other (although there is some criticism of the oversimplicity of this claim, e.g., see Hardcastle 1999). At the more serious end of the spectrum, hallucinogenic symptoms of the dissociative state have a paranormal flavor and include familiar voices, smells or tastes (Dorahy, Shannon, Seagar, Corr, Stewart, Hanna, Mulholland and Middleton 2009), ESP-type experiences, supernatural possession and spirit contact (Sar, Islam and Öztürk 2009).

In its mildest form, dissociation occurs when the normal sensory information you rely on to understand the surrounding environment is altered in some way (for example, if you're locked up in a silent, dark room for a long time). In this circumstance, you might perceive an unnatural, brain-generated representation of yourself which your brain desperately believes is the most sensible interpretation, but which is fundamentally flawed. This results in the bizarre sensation of feeling as though you are not your "normal self."

For example, most people have a representation of themselves in a "viewer-centered" perspective, but there might be occasions when this representation is mistakenly focused externally to the body in the form of an "over the head" perspective (Bensley 2007). If this occurs, the experience might be interpreted as a mystical out of body experience, rather than the strange error of consciousness that it really is. This style of dissociation linked to an actual brain disorder has been studied by Olaf Blanke and colleagues, who mapped brain areas of a 43-year-old female patient showing signs of temporal-lobe epilepsy — a condition we'll discuss in more detail in a later chapter (Blanke, Ortigue, Landis and Seeck 2002).

The mapping procedure involves attaching electrodes to the brain surface while the patient is awake and aware, with the aim of recording any seizure activity and stimulating specific brain regions that might be responsible for the dysfunction. Sometimes, artificially stimulating surface and deep brain areas can generate interesting psychological side-effects. Over an area known as the right angular gyrus, the application of an electric current in the order of 2 to 3 mA[5] led the patient to experience "sinking feelings." Increasing this current to 3.5 mA generated an phenomenological event said by the authors to resemble an out of body experience. During of these stimulation episodes, the patient exclaimed, "I see myself lying in bed, from above, but I only see my legs and lower trunk."

Further electrical stimulation generated the added impression that she was floating above the bed, close to the ceiling. These sensations are attributed to the *vestibular* (or balance-related) system, and it transpires that the brain region controlling vestibular sensations, called the vestibular cortex, is close to the right angular gyrus. The authors suggest that their artificial electrical stimulation disrupted the complex integration of somatosensory (e.g., touch) and vestibular information which normally allows a person to establish their sense of where they are. The unusual sensation that manifests as a result of this dissociation could be erroneously accepted by the patient as a mystical out of body experience.

The causes of dissociation can be varied. For example, as we've previously discovered with the case of Ruth, childhood trauma can apparently predispose a patient to serious dissociative disorder in later life (Ross and Joshi 1992). On the other hand, people who haven't suffered childhood trauma, but who also claim paranormal experience (most specifically psi experiences, spirit contact and poltergeists) are said to be experiencing normal dissociation that is common in people who score highly on a dissociative personality trait but are healthy in all other respects. Richard Castillo even suggests that quite severe dissociative states can be induced in people under the right circumstances, for example through many years of yogic meditation. This practice can lead to (and sometimes seeks to achieve) a permanently altered (dissociated) state of consciousness (Castillo 2003).

Fantasy Prone Personality

Perhaps the most widely quoted category of dissociation — based on an individual difference an linked to paranormal experience — is *fantasy prone personality* (FPP), a term coined by Sheryl Barber and Theodore Wilson (Wilson and Barber 1983). Although psychologists had studied strongly imaginative people for many years prior to 1983, FPP created a powerful heading under which the earlier findings were unified. It refers to a type of person who outwardly seems perfectly normal, but when assessed by the appropriate questionnaires, display some interesting traits. These include a history of rich childhood imaginations associated with reading stories, playing and even mystical or religious experiences (Lynn and Rhue 1986). The imagery is so intense and lifelike that it resembles a hallucination.

FPP-prone people are also likely to have had an imaginary playmate during childhood. The form of the imaginary playmate can differ widely, from another ordinary child to a human-like "fairy" (Bartholomew, Basterfield and Howard 1991). From a psychological perspective the playmate is hallucinatory, since the child really believes the experience is real-as-real, while a casual adult observer would notice there's absolutely nothing in the bedroom closet, or at the bottom of the garden (where such entities are often witnessed).

Imaginary playmates are quite common in children; however, the implication of FPP theory is that, as a form of dissociation, it lies on a continuum in the same way that other personality traits are expressed differently in the population. Thus the childhood friends of individuals scoring highly on the FPP trait are more intense than those of other children, occur more frequently and perhaps spill over into adolescence, if not adulthood.

Other hallucinatory elements of FPP include perceiving visual imagery in as much detail with the eyes closed as with the eyes open. Those who strongly possess the trait also sense imaginary aromas as real smells, actually hear imagined sounds, and imagine touch as real (Wilson and Barber 1983). For example, a fantasy prone person watching TV becomes hot, cold or even ill depending on the content of the program they're watching. It is also claimed that physical or psychosomatic states can be induced in these individuals —

for example something as extreme as *pseudocyesis* (a false pregnancy). Those exhibiting FFP might also encourage a paranormal experience through hypnosis and meditation.

Not unexpectedly, abductee and contactee claims have been attributed to FPP, as are the claims of people who honestly believe they've met an angelic being or regularly communicate with Bigfoot. A relationship between fantasy proneness and seeing ghostly apparitions has also been found (Parra 2006).[6]

The various forms of fantasy-induced hallucination are considered to be the result of cultural factors—another example of how the psychosocial hypothesis determines the structure of a paranormal experience. That is, a fantasy-prone individual hallucinates what they're brought up to see, based on everything they've been read or been told growing up. Robert Bartholomew and colleagues claim that fantasy-prone people saw fairies in the 19th century, but today they see aliens who abduct them from their beds (Bartholomew, Basterfield and Howard 1991).

As an explanation for paranormal experience, FPP is psychologically appealing because it avoids uncomfortable accusations of hoaxing by the witness, and they don't have to be mentally ill or behave that much differently to "normal" people in other aspects of their lives. Individuals who report numerous paranormal experiences, often from a young age, are particularly susceptible to being labeled fantasy-prone. These people are known as "repeaters" in the UFO literature, and their claims are often considered more critically compared with other, regular reports.

However, the news isn't all pessimistic for people who possess FPP. Clinicians who are interested in FPP frequently follow a *constructivist* approach when dealing with their clients' reports of otherworldly contact. That is, rather than treat FPP as some form of psychopathology that has to be identified and cured, the experient is encouraged to accept the occurrences as something important, albeit not objectively real. Perhaps the events the client experiences are symbolic stories they are narrating to themselves, with deep personal meaning? When diagnosed, the therapist can harness the client's energy in a creative direction with the hope they'll able to lead more productive lives — particularly if they had stressed themselves into believing they'd suffered from a long-running battle with kidnapping aliens.

Interestingly, the FPP hypothesis is not applied quite so expansively today as it was back in the 1980s and early 1990s. UFOlogists Jenny Randles and Peter Hough even mention how strong FPP proponents such as Keith Basterfield withdrew applying such a definition to all abductees after a UFO conference he attended in 1992 (Randles and Hough 1997). Perhaps this is because FPP, like any personality trait, is not so easy to define or identify, and even when the appropriate tools are used, for example the *Inventory of*

Childhood Memories and Imaginings (ICMI), there appears to be no significant difference in levels of fantasy proneness between abductees and non-abductees (Rodeghier, Goodpaster and Blatterbauer 1991).

Again, FPP theory is at its strongest when applied to repeaters rather than everyday people who have had the odd, unusual event in their lives. As a consequence, there is a massive body of experiential data unaffected by the FPP hypothesis. Furthermore, many repeaters themselves show little formal evidence of FPP. As an explanation, FPP is certainly very intriguing. However, as with any conceptual trait, it is not as concrete a concept as many researchers have assumed, and has a somewhat limited application.

"Normal" Hallucinations and Paranormal Experience

Hallucinations aren't necessarily abnormal and only suffered by patients with psychopathologies or unusual personality disorders. In fact, everyone at times can experience something that seems objectively real, but isn't, due to *normal cognitive mistakes* or *transient psychological disturbances*. Most importantly, these two possibilities are highly applicable to most common, spontaneous varieties of paranormal experience.

Normal Cognitive Mistakes

A "normal cognitive mistake" that acts like a simple hallucination and is relevant to paranormal experience is *missing time*. Probably the most notable expression of missing time is in alien abduction syndrome, although it could equally well be applied to historical cases of fairy abduction too (although these traditionally last years or centuries, rather than hours). Many abductions are reported to have happened in the bedroom at night. Therefore, if a victim experiences a complete absence of memory between midnight (when they see aliens hovering over their bed) and first morning light, then they might attribute their loss of memory to the occurrence of some nefarious event that has been erased from consciousness. A more skeptical response would be that the victim has simply fallen asleep shortly after waking from a bad dream. They don't remember what happened, because nothing happened, and they were asleep from 11 P.M. until dawn.

The other commonly reported type of abduction is the roadside kidnapping, whereby the victim is driving alone (or with passengers) at night on a deserted road and sees a strange light that appears to get bigger and ends up giving chase. The victim(s) then arrives home to find it is much, much later than they expected it to be. Two or three hours later, in fact.

In this example, the skeptical psychologist wouldn't necessarily argue that the victim has fallen asleep — driving is a bit too complicated to be performed for long distances while slumbering (although arguably a complicated, abduction-like dream might have occurred during a short "microsleep"). Instead, the skeptic is more likely to argue that a perfectly normal time-gap experience is responsible.

It so happens that the way people experience time is determined by the passing of events (Reed 1972). These events can be external, such as the ticking of the clock or the growing shadows of evening, or internal, such as a rumbling hungry stomach or the feeling of tiredness. Without these significant events, a person is less aware of time's passage. This is particularly noticeable when a person performs a task that they assume to be complex, for example driving, as opposed to something they believe is simple, such as relaxing around a swimming pool for a couple of hours on holiday.

If you drive quite a distance along a deserted road at night and there is no traffic or change of light or scenery to mark time, then it might be hard to implicitly recognize just how long the journey took. We expect to "switch off" when just lazing around doing nothing, but have a hard time believing we've done very little while driving.[7] Yet driving is a task that has a degree of automaticity associated with it (e.g., Ranney 1994). Once learned, we can concentrate on other things — such as daydreaming — while the basics are being performed. Our attention is only required when specific challenges arise, such as negotiating traffic lights or intersections.

A driver on a late night deserted road therefore shouldn't be surprised to realize they took 30 minutes more than they estimated it should have taken. Depending on factors such as prior belief in abduction by aliens — something we've covered previously — the witness might grow nervous and start asking questions about what weird thing might have occurred during the period of missing time.

Therefore, rather than generating an complicated illusion and trying to make sense of it, the victim of a roadside "abduction" may have experienced something even simpler — a period of missing time which they puzzle over. They might even make vague connections with an unusual bruise or indentation on their bodies, marks they haven't bothered to notice before. Like the victim of a paranormal illusion, the abductee might then consult a hypnotist. Once in a trance, a rambling story emerges about a mystery light landing and taking the form of a flying saucer. Saucer occupants emerge through a door in the side of the craft and approach the car. A beeping sound is heard, and then the abductee finds themselves inside the craft where all sorts of horrible things happen.

A more extreme example of missing time is a *fugue state*. This is a variety of clinical amnesia that has a rapid onset but a fixed duration — for example from dusk until dawn. It seems to be brought on by emotional stress rather than a chronic brain disorder and is characterized by a period where the patient wanders around without knowing who they are (Comparelli, De Carolis, Kotzalidis, Masillo, Ferracuti and Tatarelli 2010). We'll discuss fugues in more detail in the next chapter, but using it to account for cases of paranormal experience might be unnecessary. Missing time derived from automaticity is a much simpler explanation that simply involves the experient believing something to be the case (a short passage of time having passed) when nothing of the sort happened (they're sure a long passage of time passed instead).

Transient Psychological Disturbances

A transient psychological disturbance is just that — something that affects the human mind temporarily, is not psychopathological, and generally leaves no trace once it has passed other than a memory of something strange having occurred. Bereavement and acute illness are two examples that can make anyone susceptible paranormal experience. For example, if you report seeing the spirit of a recently departed friend, it might be because you're still affected by their loss, and the resulting subtle changes in "brain chemistry" (a convenient term for something we might not understand very well) interfere with your rational judgment of what's likely to be a completely normal circumstance.

Everyday stress is another variety of transient psychological disturbance that may lead to a paranormal experience. However, "stress" is a label that covers a complex set of physiological and psychological events, so it's a bit simplistic to think a paranormal encounter can be fully explained simply by invoking the term. Alan Murdie, writing in the *Journal of the Society for Psychical Research*, mentions the case of an elderly lady in North London who experienced recurring footsteps in her house, allegedly male and "bootlike." The lady attributed them to spirit sources, although Murdie discovered she had been threatened by debt-collectors around this time. The worry generated by the notion of bailiffs entering the house likely contributed to the auditory hallucination (Murdie 2010). This confirms that hallucinations are not confined to schizophrenics. Quite "normal" people can experience clinical-type hallucinations when highly aroused and anxious — and the anxiety causes the hallucinations, rather than the patient becoming anxious because of the hallucinations (Pauli, Badcock and Maybery 2006).

Transient psychological disturbances might even lead to paranormal hallucinations containing more intricate detail. In 1979, the French UFO researcher Michel Monnerie presented an interesting perspective on hallucinatory encounters with UFO occupants (Evans 1984). He suggested that situations might occur in which a witness sees something ambiguous in the sky. Where an easy interpretation is not forthcoming, rather than experience a "straightforward" illusion of a flying saucer, the witness is thrust into an awkward psychological state whereby their emotions swamp rationality and they experience a waking dream. Like any dream, this episode draws on stored unconscious (and perhaps forgotten) memory-material while simultaneously incorporating what's happening in the here and now. We've all had dreams where, for example, we feel we are stranded in an imaginary blizzard only to wake and find the window next to our bed is open and letting in a cold draft. In the same manner, when we're awake we might see something a little unusual, become excessively emotional then enter a creative dream using the most appropriate "dreamstuff" available to us contemporary society: UFOs and aliens!

Hypnagogic and Hypnopompic Hallucinations

A common type of disturbance that mainstream psychologists believe lead to paranormal hallucinations are alterations of natural sleep function. These might better explain the "bedroom" type abductions mentioned previously, since missing time alone can't account for aliens actually seen by the unfortunate victim standing over their bed before they black out. The same could be said for those people who report seeing a ghost hovering in their room, or a nasty little elf-like creature, or a vampire, or any other type of entity. Furthermore, the experient doesn't necessarily have to pass out or fall asleep during a bedroom encounter. They might get a fright and sit up, only to find the entity has disappeared. These are all examples of a type of hallucination intrinsically connected to the sleep cycle.

Drowsiness is a transition point between wakefulness and falling asleep, and for at least a century psychologists have recognized that the imagery and other sensations experienced during drowsiness are different from, or at least precede, the actual dreams that follow (early papers on the transition between waking and sleeping were written by Hollingworth in 1911 and Yoakum in 1912). An equivalent set of imagery can also occur when waking, and these states are called *hypnagogic* and *hypnopompic* respectively. The hypnagogic condition is better studied, probably because it's easier for investigators to question a patient about their dreamy experiences as they're falling asleep than when they're waking up.

When a person becomes drowsy there is a decrease in self-awareness and attentiveness to the external environment. Time perception becomes poor (an expression of the *missing time* phenomenon) and control over mental thoughts is lost. This altered state might explain the subsequent appearance of strange

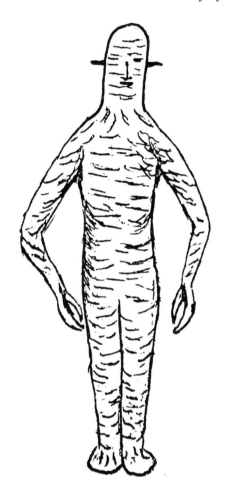

visual imagery. Examples given by Simon Sherwood, from the University of Northampton in England, include simple mists and moving clouds, to more complex objects and shapes that might be in black and white or in vivid color (Sherwood 2002). The visions might be smaller *(micropsias)* or larger *(megalopsias)* than normal, and be repetitive *(polyopsias)*. The shapes themselves could be anything from a simple geometric figure to something meaningful like a human face or a sweeping rural landscape. There might be dancing geometric forms resembling the images encountered in a drug-induced stupor, or flare-like phosphenes of light (try pressing your closed eyelids for an example of a phosphene). There might even be the feeling that you are floating and growing to an enormous size (Lachman 2002).

Examples of auditory imagery include bangs and crashes, doorbells, music, singing, footsteps, the sound of motors, scratching, humming noises, neologisms (new words) and unrecog-

Mississippi residents Calvin Parker, 19, and Charles Hickson, 41, were fishing in the Pascagoula River late one evening in 1973 when they heard a buzzing sound emanating from an egg-shaped object over the river. A door in the side of the craft opened, and three entities flew towards them. The entities, one of which is pictured here (artist unknown), had humanoid arms and legs and heads, but their hands were claws and they had no eyes or neck. They also had slits instead of mouths and objects like carrots sticking out their ears. Both men were taken into the UFO (Parker had fainted) where an eye-like device examined Hickson all over before he and Parker were released. It was suggested at the time by police and investigators that something unusual happened to the men. Just what it was is the interesting question — although simply calling it a "shared hallucination" doesn't solve anything. If a psychological solution is favored, then determining the origin of the wonderfully avant-garde entities, so different from the contemporary "Grey" alien, might require some creativity. Of course, skeptics would be comfortable with the claim that their form was nothing more than a flamboyant concoction by Hickson and Parker in an era before the homogenized Grey came to prominence (Fortean Picture Library).

nizable sentences. However, the most common example of an auditory hallucination is hearing one's name being faintly whispered as you drift off to sleep, or hearing your name called as you're waking, causing you to sit bolt upright in bed. One explanation as to why people so commonly hear their own name is known as the cocktail-party effect. The typical example is where you can be deep in conversation with someone at a party yet still hear your name spoken across the other side of the crowded, noisy room. The theory is we've developed a low threshold for the perception and processing of our personal name, even when the source is nothing more than ambiguous internal or external stimuli such as mild tinnitus, or the faint wind outside the bedroom window. We've briefly discussed how this hypersensitivity might explain why so many EVP recordings contain brief snatches of words interpreted by the listener as their own name.

So what do we make of all this strange visual and auditory imagery? If the drowsy state we enter before falling asleep generates less "volition over mentation" (as Sherwood puts it), we have no control over the bits and pieces of information that emerge from the unconscious. In our half-awake state we will undoubtedly question the origin of the material ... surely it doesn't come from within us because normally we have power to control its form and content. We might therefore construe the source of the experience to be external to us, and if the hypnagogic or hypnopompic image happens to be in the form of a person's face or body, then we might interpret as belonging to someone or something "out there." Couple this imagery with missing time associated with sleep, and we have a comprehensive psychological explanation for alien abductions and other supernatural encounters.

Sensory Deprivation

Hypnagogic and hypnopompic imagery isn't simply restricted to sleep episodes. Similar experiences can be achieved through *sensory deprivation*, where hallucinogenic symptoms can be induced by minimizing visual and sensory input (Mason and Brady 2009)—a procedure we've already seen is a component of the ganzfeld procedure in psi research. Experiments performed in the 1950s and 1960s famously deprived participants of sight (e.g., blindfolds), sound (a silent room), smell (an odorless room) and touch (e.g., padding) (e.g., Freedman, Grunebaum, Stare and Greenblatt 1962). Before long some of these people reported hallucinations, for instance simple flashes of light or basic patterns. Soon the imagery became more complex, with feelings of displacement (dissociation) also common. Indeed, what is experienced in the homogenous environment of sensory deprivation sounds similar to typical hypnopompic and hypnagogic imagery.

However, less well-known is the early finding that many of the visual sensations reported during sensory deprivation might not actually meet the criteria of a hallucination (Suedfeld and Vernon 1964). In fact, true hallucinations are rather difficult to elicit during a sensory deprivation experiment (e.g., Vernon, Marton and Peterson 1961, Solomon and Mendelson 1962). By the mid–60s, it became apparent that total deprivation — a rather hard thing to achieve in practice — is required to see the effect in full (Schulman, Richlin and Weinstein 1967). If not achieved, participants can remain in control of imagery and can prevent more extreme hallucinations from occurring.

Assuming total deprivation is accomplished, hallucinations might subsequently arise from the natural hypersensitivity of sensory receptors (in the eyes, ears and skin, for example). Weak stimuli from the visual or auditory system may be amplified into something perceptible (Yuksel, Kisa, Aydemir and Goka, 2004). Alternately, in the absence of normal environmental stimuli, participants in a sensory deprivation task might simply become aware of sensations that are always present but so subtle that they normally go unnoticed (e.g., Ziskind and Augsburg 1967, Mason and Brady 2009).

If a total lack of sensory input can lead to hallucinations, could sensory deprivation explain more complicated paranormal experiences? Perhaps an answer can be found by examining a rare, non-psychiatric disorder called Charles Bonnet Syndrome, named after an 18th century Swiss scientist who noticed the affliction in his grandfather.

The syndrome has a phenomenological diagnosis, rather than an etiological one, which simply means it's defined in terms of the experiential outcomes rather than specific damage (Halligan, Marshall and Ramachandran 1994). Sufferers of the syndrome are usually elderly, with dysfunctional visual systems, however this doesn't necessarily mean their eyes aren't working properly. They might indeed have retinal damage, but they're just as likely to have suffered destruction of neural pathways within the brain that relay visual information from the eyes to higher regions of the cortex. As a consequence, a blind spot might form in, say, the bottom left-hand corner of a patient's visual field (known as a *scotoma*). Visual information from that part of the eye might still be trying to traverse the brain as normal, but won't reach its intended cortical target. The cells in this target region, having been "deafferented" (meaning they've become separated from neural fiber input), haven't necessarily died but rather turned hyperexcitable. This overactivity, in the absence of any real neural input from the outside world, ultimately transforms into the phenomenological experience of a complex visual hallucination (Cammaroto, D'Aleo, Smorto, Bramanti 2008).

These hallucinations are derived from the actions of cortical regions that are, to put it simplistically, unaware of the damage. Even in darkness, an intact visual system will transmit a baseline signal to the cortex that is interpreted as "nothing to see." Without such a baseline, and with cortical cells behaving hyperactively, the conscious brain is free to replace the natural blackness with personal content derived from memory, a result known as the *release phenomenon* (Shiraishi, Terao, Ibi, Nakamura and Tawara 2004). Put another way, when sensory input from the outside world is no longer available, the system's ability to bring organization to what is perceived no longer occurs. Consequently, signals from deeper brain regions may be released and interpreted as familiar or novel sensory stimuli (Mahowald, Woods and Schenk 1998).

Such visual processes operate beneath our conscious awareness, so a patient with Charles Bonnet Syndrome is quite surprised at the strange and wonderful things they behold. For example, a 71-year-old man who suffered a scotoma due to diabetic retinopathy was visited in hospital by "four weird-looking people in ships" dressed in unusual clothing. When he'd returned home from hospital, an elf on thin legs would appear whenever he entered his back yard woodshed (Needham and Taylor 2000).

These types of visions have clear paranormal characteristics, and neuroscientist V.S. Ramachandran observes sourly that sightings of ghosts, UFOs and angels "by otherwise sane intelligent people" might be a consequence of Charles Bonnet hallucinations (Ramachandran and Blakeslee 1998). The paranormal is explainable, using Ramachandran's words, as an *ocular pathology*.

In "normal" people not suffering gross brain damage, longterm inadequate or monotonous sensory feedback might lead to perceptual "filling in," just like that experienced by Charles Bonnet patients. Perhaps the opaque white ghost seen briefly but in great detail at the side of a long, dark road by a shocked driver is this type of hallucination. It certain explains better than the illusionary hypothesis stories told by witnesses of ghosts with plenty of features; perhaps long dark hair, a thin, anguished face and piercing eyes.

Sleep Deprivation

A story told by a young physician working in a British hospital demonstrates how sleep deprivation can also affect a person's sense of reality. Ruth Booker recounts how it was 5 A.M. on a Monday, and she'd been on call in the casualty department and wards since 9 A.M. on Saturday. She'd had virtually no sleep during that period, and was so exhausted she no longer felt tired, or had any feelings at all. It took a huge effort to concentrate. When a young female patient was admitted, having overdosed on unidentified tablets following an argument with her boyfriend, Booker and a nurse got to work with the stomach pump. Halfway through the procedure, she noticed that the woman's head had come off in her hands. She felt not a little bit surprised, distressed or alarmed about this appalling development. Instead, with great effort she tried recalling whether she'd ever seen, or read about this type of thing happening before, and came to the conclusion that she hadn't. Soon it registered to her that the nurse was smiling, and as she focused she became aware that what she was in fact holding was the woman's wig in her hands, not the patient's head at all. This realization was met with as little relief as there was panic when the "head" initially fell off. Booker's only thought was that she wouldn't be required to re-attach the head after all, but that she should look into how it was done, in case it ever really happened when she was on duty (Booker 2002).

Turning to the paranormal, Michael Shermer claims to have had an "alien encounter" while endurance bike riding. Early one August morning while riding in Nebraska he spied a large craft with bright lights. It overtook him and forced him off the road, before alien beings emerged from the craft and abducted him for 90 minutes. Next thing he knew, he was riding back along the road with no memory of what happened during that time. He recounted the incident to a film crew not long afterwards, citing it as a perfect example of a complex hallucination brought about by the psychological disturbance of sleep deprivation (Shermer 2005).

Sleep deprivation appears to throw the brain into an altered state of consciousness, similar to hypnosis. A neuropsychological reason given for these hallucinations is that when sleep deprived, executive control regions in the prefrontal and parietal cortex of the brain (shorthand for your "ego") are deactivated (Fosse, Stickgold and Hobson 2004). Ironically, this is the same process that occurs when a person is drifting off to sleep. Deactivation means less control of thought content and the release of strange, unfamiliar imagery and semantic narrative from somewhere deep in the unconscious brain. If on a roadway at night, the sleep-deprived traveler can't help interpret this information in the context of what Shermer believes is so popular modern culture — abduction by space aliens (Shermer 2005). In a different context, a hospital, the sufferer might instead see the disembodied head of a patient.

Sleep Paralysis

Arthur Conan Doyle, the author of the Sherlock Holmes stories, wrote in his 1930 book *The Edge of the Unknown* about a ghostly bedroom encounter he experienced in his house at Crowborough, East Sussex. He woke one night, plainly aware that there was someone in the room with him, and that the presence was unworldly. Yet he couldn't move — he was completely unable to turn his body to see what it was. He heard footsteps across the floor, and became aware of someone bending over him and whispering in his ear "Doyle, I come to tell you I am sorry." Immediately his faculties of movement returned and he was able to move, but there was nothing in the still darkness to suggest a visitor had ever been. His wife hadn't woken, and there was no evidence that anything untoward had happened. At the time, Conan Doyle assumed he'd experienced an actual haunting (Keel 1971).

Today, if someone presented themselves to a clinician with a similar tale a very different explanation would be given, and they would likely be referred to a sleep disorders clinic. The episodes would be documented in a medically sound manner — with records taken of the bedroom environment and the fact that the victim was lying on his back, awake, but couldn't move. Notes would be written regarding the supernatural noises, the rapid return of normality, and the revelation that a nearby companion was completely unaware of the experience.

Professionals at the clinic might further explore whether the encounter occurred at sleep onset or offset (or both) and its frequency over a set period of time. Information might be gathered as to whether the experiences were scary — scary enough to make the patient wary of falling asleep on successive nights. Furthermore, the degree of immobility in the patient would be assessed, and what kind of visual imagery emerged. In one case at a British hospital, a patient reported the image of a normal but unfamiliar boy who consistently appeared at the foot of the bed. Sometimes the boy would climb onto the bed, sit on a pillow, and even talk to the sufferer. At first the conversation was friendly, but as the episodes recurred the exchange became menacing and the boy would climb onto his chest, causing breathing difficulties. If the conversation went badly, and the sufferer didn't give the boy an acceptable answer, a punishing "electrical shock" was delivered. This made the patient suspect the boy was a demon (Stores 1998).

This clinical tale has elements very similar to Conan Doyle's, although it possesses the added feature that the entity was actually seen, and over many consecutive nights. There is also the aspects of suffocation and malevolence — the entity had, in the patient's opinion, "an evil intent." Not surprisingly, since the patient was referred to a sleep disorders clinic, they were diagnosed with a sleep disorder. And over the last 20 years, one popular disorder that accounts for all the elements of Conan Doyle's encounter, and the vision of the demonic child discussed by Gregory Stores, is *sleep paralysis*.[8] Sleep paralysis has a more intense quality than simple hypnagogic and hypnopompic hallucinations, and is well suited to the prototypical paranormal bedroom experience. While sleep paralysis appears to be a response to ambiguous stimuli, and has a lot in common with an illusion, the condition's multiple facets and intensity (as we'll discuss soon) suggests to many researchers it's a type of hallucination (e.g., Cheyne and Girard 2007).

To understand a more about sleep paralysis we need a brief understanding of *rapid-eye movement* (REM) sleep, because sleep paralysis is intrinsically related to this form of sleep state. The most scientific way to imagine REM is that it is represented by a type of EEG wave that is different from the waves representing other types of sleep.

Wakefulness is characterized by an EEG recording that displays *alpha* activity and *beta* activity. Alpha activity tends to occur when a person is mentally resting and has their eyes closed. The waves recorded on a computer screen are regular in shape and of a medium frequency, meaning their pattern is not completely squashed together (indicating high frequency), nor is it too stretched out (indicating low frequency). On the other hand, beta activity is associated active thinking and alertness, and is represented by an irregular wave pattern of a higher amplitude and slightly higher frequency than alpha activity. A wave's amplitude simply refers to its "electrical" height, and in the case of beta waves it's convenient to equate the "messiness" with "thought processes."

When you nod off and fall asleep, lower frequency *theta* waves start to appear on the EEG recording and these have slightly higher amplitude than alpha waves. This is called *Stage 1 sleep*. EEG waves with these characteristics represent synchronous neural behavior, meaning the cells in some brain regions are acting in a similar way — something that makes sense when falling asleep. *Stage 2 sleep* begins about 10 minutes after *Stage 1*, and the EEG pattern becomes more irregular again. It resembles theta activity, but bursts of high amplitude waves called *K complexes*. The subject is fully asleep, yet if they're awoken they will claim never to have been asleep (Carlson 2005).

Around 15 minutes following Stage 2 sleep, *delta* activity is recorded. This type of pattern possesses high amplitude and low frequency and characterizes *Stage 3* and *Stage 4 sleep* (with more and more delta activity). The low frequency of the wave is the reason why it is more commonly called *slow-wave sleep*.

As sleep continues, the pattern of *Stage 4* will change back into a combination of active, irregular theta and beta activity. This is labeled *REM sleep* because the eyeballs behind the closed eyelids begin to dart around as though the sleeper is awake and responding to a visual scene. REM sleep occurs around 90 minutes after going to sleep, and recurs at 90 minute intervals throughout the sleep cycle (Nishino, Riehl, Hong, Kwan, Reid and Mignot 2000).

One of the most obvious features in REM sleep is *muscle atonia* — the paralysis of all voluntary musculature (sparing the diaphragm muscle below the ribs, which is crucial for breathing). This occurs for the obvious reason of preventing the sleeper from acting out their dreams (Mahowald, Woods and Schenk 1998). Other quite understandable changes to waking activity include alterations in heart rate and respiration, because the sleeper's cells do not require as much oxygen as they do when awake. There's also *gating* (lowering) of sensory input, which reduces the sleeper's knowledge of what's happening in the outside world (Cheyne, Rueffer and Newby-Clarke 1999). Other less obvious events include eye and middle ear movements. Overall, REM sleep is characterized by a loss of self-awareness and an increased absorption in mental imagery that is commonly considered to be dreaming.

Sleep Paralysis as a REM Disorder

On rare occasions, people fall asleep and pass from waking straight into a REM state (sleep-onset REM). Similarly, when they wake up they can pass directly from REM to full consciousness (sleep-offset REM). Why might such an imbalance occur? Here's what is conjectured, although researchers aren't really too sure of the exact mechanism.

At the very bottom of the brain, where it becomes the brainstem and the start of the spinal cord, is a region with the anatomical label *pons*. Collections of cells within the pons have been identified by neurophysiologists as either *REM-on* and *REM-off*, and these cells have to work together for the wake/sleep or sleep/wake transition to occur. However, if the REM-on cells are hyperactive or the REM-off cells are hypoactive (under active) when falling sleep, the resultant lack of neural cohesion might cause us to dream "too early."

The most significant *psychological* side-effect of this dysfunction would be the retention of self-awareness as we pass straight into REM sleep, or the "early start" of self-awareness when emerging from REM sleep (Gangdev 2004). Under such circumstances, the sleep paralysis sufferer would be conscious of what is happening to them and find their experience to be highly unusual. Characteristics mentioned previously include paralysis (the *atonic* condition) as well as awareness of low-level exogenous (external) and endogenous (internal) stimuli. These could include the "noise" detected from inner ear movements. There might also be a feeling of a *sense of presence* that someone or something is standing or hovering nearby (Conesa 2000). This aspect of sleep paralysis has been labeled *Intruder* (e.g., Girard and Cheyne 2004), because the feeling is commonly interpreted by the sufferer as the presence of an intruding demon, monster, witch or extraterrestrial alien.

The REM state also involves input from a brain region called the *limbic system* (Hobson, Stickgold and Pace-Schott 1998). Normally, the REM-on cells in the pons activate regions in the higher cortex via a relay nucleus called the *thalamus*. The thalamus also projects fibers to the nearby *amygdala*, a part of the lobes near the temples that are anatomically connected to the limbic system and associated with emotional states, particularly reaction to fear-inducing stimuli (LeDoux 1994)[9].

Therefore, if you suffer a sleep paralysis episode and remain aware of what's happening, and experience the strong emotions derived from amygdala activation, you're going to try to make sense of the fear you feel. You might analyze any available, meaningful information to determine the source of the emotion, and come to the conclusion that the vague, whispering sounds you hear coming from the dark, or the shadow that hovers over the side of your bed as your eyes frantically dart from one side of the room to the other, are supernatural (e.g., Cheyne, Newby-Clarke and Rueffer 1999).

You're also likely to question why you can't move, and reach the conclusion that it's because a horrible creature is holding you down and preventing you from breathing. This "explanation," coupled with the dream-like imagery that's flashing through your mind, turns the dark shadow hovering over you into a witch, crushing your chest and trying to suffocate you. Overwhelmingly, sufferers report a real event is happening to them, rather than rationally judging that the experience is some kind of transient psychological disturbance (Cheyne and Girard 2004). The attribution of the experience to external, supernatural causes can also occur *after* the event, when the victim has woken, regained control of their limbs, and is groping for explanations. Furthermore, since sleep paralysis is highly unpleasant, the supernatural cause will be similarly distasteful, such as a demon or an alien (Banaji and Kihlstrom 1996).

Sleep paralysis sufferers differ greatly in their interpretation of their experiences, and cultural reactions to claims of bedroom encounters with the paranormal can differ greatly, too. In the early 1980s, the folklorist David Hufford wrote an influential book called *The Terror that Comes in the Night* detailing, among other events, the night-time attacks by "The Old Hag of Newfoundland." Early in the flap, victims reported waking in the night, immobile and feeling a heavy weight on their chest, attributed to an ugly (supernatural) hag. Knowledge of the phenomenon spread locally, and as more and more people heard of the attacks, more and more people reported having them — a function of *social contagion*. Similar types of oppressions have since been formally documented, both historically and in the present day, in places as diverse as Sweden, Japan, India, Thailand, Mexico and Alaska (Spanos, McNulty, DuBreuil, Piries and Burgess 1995). In a Chinese population, this type of night terror it is known as *ghost oppression* (Wing, Lee and Chen 1994), in Japan *kanashibari* (Wing, Chiu, Leung and Ng 1999), on Baffin Island *uqumangirniq* (Law and Kirmayer 2005) and in medieval Europe the *incubus* and *succubus* (male and female vampire-like entities respectively).

Interestingly, the Japanese generally believe the phenomenon to be something real, assisted by their cultural framework of the *kanashibar*, whereas

Canadians, despite the "real-as-real" quality of the encounter, are more likely to accept their experience as a dream (Fukuda, Olgilvie and Takeuchi 2000). Psychosocial factors are therefore considered to be a crucial difference in perceiving the experience as a demon, an alien or even the distorted memory of childhood sexual abuse (McNally and Clancy 2005). To complicate things more, some fortunate sufferers don't actually experience the fear component. Rather, they interpret the abnormal vestibular (balance) sensations associated with the sleep paralysis state as floating. An explanation of some people's reports of OBEs, perhaps? Other suffers, however, report sinking

An incubus in the form of a bird perches upon its helpless victim (artist Charles Bilbert, 1873–1929). Mainstream psychology considers these intruding bedroom encounters — whether historical or contemporary — as derived from isolated sleep paralysis. In this condition, atypical brain processes derived from sleep dysfunction manifest as a range of symptoms reported by sufferers. The symptom represented in this dramatic illustration is the dampening of respiratory muscle activity, which the victim might perceive as pressure on the chest derived from an external, malevolent agent such as a crouching vampire, demon or witch (Mary Evans Picture Library).

feelings (Conesa 2000), which a psychologist might apply to the experiences of a British long-term alien abductee called Jayne (Hough and Kalman 1997), who reported occasional, terrifying "sucking down" sensations when in bed.[10] The explanation of sleep paralysis has also been applied to paranormal experiences outside the bedroom. In one study, a group of Japanese medical researchers assert that roadside ghost experiences (which they call *highway hypnosis-like ghost tales*) occur when drivers nod off at the wheel and immediately enter REM sleep (Furuya, Ikezoe, Shigeto, Ohyagi, Arahata, Araki and Fujii 2009). A little confusingly, this explanation opposes the sleep deprivation theory of roadside hauntings, whereby drivers who are sleep deprived are considered to be still awake when hallucinating their apparition. The same core experience can therefore be derived from two different states of consciousness, a situation that is somewhat perplexing — a person can see a "phantom hitchhiker" when they're awake, but they can also see them when they're asleep and dreaming.[11] Furuya and colleagues further propose that the apparition in a highway encounter is "usually clear but sometimes vague," which also tends to hedge bets since it could account for just about any roadside report of paranormal phenomena. That's perhaps not surprising, since these Japanese researchers have no time for things paranormal, confidently believing that few people in the world believe in ghost stories, and that most of these stories are attributable to neurophysiological, neurodegenerative or psychological disorders.

The Pervasiveness, and Treatment, of Sleep Paralysis

Sleep paralysis is highly prevalent in humans. Researchers from the Kurume University School of Medicine found that of over 8000 Japanese questioned, 39.6 percent reported at least one episode in their lives that these researchers relate directly to sleep paralysis. Elsewhere, figures of between 10 and 30 percent are quoted for sleep paralysis "signs" (e.g., inability to move, or pressure on the chest) in samples drawn from a variety of cultures (Awadalla, Al-Fayez, Harville, Arikawa, Tomeo, Templer, and Underwood 2004). In terms of treating the condition, Gregory Stores suggests a combination of explanation, support, self-relaxation techniques and regular sleep patterns to re-instate normal sleep, and drugs (e.g., antidepressants) to increase the brain neurotransmitter serotonin and alleviate stress (Stores 1998). One theory is that sleep deprivation coupled with stress increases sleep-onset REM activity, and this in turn leads to sleep paralysis symptoms (Spanos et al. 1995). Another variable associated with sleep paralysis is that the sleeper is frequently lying on their back (Cheyne 2002), just the position Conan Doyle found himself in when he experienced his own ghostly bedroom encounter.

Criticisms of Sleep Paralysis Research

A psychologist investigating sleep paralysis would typically administer questionnaires with names like the Waterloo Unusual Sleep Experiences Questionnaire, or Sleep Questionnaire of Alertness and Wakefulness to a group of experimental participants. These instruments ask the participants questions such as "Have you ever awakened in the morning and found yourself unable to move (paralyzed)?" (e.g., Ohayon, Zulley, Guilleminault, Smirne 1999). Other researchers might include vignettes in their research programs. Vignettes are descriptive passages that might describe core elements of the sleep paralysis state, such as drowsiness, feeling paralyzed, self-awareness and knowing that the experience isn't a dream (Spanos et al. 1995).

Participants read the vignette and can agree to having experienced a similar range of incidents, adding information about whether they've sensed an unseen presence or seen an actual entity, felt pressure on the chest or endured a "floating feeling." Participants also inform the experimenter about other aspects associated with the episode, such as the position they were sleeping in when they had their encounter (e.g., back or stomach), and their psychological state at the time (for example, were they overly emotional?).

A participant who answers "yes" to most or all of these symptoms is labeled as having suffered from sleep paralysis. These sufferers might then be administered a battery of personality tests of the type we've discussed in previous chapters, with subscales measuring traits such as depression, psychoticism, phobic anxiety, magical thinking, fantasy proneness, perceptual aberration, paranormal belief and imagery vividness. Using a variety of statistical techniques, a relationship might then be demonstrated between sleep paralysis and one or more of these psychological variables. For example, Nicholas Spanos and colleagues from Carleton University show a significant relationship between the intensity of a sleep paralysis episode and traits of psychopathology, imaginativeness and hypnotizability (Spanos et al. 1995). These authors suggest that while sleep paralysis is common in the general population, those who are naturally imaginative are likely to experience more vivid imagery. As a consequence, they are more motivated than "normal" people to try and to move in bed and escape the threat, subsequently perceiving themselves to be paralyzed. It is this category of people most likely to report having a "night terror" caused by sleep paralysis.

Perhaps a little unfairly, a participant who reports having any type of bedroom encounter will therefore be categorized as a sleep paralysis sufferer. The psychological assumption is that there's no room for the possibility that the paranormal experience was objectively real. The more symptoms you report, the higher your score in the "sufferers" category. There's simply no such thing as a victim who recounts a night-time, "paranormal" episode that cannot be labeled as having had sleep paralysis. And any "elevated" personality variables the sufferer exhibits are assumed to contribute to the paralysis episode, rather than the episode being real and mediating personality changes.

Nonetheless, sleep paralysis is a powerful psychological explanation for paranormal encounters. It isn't some fuzzy theory that might happen in people, but a legitimate sleep disorder which is proven to result in a variety of strange perceptions. I personally remember a one-off episode that happened to me years ago, waking up to a sunny morning and feeling very strange. I was unable to move for at least a minute, and felt as though I was in the presence of *something* that wasn't nice. Yet the benign, comforting environment I was in, accentuated by the fact that it was such a beautiful day outside, allowed me to reach to the logical conclusion that there was nothing to worry about, and soon found I could move. Had it been night-time? Perhaps I would have interpreted it differently, and truly believed I'd experienced a horrifying spirit oppression. Sleep paralysis can sensibly account for a large number of supernatural encounter cases — perhaps a vast majority. Yet it might be unwise to assume it explains all cases — as the psychological research often takes for granted — since that surely would stifle consideration of other possibilities, however awkward they might seem.[12]

A Review of the "Hallucinatory Hypothesis" of Paranormal Experience

The hallucination hypothesis for paranormal encounters, whether associated with sensory deprivation, sleep deprivation or sleep paralysis (if designated a type of hallucination), has an advantage over the illusion hypothesis in that it can account for stories with more rich and detailed content. If the witness claims to have seen a ghostly lady hitchhiking at the side of the road — a hallucination. If Doreen Kendall sees a detailed UFO hovering outside the hospital window — a hallucination. If an abductee is taken on board a UFO and meets its occupants — a hallucination. If the witness is frozen in bed with a ghastly demon on their chest — a hallucination. The difficulty for the psychologist is explaining how it all happens "neurophysiologically," although some wonderfully sophisticated models have been developed. Nevertheless, it would be nice to be able to map the underlying brain events generating these experiences to the extent where the events could be predicted in advance or even induced in a laboratory. This is an issue raised by Marcello Truzzi, who complains that the scientific explanation for a paranormal event is often as unknown and as far-fetched as the paranormal "cause" (Truzzi 2001). For

example, it might be argued that NDEs are caused by verbal messages —
received while the patient is unconscious — that are converted into visual
imagery. That's all very interesting, but *how* does this happen? Such an explanation is still highly descriptive.

Luckily, there are theories that don't just label intense paranormal experiences with scientific-sounding words, or even map the neurological processes
using impressive anatomical names, but try to explain them to the point of being
able to induce them in real people. This is the subject of the next chapter.

CHAPTER 5

Witnessing the Paranormal: Neurological Dysfunction

We've discovered how the illusion hypothesis asserts that mundane ambiguous stimuli are mistakenly interpreted by our perceptual systems as something paranormal. Alternately, the hallucination hypothesis claims that there is nothing truly external to us, but for a variety of natural psychological and physiological reasons we might encounter something we consider paranormal. Although it's suggested that certain dysfunctional people might have a propensity towards these encounters due to personality and cognitive disorders, both theories emphasize that anyone might be prone to paranormal experience.

In this chapter, we will take the hallucinatory hypothesis a bit further, exploring a theory of paranormal experience related to more serious brain dysfunction. Then we'll examine a second more controversial theory that, to a certain extent, combines the illusionary, hallucinatory and brain dysfunction hypotheses. Both these theories are popularly equated with a professor of psychology at Laurentian University in Canada called Michael Persinger, and have been widely quoted not only in scientific literature but also in the wider popular media. On account of this iconic status it is important to explore Persinger and his co-workers' theories in detail, while acknowledging that some researchers do have reservations about their findings.

Epilepsy

For decades, there has been speculation that many intense paranormal encounters are caused by epilepsy. The epilepsy most people are aware of is the grand mal type,[1] characterized by muscle convulsions and loss of consciousness (Blumenfeld, Varghese, Purcaro, Motelow, Enev, McNally, Levin,

Hirsch, Tikofsky, Zubal, Paige, and Spencer 2009). The seizures occur when cells in the limbic system, particularly in the associated hippocampus, become abnormally active and fire synchronously, spreading their signals to a higher brain region called the motor cortex. Cells here have direct control of the muscles we use to move around. Under normal circumstances, when our "smart" brain regions require muscle movement, a signal passes to the motor cortex, which then activates the appropriate motor cells and a muscle contraction occurs somewhere in the body. Should cells in the motor cortex become abnormally active — known as epilepsy — the consequence can be uncontrolled muscle movement that manifests as gross muscle spasms. The term for cells that show this abnormal activity is *labile*. The electrical activity these cells display show a repetitive and synchronous discharge when measured using EEG, which doesn't resemble the complicated wave patterns seen in normal waking life.

A lesser known type of epileptic seizure is not of the grand mal variety that affects motor regions of the brain. Rather, the typical foci (or place of origin) for this alternative epilepsy are the temporal lobes (underlying the temples) and nearby limbic areas.[2] I use the word foci, the plural of *focus*, because the brain has two sides known as hemispheres. Thus there is a left and right temporal lobe, just as there is a left ear and a right ear and a left and right motor cortex. Both hemispheres are connected by nerve fibers, so communication between the left and right temporal lobes is normally constant.

The temporal lobes have been described as "a monumental library equipped to catalogue, store and retrieve the experiences of a lifetime" (Zeman 2005). This implies that a focal seizure from here will have profound experiential implications for the epileptic, because this "library" stores imagery, and as we've learned, imagery is a big component of hallucinated paranormal experience.

In common with neurons (nerve cells) of the motor cortex, cells in the temporal and limbic areas are particularly labile. For example, the hippocampus is a limbic structure beneath the temporal lobes and is extremely sensitive to changes in blood flow (Persinger and Makarec 1986). If such alterations occur — perhaps due to stroke — it can trigger abnormal hippocampal activation. This activation could be bilateral, affecting both lobes, or it could also be unilateral, affecting only one side. However, the ability of the lobes to communicate using pathways such as the corpus callosum — the bundle of nerve fibers that connects both hemispheres — means that the psychological manifestation of a unilateral seizure can subtly influence the unaffected side too.

When the focus of abnormal neuronal activity in the temporal lobes is small it's termed a *simple partial seizure*. Because of the size, such a seizure often can't be detected by surface measuring equipment such as the EEG because the abnormal activity is hidden among all the messy noise generated by the rest of the brain. Psychological symptoms of simple partial seizures tend to be unidimensional, that is, a single incident of any of the manifestations discussed below.

Seizures with a larger focus are called *complex partial seizures*, and in their extreme form often encompass part or the whole of the temporal lobes. This is known as temporal lobe epilepsy (TLE).[3] More specifically, medial temporal lobe seizures are associated with deep limbic structures, and lateral temporal lobe seizures with the overlying cortical structures (Maillard, Vignal, Gavaret, Guye, Biraben, McGonigal, Chauvel and Bortolomei 2004). These temporal lobe seizures frequently lead to a complex set of symptoms associated with whatever function the cortex and/or the adjacent limbic system has. Furthermore, unlike simple partial seizures, complex seizures can be identified using EEG measurements. The unusual "spike" discharges representative of temporal lobe epilepsy are large enough to appear amid the background electrical activity of the brain[4].

Symptoms of Temporal Lobe Epilepsy

Temporal lobe seizures often occur for longer time periods than grand mal seizures, and — more importantly for our interest in paranormal experience — patients with TLE do not show convulsive behavior. This is significant in the context of paranormal experience because it suggests that people endure an intense epileptic seizure without anyone around them necessarily noticing it's taking place. While there is the occasional loss of consciousness during a seizure, very often the patient remains aware of themselves and their subjective experiences. These symptoms are known as *signs*, and some of these signs involve the basic senses of vision, audition, gustation (taste), olfaction (smell) and the vestibular system (balance). Let's look at these in more detail.

Olfactory signs— Hallucinatory smells are often reported by patients suffering temporal lobe epilepsy, and this symptom is termed *olfactory reference syndrome* (Devinsky, Khan and Alper 1998). The presence of olfactory hallucinations makes anatomical sense because the limbic system is part of a broader structure known as the *rhinencephalon*. This name matches the olfactory role the limbic system is thought to have controlled in ancient times.[5] Over the years, the function of the human rhinencephalon is thought to have been subsumed by emotion, perhaps to the detriment sense of our sense of smell. Nevertheless, the overlying piriform cortex still has an olfactory role. The characteristics of odors reported by patients experiencing a seizure range from acrid and pungent (Servan-Schreiber et al. 1998) to pleasant and perfumy (Neppe 1983).

Gustatory— Since they are both chemical senses, olfaction and gustation are closely related to one another.[6] Nevertheless, gustatory hallucinations are less common than olfactory hallucinations, although some temporal lobe epilepsy patients have reported bitter and metallic tastes (Servan-Schreiber et al., 1998), while others report unpleasant tastes with odorous characteristics similar to rotten fish and fruit (Chen, Shih, Yen, Lirng, Guo, Yu and Yiu 2003).

Visual— Visual hallucinations typically arise following abnormal activation of the occipital lobe, an area very distant anatomically from the temporal lobes but one associated with visual processing. These sensations, however, tend to be quite simple. On the other hand, epileptic patients undergoing electrical cortical stimulation of the amygdala and hippocampus experience more complicated visual experiences such as seeing children dancing or castles (Blanke, Landis and Seeck 2000). Therefore — and unusually — it seems that complex visual hallucinations are more a characteristic of temporal lobes seizures than occipital lobe seizures (Cummings 1997, Bien, Benninger, Urbach, Schramm, Kurthen and Elger 2000). In one instance, a 54-year-old woman with multiple sclerosis of the temporal lobes[7] causing seizures reported seeing fantastic Lilliputian (tiny) hallucinations in her peripheral vision. The images were of small objects, animals and people that either made sounds, spoke or even sang to her (Jacome 1999). Therefore, while not considered a primary symptom of temporal lobe epilepsy, hallucinated imagery is a component of some temporal lobe seizures.

Auditory hallucinations—*Heschl's gyrus* (a part of the wider auditory cortex in the temporal lobes) is a region of the brain that processes sound. In the left hemisphere, the meaning of the sound is determined by the adjacent Wernicke's area. Consequently, a seizure close to left superior temporal gyrus may result in auditory hallucinations and a loss of speech — known as *aphasia* (Zeman 2005). Often these hallucinations are crude, for example when associated with tumors of the temporal lobes (e.g., Keschner, Binder, and Strauss 1938). Alternately, auditory hallucinations may involve spoken language if the patient suffers from the more subtle dysfunction associated with epilepsy. For instance, a female Japanese epileptic patient with seizures originating in the medial temporal lobes displayed rigid facial expressions and frequently engaged in a monologue to nobody in particular. She also reported an auditory hallucination of her parents' voices, although they were not present at the time (Takeda, Inoue, Tottoi and Mihara 2001).

Vestibular hallucinations— Feelings such as floating, similar to an OBE, have been reported by temporal lobe epilepsy patients. Knowledge of these seizures and their relationship to the sensation of being "out-of-body" go as far back as the famous experiments of the 1940s conducted by the neurologist Wilder Penfield. These experiments involved electrical stimulation of the cortex (the outside surface of the brain) and developed the notion that specific brain areas regulate awareness of the various sensations derived from the body, in a topographic (map-like) manner. Cortical stimulation on patients has since found that stimulation of the right superior temporal gyrus of the temporal lobes creates a "mental diplopia," or the feeling in the patient that they are present in one place (here and now) but also the weird sensation of being elsewhere at the same time (Tong 2003).

Heightened emotion and cognition— The abnormal activity of the amygdala in patients with temporal lobe epilepsy has been associated with feelings of personal significance, "cosmic awareness" and enhanced meaning in the events that surround them (Persinger and Makarec 1986). Outwardly, these people are often humorless, and feel that they have been selected and guided by one or more divine beings (Zusne and Jones 1982).

Cardiovascular elements— The amygdala sends projections to the hypothalamus and deeper cardiovascular centers of the brainstem which control autonomic aspects of the conditioned fear response. Amygdaloid seizures might therefore cause patients to experience changes in heart rate, respiration and blood flow (flushing) which they attribute to external causes (van Paesschen, King, Duncan and Connelly 2001)— possibly supernatural.

The Sense of Presence— Recall that the brain is divided into two sides called hemispheres, and while many of the functions of each mirror-image brain area are the same, notable differences do exist. One popular argument is that the left hemisphere dominates self-awareness because language is located here.[8] Self-awareness is therefore linked to linguistic concepts and categorical thinking (Booth, Koren and Persinger 2008). On the other hand, the right hemisphere is often viewed as the silent partner in the brain, and its influence tends to be more "unconscious," with less emphasis on cognition and more on spatial awareness, intuition and emotion (Booth et al. 2008).

From the perspective of temporal lobe seizures, unilateral or bilateral dysfunction[9] might unbalance the standard one-way dominance of the left temporal lobes over the right temporal lobes, and allow the latter to exert a greater than normal influence on waking consciousness. Persinger describes this as the unexpected entry of "a pattern of neuroelectrical activity" (Persinger 2003). It is famously argued by Persinger and colleagues that one of the fundamental aspects of consciousness is the sense-of-self, which is mediated by the left hemisphere. If an intrusion by the right hemispheric equivalent of the sense-of-self occurs because of a lifting of "commissural inhibition" and less dominant left hemispheric activity (Persinger 1994), the patient will have a hard time understanding the unusual sensations and feelings they experience. The phenomenological outcome of right hemisphere intrusion is difficult to conceptualize — it can only be speculated that something "psychological" occurs that feels different from normal.

Should such an intrusion occur (and be aware that there's plenty of speculation as to whether this happens, and what the effects would be), then the patient might experience a strange and nebulous sense of presence. That is, they have the feeling that "something" is nearby but they don't know who it is, and can't see anyone. During a more extreme seizure, they might visualize the unusual intrusion of their right hemisphere sense-of-self as something external to them but still very personal,[10] such as a guardian angel, spirit guide or even a doppelganger (a person's "double," or own self externalized). While the thought of meeting yourself as a double seems ridiculous, there is the occasional historical and contemporary case of people who report coming face-to-face with themselves in public locations, in broad daylight. However, meeting a doppelganger in broad daylight is not unexpected, since TLE seizures don't have to always occur in specific locations such as the bedroom at night as you drift off to sleep (the time and place where many paranormal experiences do occur).

The intrusion of right hemispheric content into left hemispheric self-awareness could also be experienced as something more sinister than an angel or doppelganger. Due to individual difference, cultural upbringing and neurological factors (e.g., amygdaloid activation) the resulting interpretation of an epileptic episode by a patient might be anything from an evil demon to a terrifying extraterrestrial alien. Persinger calls such a model *vectorial hemisphericity*, which manifests as a primarily unpleasant "ego-alien" intrusion (Persinger 1993) — meaning you perceive your own self as something that's not actually "you" at all!

Visceral impressions — An unusual element of simple partial (epileptic) seizures are "thoughts" coming from the stomach of a patient (Manford and Shorvon 1992). Such a symptom implies that the brain is confusing physiological and psychological modalities — in this case mistaking the awareness of autonomic (gut) events with cognitive processes from the higher brain. Another type of visceral impression experienced by some female patients with temporal lobe foci (usually localized in the right hemisphere) are sexual auras and ictal orgasms (Cummings 1997).

On occasions, visceral impressions such as *pseudocyesis* have been linked to temporal lobe epilepsy (Persinger 1991). Pseudocyesis has a range of physiological symptoms including enhanced awareness of abdominal sensations (the imaginary baby), *hyperprolactinemia* (high production of a protein necessary in pregnancy for breastmilk production) and *amenorrhea* (the lack of a menstrual cycle), as well as a more complicated range of psychological symptoms. From an anatomical perspective, a temporal brain region known as the *insular cortex* (or insula) has connections to visceral areas including the uterus. It also projects to the amygdala,[11] which in turn send fibers to autonomic regulatory areas such as the hypothalamus (Persinger 1996).

Persinger argues that a labile female who is prone to TLE and upset about their personal relationships could set off a train of neurochemical events in their limbic-hypothalamic pathway which results in the appearance of an imaginary pregnancy. Naturally, a pregnancy is a complicated affair and cannot be sustained for long simply because of hyperactivity of a single, functional brain system. As Persinger suggests, the transient nature of pseudocyesis would explain the "stealing" of the imaginary baby by traditional fairies or perhaps more contemporary aliens, depending on the cultural conditioning of the patient.

Finally, in some patients the visceral expressions of temporal lobe seizures have a truly unpleasant quality. For example, one patient with epilepsy of the limbic system suffered a hallucination in which his body felt as though it were cut into pieces in preparation for cannibalism! (Pontius 1996).

Déjà vu and auras— In *déjà vu* an individual experiences intense familiarity of a present environment, and believes they've experienced the same scene at some undefined time long ago (Brown 2003). From a paranormal perspective, déjà vu is most commonly linked to reincarnation, but of course a psychologist's attitude to déjà vu doesn't include the rekindling of a true, past-life memory but rather neurological dysfunction. Regions of interest include the temporal lobes, on account of their importance in processing autobiographical memory. In a very simplistic way, you might say the memories of your past are stored here. It's argued that if there is false activation of the normal connection between these temporal lobe areas and the cortical areas involved with perceiving the "here-and-now" of everyday life, then what a person sees through their eyes, for the first time, might be misinterpreted as something familiar (Spatt 2002).

In support, there is evidence that patients suffering seizures of the temporal lobes report déjà vu sensations (Bancaud, Brunet-Bourgin, Cahauvel and Halgren, 1994). Recent findings further suggest that hypoactivity of perirhinal and entorhinal regions within the medial temporal lobes are the focus of the seizure-generated déjà vu episodes. These specific areas are important in discrimination of familiarity (Guedj, Aubert, McGonigal, Mundler and Bartolomei 2010), so if they're not working correctly, any normal memory the patient encounters might not be matched with a sense of recognition. For example, a location might not be explicitly remembered by a patient, even though they've been there before, yet it still feels familiar. Alternately, in healthy people déjà vu experiences might be due to temporary alterations of the temporal lobe memory pathways, for example during drowsiness when the connectivity between temporal and cortical brain areas are more active in preparation for memory consolidation processes believed to occur in sleep (Spratt 2002).

A related phenomenon to déjà vu is the epileptic *aura*.[12] An epileptic aura is a precognitive sensation that is a product of a partial temporal lobe seizure (Kasper, Kasper, Pauli and Stefan 2010), and manifests as a profound sense that an event will occur imminently (Sadler and Rahey 2004). For example, a patient who worked at a suburban music store related both déjà vu and aura sensations at their workplace — a "rising feeling" in the stomach followed by a déjà vu–like knowledge that what was about to happen had happened before. The patient believed they could predict what a customer would say next, or what compact disc they were about to pick from the shelf.

Additional Temporal Lobe Epilepsy Symptoms
Involve Amnesia and Unconsciousness

Amnesia— The hippocampus helps consolidate sensory information (sight and sound) from short term memory into long term memory. This hippocampal activity can be temporarily disrupted during a temporal lobe seizure, hence no memories of what happened during the seizure will be formed. As a result, the patient might seem perfectly lucid and self-aware during the seizure but will have no memory of anything that happened to them. Where simpler explanations for a person claiming to have experienced a period of "missing time" cannot be found, a psychologist might attribute a patient's paranormal encounter to an acute temporal lobe seizure.

Absence seizures— In *petit mal* epilepsy (also called *absence seizures*), patients lose consciousness and may display the outward behavior of staring and unresponsiveness. There is no accompanying subjective experience, and the patient reports a "blackout" (Monaco, Mula and Cavanna 2005). While this epileptic loss of consciousness is caused by very different processes from other types of unconsciousness — for example deep sleep, coma, and drug-induced general anesthesia — all states are characterized by a brain-wide electrical activity that's slow and synchronized, and very different from the fast and flexible pattern typical of consciousness (Monaco et al. 2005).

One theory is that no information processing is allowed to occur in the frontal lobes because of changes in blood flow or metabolism brought on by the seizure. The lack of information processing means no resultant self-awareness. Another possibility is a seizure-induced lack of functional activity in the connection between the thalamus and the cortex. If information from the senses (which necessarily passes through the thalamus) never reaches the cortex, then the patient will be cut off from the outside world while undergoing their epileptic seizure.

Fugue states— Though rare, the *fugue* state is a fashionable topic of discussion because it is so intriguing. Once famous example (alleged to be caused by temporal lobe epilepsy) originates from a Friday evening 1896, when Henry T. Clarke left his home in New Haven and headed to the railway station, where he worked for a baggage transfer firm. Based on his police statement, his next memory was when he woke alone in a strange bed and found his clothes were different from what he'd been wearing when he left for work. His wife was nowhere to be found. Exploring further, he discovered he was booked into a lodging house in San Francisco, his name was now A. Walker, and eight weeks had passed. Clarke was aware that he'd suffered similar amnesic episodes when in his home town, although these usually only lasted a few hours. He'd even been supplied with a medical diagnosis for his condition when attending university — namely "congestion of the brain" (Schnabel 1995). Although it sounds a rather silly label, it does hold some charm and is perhaps more evocative of the source of the amnesia compared with the somewhat cold description of Clarke's disorder as an "epileptic fugue state."

The reason a fugue is not simply a case of amnesia is that the sufferer behaves in ways that outwardly seem quite sociable, but isn't normal with respect to their own personality or life experiences. It turns out that Henry T. Clarke had stolen money from his employer before the amnesia and this was quite uncharacteristic for him — or so we are told, the assumption being he wasn't just using the fugue excuse as a means of escaping punishment for a planned crime.

An alternative label for the fugue state is *zombie mode* (Koch and Crick 2001), whereby the individual is said to lack *qualia*, or the phenomenal feeling of consciousness.[13] Nevertheless, patients retain cognitive consciousness so they can still be seen by others to behave normally even though they are in essence only responsive automatons. Why people in fugue states behave so differently to their normal selves is not known.

Trances— Some people with temporal lobe epilepsy also display *dissociative trance disorder*, whereby they fall into a trance after a specific external cue. For example, a Japanese patient who had a reputation of mediumship would hear the name and birthdate of a client during a sitting, then quickly fall into a trance, chanting prayers (Ogata and Miyakawa 1998). It is this type of nonordinary behavior (chanting and so forth) that distinguish trances from absence seizures, fugues or amnesic states. This behavior also bears some similarity to the auditory hallucinations experienced by the female Japanese epileptic patient discussed previously, although the woman in this earlier example had some recollection of the event after returning to consciousness.

As an aside, trances are not the only temporal lobe symptom associated with religiosity. Christian epileptic patients display a greater intensity of spiritual experience than non-epileptic churchgoers. This might involve the patients' encountering a great spiritual figure, or an angel, or a spirit guide during their lives (Trimble and Freeman 2006).[14]

When Symptoms Combine

Temporal lobe epileptics can experience a combination of temporal lobe signs. For instance, a patient visiting the consultant neurologist Adam Zeman reported at the onset of an epileptic episode the sense of an "indefinable" smell or taste coupled with a memory lingering on the outskirts of consciousness, as well as sexual arousal. On one occasions, this culminated in a "graceful" collapse to the floor, and a short period of unconsciousness (Zeman 2005).

Temporal Lobe Signs and the "Normal" Population

It might seem a little off topic that we've spent so much time examining the symptoms of a neurological disorder such as temporal lobe epilepsy, since the emphasis of the book so far has been that paranormal experience is overwhelmingly reported by people not suffering from any overt mental illness or brain dysfunction. However, Persinger, his colleagues, and supporters of his thesis argue that microseizures of the temporal lobes can generate a kind of "mini" epileptic event. Furthermore, these incidents are common in all people at all times, particularly when they're asleep, but only manifest as an unusual subjective experience when a number of microseizures combine to create a seizure focus. The word "coherence" is often used in this context, meaning hyperactivity of different temporal lobe regions occurs simultaneously or coherently. As the proportion of neurons affected increases, clinical symptoms begin to appear (Persinger and Makarec 1993).

Temporal lobe epilepsy is therefore not an "all-or-nothing" state only suffered by epileptics. Rather, temporal lobe lability (or hyperactivity) is said to exist along a continuum in the population in a similar way to fantasy prone personality or any other personality trait we've discussed. In fact, some temporal lobe signs or transients caused by mini-seizures are even considered desirable. Poets, for example, show more temporal lobe signs than "normals" (Persinger and Makarec 1993). However, the more extreme manifestation of temporal lobe lability is indistinguishable from temporal lobe epilepsy proper, and apparently can lead sufferers to social withdrawal, suicidal ideation and a fantasy life that interferes with their normal social functioning.

Nevertheless, most people who claim paranormal experiences cannot be classified as mentally ill. Nor do they display overt signs of epilepsy. Consequently, a label such as temporal lobe lability is attractive to psychologists because it neatly describes how outwardly normal, healthy individuals can experience extraordinary paranormal episodes.

What "Normal" Events Might Cause Temporal Lobe Lability?

A perfectly normal event that might encourage right hemispheric dominance is *dream sleep*, although this was disputed some time ago by researchers Howard Ehrlichman, John Antrobus and Marjorie Wiener, who showed using EEG that there is no dominance by either hemisphere in dreaming (Ehrlichman, Antrobus and Wiener 1985). The original claim derives from studies on epileptic patients, the results of which suggests this disorder might drive an actual "right hemisphere–dream focus" (Serafetinides 1993).

Alternately, it has been argued that emotional stress from bereavement (Persinger and Makarec 1987), or metabolic anomalies such as fasting or hypoxia, also permit right hemispheric intrusion or other temporal lobe signs. Even meditation might encourage interhemispheric coherence (Cook and Persinger 1997). On a related note, induced trance states are an ancient religious and spiritual practice and are generated from activities such as forced starvation, hypoxia, stress and drug use. In fact, the whole gamut of paranormal and mystical experiences — from psi to OBEs and NDEs to encounters with the entities and the divine — can be generated from drug ingestion.

In particular, entity encounters are strongly associated with the chemical N, N-dimethyltryptamine (DMT) and it variants. DMT is a natural component of some psychoactive plants and concoctions made from these plants, such as the South American *ayahuasca* brew (Luke and Kittenis 2005, Hancock 2005). Obviously mainstream psychologists don't believe these drugs actually open hidden communication channels in the brain to other transcendental realms.[15] Instead, they might see evidence of hemispheric coherence that leads to hallucinations interpreted by the drug-taker as encounters with aliens, intelligent plants, or God.

Temporal Lobe Lability and the Paranormal

So far we've learned of the contentious proposition by Michael Persinger that a sense of presence, caused by a temporal lobe transient, is a neat explanation for alien or ghostly encounters. The chemical, pungent and burnt odors that are a documented characteristic of a microseizure succinctly explains the smells often reported inside alien spacecraft during an abduction (e.g., Rullán 2000[16]). Fugue states cause "missing time." Trance states become "spirit channeling." The sexual and visceral elements of a temporal lobe seizure explain reports of extraterrestrial aliens taking sperm samples, indulging in "anal probing"[17] and fetus removal. In another cultural setting temporal lobe symptoms would account for alleged rape by demonic beings, while déjà vu and auras solve the mystery of reincarnation stories and psychic experiences such as precognition. The heightened emotion and cognition brought on by a seizure explains the deep instructions or advice given to abductees by their aliens hosts, or to those who interact with angelic beings.

Occasionally, a paranormal case stands out as obviously sincere but patently unreal, in the sense that the contact reported by the victim with an extraordinary entity has been observed by impartial witnesses to be anything but physical. One classic example is the experience of Australian woman Maureen Puddy. Narrated by Judith Magee, one of the original investigators, the story goes that one evening in July 1972 Maureen was driving along a road on the outskirts of the city of Melbourne when she saw a blue light in the sky. She stopped the car and got out to have a closer look, and reported that she saw a 100-foot long, blue-colored UFO hovering ahead. She quickly jumped back in the car and drove off, but the UFO followed her for a short time before streaking away. A few weeks later she was on the same road, at about the same time of night, and saw the same UFO. Her car engine stalled and although frightened, Maureen was reassured by a voice in her head that told her, among other things, "We mean you no harm."

Later in February 1973, Maureen received a telepathic message telling her to return to where she saw the UFO in order to gain further information from the visitors. Magee and colleague Paul Normal met Maureen at the original site, and found her in an agitated state. Apparently, an entity wearing a suit made out of material resembling gold foil had materialized in her car, then disappeared again. Sitting in her stationwagon and talking to Magee and Norman, Maureen then claimed she could see the entity again, this time walking towards the group. Neither investigator saw anything unusual, although they acknowledged that Maureen was sincere in expressing anxiety over what she was witnessing — Magee assumed the communication was equivalent to a private "closed circuit television" message between the entity and Maureen. Maureen then entered a type of trance, when she began describing the interior of the UFO in which she and the entity now stood, the entity pointing towards a mushroom-shaped object in the middle of a room, with the consistency of jelly, that might have been something like a compass. Maureen eventually awoke from her stupor and explained that the entity had departed. Of course, all this happened despite the fact that Maureen never left her car seat.

Viewing the case after nearly 40 years, the contemporary psychological explanation is that Maureen Puddy's encounter with aliens derived from persistent epileptic seizures of the temporal lobes.

CHAPTER 6

Witnessing the Paranormal: The Induction of Hallucinatory Encounters

Having examined some of the internal origins of temporal lobe seizures that cause paranormal experience, it's interesting to discover that researchers have also identified possible external causes for transients too. One theory combines the features of temporal lobe lability with the claim that transients can be induced in the brain by environmental events. External causes that have been implicated include natural earth and meteorological events. This theory is reliant on the fact that information processing in the brain is electrochemical, and these subtle processes could be affected by outside electromagnetic forces. However, before we examine the theory any further we need to understand exactly what "electromagnetic" and "electrochemical" processes are.

Electromagnetism

The electrical or magnetic influences on a person (or anything else in nature for that matter) can be described in terms of the word *field*, which has both a magnitude (strength) and a direction.

Some electric and magnetic fields that surround a source, such as a battery or a magnet, are stationary and don't vary over time. In other words, the strength of the field varies depending on where you are standing relative to it, since fields weaken the farther away you move from the source. Alternately, if you stay in the same spot and don't move, the field won't change its magnitude. Imagine of a metal magnet lying on a table and you've envisaged a stationary magnetic field.

However, it's possible for electric or magnetic fields to fluctuate over time, so at any point in the field the nature of influence over a person in that field varies. Under these circumstances, magnetic and electric fields are very closely related. That is, an alternating electric field (changing over time) will induce a magnetic field. Very simplistically, we can also imagine electric and magnetic fields merging to become an electromagnetic wave, such that it has both an electric component and a magnetic component. It's a termed a wave because it can be drawn like a wave — the electric and magnetic components oscillating at any point along it (with peaks and troughs like waves on the ocean).

Moreover, the electromagnetic wave radiates out from its source at the speed of light, hence the use of the term electromagnetic radiation. Visible light is a form of electromagnetic radiation we're all familiar with.

Sources of electromagnetic radiation can be anything from vibrating molecules giving off heat energy (infrared electromagnetic radiation), to nuclear decay (gamma rays) (Cutnell and Johnson 2006). The electromagnetic wave also carries energy, which is obvious if you think of the heat that's present in the sun's rays — another example of electromagnetic radiation. The source of the electromagnetic wave will determine how much energy it carries. For example, radio frequency waves from a radio transmitter carry little energy compared to a gamma ray. A good way to envisage this energy is as a wavelength or a frequency. Imagine a slice of wave with a single trough and two half-peaks on either side. This is one wavelength. If we represent the two half-peaks and trough as a graph with time drawn on the horizontal axis, then this waveform will possess a lower frequency than a wave with 10, or 50, or 10,000 peaks and troughs squashed up in the same space. Consequently, radio frequency waves have low energy because they have low frequency, whereas gamma waves have very high frequency and are packed with energy.

Notably, the energy possessed by an electromagnetic wave weakens as it travels through the environment. If you imagine a "piece" of radiation emitted from a single source, it actually travels as a thin expanding sphere away from that source. Since a fixed amount of energy was given off to start with, as the sphere grows, any "place" on the sphere has less and less energy. The energy has to be shared across more and more space on the surface of the invisible sphere. To get a better idea, think about a growing bubble made of blue ink. The amount of ink is fixed. The small bubble of ink is dark blue, but as it grows it gets lighter and lighter, as the ink gets shared around. Another way to think of the decreasing intensity of the wave is to imagine the magnitude of the electric and magnetic waves decreasing.

Electromagnetism and Paranormal Experience

It's all very well to describe electromagnetic radiation, but the question remains: how can this radiation influence people, and what's this got to do with paranormal experience? One suggestion might be as a transfer of energy. If electromagnetic radiation hits a person, the energy contained in the wave dissipates, and if there's enough energy, the area affected can heat up rapidly. In fact, if the electromagnetic wave is energetic enough the atoms that make up the molecules in a person's body can be ionized. That is, some of the electrons are knocked out of them. Electrons are very important in the stability of molecules, yet when loose they become a sort of local electric (eddy) current, and having a sea of free electrons loose inside the body isn't healthy.

Another, more subtle aspect of the interaction between electromagnetic radiation and the human body is the effect the electric and magnetic fields can have on the normal operation of neurons in the brain. To appreciate this process, let's look at how neurons actually work.

Neurons

Neurons are a type of cell that are hugely larger than the atoms or molecules they are built from. Nevertheless, the electrical charge of these ingredients (either positive or negative) is important in determining how neurons work. Specifically, there is normally more negatively charged material inside the cell than there is in the fluid they float in (called interstitial fluid). For a neuron to become active and send a message to some other part of the brain or body, a localized region of holes (called channels) which transverse the surface of the neuron must open — they are normally shut. Typically, the opening of channels is caused by the arrival of a chemical (a neurotransmitter or hormone) from somewhere else in the body. In one common circumstance, the opened channels let some of the positive charge (sodium ions) from the surrounding fluid into the neuron.

The entry of this positive charge opens up adjacent channels which also let in more positive charge, which then open up adjacent channels and so on, down the line. As a result, an electrochemical message is transferred along the length of the neuron to some distant place where another neurotransmitter might be released from the nerve's "tail" (or terminal). The word *electrochemical* is used to describe this process because there is an electric component (the charged particles traveling in and out of the cell, both positive and negative) and a chemical component (the physical movement of charged atoms such as sodium).

Placing charged particles, such as sodium ion, in the fluctuating field of an electromagnetic wave will influence the way they behave. In turn, the normal operation of a whole neuron (which depends on the charge movement to function correctly) might be affected, leading to all sorts of microscopic physiological consequences[1] (Frankel and Liburdy 1996). The question is, can the operation of the whole brain — a huge collection of neurons and other supporting cells — be coherently influenced by subtle changes in external electromagnetic radiation? Put another way, can electromagnetic stimulation cause collections of cells to alter their function, yet leave the brain physically undamaged? Electromagnetic radiation can certainly damage the body outwardly (think of sunburn), and while electric fields tend not to penetrate the human body to any great depth, magnetic fields are not inhibited nearly as much. As a result, a popular notion is that fluctuating magnetic fields on their own (disconnected from any electrical component) can influence human behavior by delicately influencing brain activity.

The Potential Influence of the Earth's Magnetic Field on Human Behavior

As might be expected, Michael Persinger and co-workers have endorsed this possibility and published a huge amount of scientific papers prefaced with the title *Geophysical Variables and Behavior*. This shows they hold a strong suspicion that the physical fields and energies emanating from the earth might interact with the brain and influence behavior, hence the "geo-" part in the word *geophysical*.[2] They believe one of the main culprits is the weak magnetic field of the earth, also called the *main field*.

The main field emanates from the earth's liquid core, which is in constant flux (or change). Movement of countless charged particles in the core creates a huge electric current, and this in turn induces a magnetic field with a north pole (the actual Magnetic North Pole) and a south pole (the actual Magnetic South Pole)[3] in the way that a simple bar-shaped iron magnet has a north pole and south pole. The main field covers the earth like a spherical glove and — this is the important bit —fluctuates over the short and long term. The field is also influenced by electrical currents that dance around in the upper atmosphere. These atmospheric currents are generated by streams of radiation emitted from the sun (called solar flares) which ionize particles in the earth's upper atmosphere. Ionized particles, such as protons and electrons, are also emitted on occasion from the sun itself, an event known as the solar wind. The solar wind is so influential it can distort the normally spherical shape of the earth's magnetic field into the shape of a teardrop! These cyclic periods have the dramatic name of *geomagnetic storms* (Gonzales, Joselyn, Kamide, Kroehl, Rostoker, Tsurutani and Vasyliunas 1994).

Other, earthbound factors can also affect local and global measures of geomagnetism. These include geological features under the earth's surface — most notably rocks formed millions of years ago that have strong magnetic properties. Subsequently, certain places on earth can experience a magnetic field far more intense than neighboring regions. Under-surface channels of earth and rock can also be high in electrical conductivity and can affect geomagnetic activity (Campbell 2003).

From this physical evidence, it's interesting to postulate whether any of this natural geomagnetic activity influences human behavior. There's quite a lot of evidence that animals such as bees and pigeons interact with the Earth's main field and perform impressive navigational feats. However, less is known about the reaction of humans to the field. Nevertheless, associations have been proposed that are detrimental to human thinking and behavior. Before examining these theories, it would be remiss not to appreciate a rare, controversial positive geomagnetic influence. In a study by John Palmer and colleagues from the Rhine Research Center in Durham, North Carolina and Liverpool Hope University in England, it is proposed that the Earth's geomagnetic field increases human electrodermal activity (e.g., perspiration). According to these researchers, this in turn might account for various psychokinetic and psychic healing effects on the body, with the sensitive human "agent" recruiting the energy in a particular location to assist them in their tasks (Palmer, Simmonds-Moore and Baumann 2006). The mechanisms of this proposed effect remains, not unexpectedly, a mystery.

Returning to the alleged negative consequences of changes in geomagnetic activity on humans, epileptic seizures and accounts of ghostly apparitions are reportedly more frequent in places where geomagnetic activity has increased (Booth et al. 2005), for example after a geomagnetic storm. The way differences in this geomagnetic activity are measured is through the calculation of indices of disturbance. One is the K-index, which is derived from the main field and is calculated daily, as the overall global index, from measurements obtained from various magnetic observatories world-wide (Haraldsson and Gissurarson 1987). Once the interested psychologist has collected this data, they can correlate global and local geomagnetic measurements with whatever paranormal variable they're interested in — a rash of UFO sightings perhaps, or poltergeist disturbances, or manifestations of the Virgin Mary. If a significant statistical relationship is found, then it might be argued that something resembling temporal lobe lability has been induced geomagnetically in enough people to explain the hysteria. Some communities will see UFOs in the sky, while others might witness religious symbols from Heaven. The differences in reported phenomena are explained offhandedly as "cultural" or "psychosocial."

Local Earth Energies

Another external influence said to affect the human nervous system is that generated intermittently and locally through movement of the Earth's surface. When the Earth's huge tectonic plates shift during an earthquake there are many stresses and strains on the surrounding rock, just as there are when volcanic activity injects hot fluids and gasses into them. It is proposed that both types of events can change local magnetic and electrical fields (Johnston 1989). For example, in certain rocks placed under pressure, the resultant change in internal structure creates small magnetic alterations in the order of tens of nanotesla (nT)[4] compared to the normally stable, surrounding magnetic field (Martin-Del Pozzo, Cifuentes-Nava, Cabral-Cano, Sánchez-Rubio, Reyes, Martínez-Bringas, Garcia and Arango-Galvan 2002). Rocks showing this property are called piezomagnetic. It has even been alleged that such changes might be large enough to induce changes in a person's labile temporal lobes if that person is standing close to these rocks. In an early paper on the subject, Michael Persinger also refers to the extremely low frequency electromagnetic radiation created by weather events such as frontal activity and thunderstorms. The energy in these natural events possesses wavelengths approximating the circumference of the Earth[5] and has both penetrating ability[6] and ranges with power peaks resembling waveforms in the human brain (Persinger 1975).

Tectonic Strain Theory

The proposal that the earth's moving crust can alter human brain function, leading to all sorts of weird and visionary experiences, is known as *tectonic strain theory*. These strains are barely perceptible as actual earthquakes, yet manifest neurologically as UFO reports (Persinger 1979).

According to the theory, even a weak display of seismic activity across a large region of land will contain pockets of high activity that is cancelled out, across its expanse, by other sections of the fault where no activity is registered. However, a tiny human in one of these intense sections will encounter the psychological manifestations of field exposure (Persinger 1990). Conveniently for the theory, this effect won't be noticeable at the regional level, hence residents in the surrounding districts will be completely unaware of the geomagnetic cause of the paranormal experiences reported nearby. In the 1970s and 1980s, Persinger and colleagues wrote a number of articles claiming that correlations exist between seismic activity and reports of UFOs. These reports are the cornerstone of the tectonic strain theory because they allow the possibility of prediction, something eagerly sought for a scientific theory.

Ball Lightning and Earthlights

Interestingly, it is not only invisible geomagnetism that allegedly induces paranormal experiences. There is some evidence that volcanoes and earthquakes might produce actual luminous phenomena that people can see with their own eyes and that lead to reports of UFOs or other weird phenomena. For example, multiple eyewitness reports of strange lights were made by fishermen shortly before an earthquake struck at Kobe, Japan, in 1995. These men saw a large glowing orange ball move from an island in the Osaka Bay to Mt. Rokko, near Kobe, and strike the mountain, causing a fall of lightning (Kamogawa, Ofuruton and Ohtsuki 2005). How lightforms (commonly called *earthlights*) of such size and persistence can be created is not well understood, although one suggestion by these scientists is that the emission of electrons from crushed rocks within the fault excites air molecules enough for them to emit photons of visible light. Alternately, if the disturbance of the earth's fault is considerable it will produce a voltage between the cracks that's large enough to give off energy in the form of electromagnetic waves such as infrared radiation, or even visible light radiation (Rutkowski 1983).

According to the theory, invisible magnetic fields subtly shape the brain's neural activity and can generate acute, epileptic-like seizures that produce a variety of paranormal experiences. Alternately, the Earth's geomagnetic forces might simply create a natural lightform in the absence of earthquake activity or even the hint of a volcano, and these physical events are witnessed from afar and interpreted as anomalous.

As mentioned, these lightforms are commonly associated with seismic or volcanic activity. Some lightforms are also associated with simple storms. Ball lightning, for example, is a variety of free floating lightning behaving in erratic ways (Wessel-Berg 2003). It might comprise ionized plasma which has been created in the aftermath of a lightning strike, whereby the energy dispersed across a storm cloud becomes highly localized in the form of a small glowing globe temporarily protected from rapid decay. Separated from the normal atmosphere surrounding it, two distinct phases co-exist, which gives it a strange appearance. For many years ball lightning was considered an optical illusion because of its bizarre behavior and longevity, so different from "normal" lightning that lasts only an instant before it dissipates.

Some weird properties of ball lightning summarized by physicist David Turner include a spherical shape — from one centimeter to over a meter, an ability to emit light, the apparent coolness of its surface, its physical stability (surviving for as long as 100 seconds), erratic motion and its association with stormy weather (Turner 1998). Also interesting is its capacity to interfere with radio reception, and the way it can cause bizarre damage. In one example, ball lightning punctured a hole through a glass window pane, leaving perfectly fitting glass disc on the floor nearby (Corliss 1983). Perhaps most strangely of all, ball lightning has a tendency to be drawn inside buildings, but at the same time it appears to avoid obstructions as it travels. The seemingly "clever" behavior gives ball lightning something of a mystical status. In fact, the weirdly behaving earthlights associated with seismic rather than storm, activity has a reputation for intelligence!

Referring to paranormal encounters with earth energies and associated earthlights, Jim Schnabel elegantly summarizes how the light phenomena "swerve and swoop crazily" in the night sky, affected by changes in the invisible electromagnetic topography of the atmosphere. At the same time, radios and televisions crackle with interference, compasses spin and animals and humans "howl and hallucinate" respectively — the outcome of a temporal lobe micro-seizure. Earthlights don't disappear in the daytime, either. They might be a little harder to see, but a witness could still perceive the boundary between

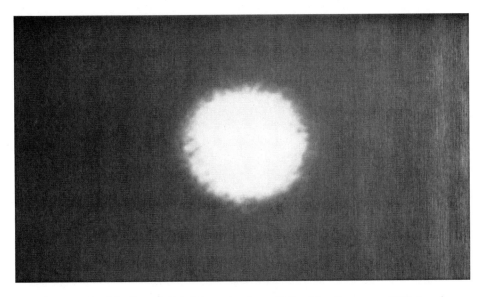

A photograph of the "spook light" haunting Long Valley, New Jersey, ca. 1970. Local legend says it is a lantern swinging from the hand of a long-dead railroad conductor known as The Hookerman. An earthly explanation for this phenomenon was provided in a 1976 investigation, when the light was determined to be a gaseous plasma produced by seismic activity in the locale. From a broader sociological perspective, various U.S. states have a shared mythology of spook lights associated with dead railroad workers — which is just as intriguing as their straightforward, scientific explanation (Fortean Picture Library).

air and the ionized plasma in strange ways, perhaps as a metallic object ... an extraterrestrial flying saucer? (Schnabel 1995).

Apart from the initial hallucination, any additional symptom the witness reports — from bruising and radiation sickness to a changed view on life and the universe — can by explained as a combination of external exposure to damaging electromagnetic energies and the internal effect of a temporal lobe transient. All in all, we have a popular theory which skeptics (and psychologists) admire because of its technical foundation and its comprehensive ability to account for all facets of intense paranormal experience.

Geomagnetic and Technological Induction of Paranormal Experience Within Buildings

Not only are UFO reports explained using theories of tectonic strain and temporal lobe lability. Recall that hauntings inside buildings include reports of ghostly apparitions, voices, raps, various noises, movements of objects, smells, cold breezes, luminous phenomena and disturbances of electrical equipment (Alvarado and Zingrone 1995). You'll notice that many of these events could also be attributed a geomagnetic origin, with accompanying temporal lobe symptoms. Therefore, we shouldn't be surprised to learn that some researchers believe geomagnetic fields might be associated with haunted houses too. Jason Braithwaite and colleagues from the Behavioral Brain Science Centre at the University of Birmingham in England refer to "experience-inducing fields" which increase brain activity in sensitive people — leading to seizures and stories of ghostly encounters (Braithwaite, Perez-Aquino and Townsend 2004).

The fields might be natural and have no problem penetrating the walls of a house. Normally, the earth has a static average magnetic field approximating 50,000 nT, but this value can change by 40 or 50 nT in as little as four minutes due to natural variations. Although this seems small compared to the overall field size, it is this complex variation, rather than the absolute strength of the field, which is said to be crucial in generating phenomenological haunting experiences. Such a change is alleged to be large enough to influence normal brain function, and Persinger believes field fluctuations exceeding 30nT can increase night-time temporal lobe seizures (Persinger likes to use the expression "between 2 A.M. and 4 A.M.").

Seizure prevalence is apparently due to the magnetic field decreasing levels of a brain chemical called melatonin, in the absence of which another epileptogenic (epilepsy-causing) chemical, corticotropin releasing factor (CRF) is increased. Therefore, it is argued that microseizures of the temporal lobes are more likely to occur in the early morning, and particularly during a period of bereavement when a person is mourning the loss of a loved one. Their disrupted sleep patterns ultimately lead to elevated amounts of CRF and the increased possibility of a transient episode (Persinger 2001, Lange, Houran and Harte 1996). Taking this to its logical conclusion, it appears that that bereavement, the early morning and sleeplessness, coupled with a fluctuating magnetic field close by, all combine to create a potential ghost sighting.[7]

Actual incidents of this type of occurrence have been investigated by Persinger and his co-workers. Claims of strange lights, shadowy forms, odd noises and a feeling of fear in a residential building in Sudbury, Canada, were linked to geomagnetic pulsed electromagnetic bursts occurring over successive nights in the vicinity of the building (Persinger and Cameron 1986). Explaining another type of paranormal event, the authors suggested that objects allegedly moved by spirits in poltergeist cases occur when the claimant enters a trance like "automatism" as a function of a temporal lobe transient. Naturally, they move the objects themselves in their trance, and when they return to waking consciousness they are at a loss to explain how object shifted its position.

Buildings are full of electrical and magnetic "noise" — typically emanating from electrical appliances — with the impressive title of man-made power-frequency electromagnetic fields (Braithwaite 2005). Various other energies present are ionizing radiation, and ultrasound (Lange, Houran and Harte 1996), which have also been linked to the development of labile states and even sleep paralysis (Conesa 2000) and, ultimately, haunting and poltergeist experiences. Persinger describes one case involving a young couple in their home. Both apparently displayed heightened temporal lobe sensitivity (meaning they were prone to seizure activity) and reported being woken by an apparition after midnight. The experience included hearing breathing near their bed and the feeling of apprehension and "sense of presence." Persinger and colleagues monitored the couple's "electronically dense" house over a number of nights and discovered fluctuating magnetic fields, due to poor electrical grounding, that coincided with the reports of the ghostly encounter. Paranormal case solved (Persinger 2001).

In another example, they investigated the case of a young female who had been referred to a psychiatrist because she'd witnessed apparitions, felt a phantom stimulation of her vagina and uterus, and sensed the presence of a baby over her left shoulder — all in the early morning while she was still in bed. The patient's interpretation of these events was religious, rather than paranormal. Persinger's interpretation, as expected, was very different from the patient's. Apparently the girl had suffered damage to her frontal lobes as a younger child, although this injury did not manifest itself outwardly as a change of behavior. Nevertheless, the implication was that her brain might have been more "labile" than normal, and further investigation uncovered a pulsed magnetic field from an electronic clock that sat inches from her head as she slept. Putting all this evidence together, it was determined that the magnetic field suppressed nocturnal melatonin levels, which in turn increased the likelihood of temporal lobe seizures. The religious interpretation, one again, was attributed to cultural conditioning.

Testing the Electromagnetic Hypothesis: Experiments in Real Haunted Houses

In a detailed set of experiments, Richard Wiseman and colleagues sought to test the electromagnetic hypothesis by measuring the variables of magnetism and radiation at a "haunted" location[8], and chose the famous Hampton Court Palace in Surrey, England (Wiseman, Watt, Greening, Stevens and O'Keefe 2002). Two "haunted" sections of the palace were chosen for the experiment; the Haunted Gallery (labeled "A") and the Georgian Rooms (labeled "B"). Then they chose participants from tour-groups visiting the palace and divided these tourists into two groups — one group was subtly informed that A wasn't haunted but B was, and the other group was told that B wasn't haunted but A was. Recall that this is the method of suggestion, whereby a participant's later memory of an event can be altered by the information they receive before or during the event.

Wiseman and colleagues also determined whether the participants were believers in ghosts, and whether they had any prior knowledge of the haunted reputation of Hampton Court. This was to establish whether their subjects would assign special significance to the allegedly haunted areas of the palace as a consequence of the experimenters' suggestions, and subsequently report symptoms of haunting such as increased emotions, a sense of presence, temperature changes, dizziness, or unusual smells, sounds, visions and tastes.

Once the tour was finished the participants' experiences were analyzed, and Wiseman and colleagues found more symptoms of ghostly presence in believers compared with non-believers. As we've seen, psychologists would attribute this to believers' proneness to cognitive mistakes or psychogenic sensitivity. Alternately, it might be because they are more sensitive to real-life ghosts. In contrast, there was no influence of suggestion on its own. That is, the group of participants who were told that area A was more haunted than area B didn't necessarily experience more ghostly signs in A, regardless of whether they were believers or not. The same applied to the group told area B was more haunted than area A.[9]

Wiseman and colleagues also learned that strange (ghostly) experiences were positively related to local magnetic fields detected in certain parts of the building. This relationship was also independent of belief, suggesting believers aren't necessarily more sensitive than non-believers to invisible fields. In a follow-up study, these researchers more accurately pinpointed the areas of the palace that were believed to be haunted, and tested whether visitors were more likely to report their experiences in these known haunted areas (Wiseman, Watt, Stevens, Greening and O'Keefe 2003). Participants were required to individually rank the "haunted feel" of different areas in the palace, while the strength and variance of local magnetic fields in their vicinity were recorded.

It transpired that participants were significantly more likely to feel temperature changes, dizziness, headaches, shortness of breath, foul odors, sensed presence, intense emotions and sickness in the traditionally haunted locations compared to non-haunted "control" locations, regardless of how much they consciously knew about the history of the palace. These haunted locations also possessed local magnetic fields displaying significantly more variation than control areas. However, before jumping to a Persinger-like conclusion about the magnetic origins of the paranormal experience, Wiseman's group conceded that other, simpler variables exist alongside fluctuating magnetic fields which are stronger candidates in explaining the ghostly sensations.

These include prior knowledge of the haunted area (as we've discussed) but also subtle draughts or natural odors, the presence of low frequency sound waves and a lower level of light which make the location feel eerie. For example, a specific corner in the palace's Haunted Gallery was frequently chosen by visitors as a site where they experience "funny feelings." It also showed an unusual magnetic field variation. Yet when examined more carefully, it turned out the corner was actually the darkest spot in the gallery and that's what makes people feel creepy. These embedded cues certainly confound the experimental results, making it difficult to determine what the source of the haunting experience actually is. So, in a follow-up study the influence of these additional variables was closely examined (Wiseman, Watt, Stevens, Greening and O'Keefe 2003).

To avoid the possibility that visitors to a "haunted" location change their behavior explicitly (or unconsciously) because they're aware of its history, Wiseman and colleagues now chose the South Bridge Vaults for their experiment. These vaults are a reputedly haunted array of rooms built into the arches of a late 18th century bridge in Edinburgh, Scotland. Although publicized locally as a haunted site, the specific details of where the "ghosts" actually reside is less well known. As in earlier experiments, participants were required to individually rank the "haunted feel" of different areas of the vaults, but on this occasion a wider range of physical variables were tested, not simply the strength and variance of local magnetic fields.

These additional variables included air temperature, air movement, outside lighting in the corridors, a vault's interior lighting, its floor space and ceiling height. Remarkably, the results gathered by Wiseman and his colleagues showed that participants did report their ghostly experiences in the areas traditionally identified as "haunted." However, while this implies a consistency of experience among participants, it doesn't necessarily mean they were sensing actual ghosts in the vaults. To the investigators, it was more likely that the participants were sensitive to environmental variables in those areas, such as cramped floor space and the very low ceiling height of the vaults. Unfortunately for the geomagnetic theory of paranormal experience, fluctuating magnetic fields were not correlated with visitors' haunt experiences.

Wiseman is not the only researcher to investigate haunted houses and publish the findings in reputable journals. Earlier studies have been performed by Michaeleen Maher, for example, at Pennsylvania's General Wayne Inn in 1988 (Maher 2000). For many years, Maher has led "sensitives"[10] and skeptics through haunted locations to identify individuals who could "pick" where an apparition or poltergeist was known to reside (Maher and Schmeidler 1975, Maher and Hansen 1992, Maher and Hansen 1995).

The General Wayne Inn study recruited three sensitives and three skeptics who were led through the building, their task to locate the haunted sites and dismiss the non-haunted areas. Magnetic field strengths were measured in each location[11], and photos, videos and sounds were also recorded. Of the five remaining participants supplying data (one skeptic did not), only one "sensitive" performed better than chance on the task. Furthermore, there was no relationship between the magnitude of magnetic field measurement and a chosen "haunted site."[12] Results such as these, and Wiseman's from the United Kingdom, therefore suggest that ghostly encounters are not necessarily a function of a seer's ability to unconsciously detect natural but invisible magnetic stimuli in the surrounding environment.

To be fair, other studies come to different conclusions. In one example, Jason Braithwaite and team chose the haunted site of Muncaster Castle in Cumbria, England, and did find magnetic differences between the pillow area of a bed located in the castle's haunted tapestry room (where ghosts are traditionally seen at night) and the surrounding environment. These included higher magnetic baseline levels coupled with the occasional magnetic burst lasting a number of minutes. Braithwaite argues the presence of these weak magnetic anomalies across any night, coupled with the susceptibility of the sleeper to labile episode, their expectations of seeing ghosts and their level of arousal, were responsible for the paranormal reports. The origin of the static field disturbance was attributed to the bed's magnetized metal mesh, on which sleepers move around (Braithwaite and Townsend 2005, Braithwaite and

Townsend 2008). In addition, the field changes in the remote castle were actually greater than what is normal in a built-up, high population area, hence there might be a geological source to the field rather than a technological (electronic) one. Braithwaite suspects the castle was built on natural magnetic materials called specularite and magnetite, and the site is also located in the vicinity of two fault lines.

Furthermore, in cases where magnetic field measurements don't correlate strongly with paranormal phenomenon, it might be due to the different way these measurements are taken (Braithwaite 2005). To correct this perceived problem, Braithwaite developed the magnetic anomaly detection system, or MADS for short, which he hopes will allow consistency in the way hallucination-inducing magnetic fields are measured in haunting cases. The MADS is a bit like an EEG recorder, although it gathers data across time for magnetic fields in local environments, rather than the electrical signals emanating from the brain.

Transcranial Magnetic Stimulation

It is one thing to speculate that a relationship exists between "energies" in natural or built locations and paranormal experiences. It's another thing to formally test this putative relationship. In an attempt to perform such a test, Persinger and his research group constructed a helmet attached with wire coils that generates a complex, weak magnetic field similar in strength to that given off by a computer screen (Persinger 2001). This technique they label *transcranial magnetic stimulation* (TMS) and the researchers believe it to be a non-evasive way of influencing cortical neurons. When an alternating electric current is run through the coils, it produces a magnetic field that passes through the skull and allegedly induces tiny electric currents in the brain that locally affect cortical processing. For example, if speech areas of the left hemisphere are targeted by stimulation, there can be speech arrest (Wassermann, Blaxton, Hoffman, Berry, Oletsky, Pascual-Leone and Theodore 1999).

In one typical case, Persinger and co-workers claim that a man who had experienced a haunting at his residence reported the same fearful sensations when a special "recipe"[13] of TMS was applied to his right temporal lobe in the laboratory. In order to understand what the magnetic stimulation was actually doing to his brain, simultaneous EEG readings showed paroxysmal (meaning frequent and rapid) activity in this location (Persinger, Tiller and Koren 2000). Of course, one could argue that the laboratory-based stimulation simply set off the same phenomenological sensation, such as a memory, that the original haunting created. By analogy, an electrode directly stimulating

A young Michael Persinger photographed during a break at a scientific conference during the 1970s. Persinger, backed by a strong research team, would surely be the most prominent investigator of brain-focused psychological causes for paranormal experience, having published a huge range of scientific studies from the 1970s through the present. Over the last few years there has been some criticisms of certain findings from his group, particularly those related to the impact that fluctuating magnetic fields have on the generation of anomalous experience. However, this doesn't seem to have negatively impacted his research program, which appears to be as busy as ever — although the written output is perhaps worded with a little more caution (Fortean Picture Library).

the limbic system can elicit fear in a patient, but that doesn't prove that a fearful response is a meaningless artifact and nothing real can ever create it with purpose.

Putting this criticism to one side, Persinger instead suggests that TMS helps generate intercalation of hemispheres and allows the intrusion of right hemispheric processes into waking consciousness — a process we've previously discussed. A more recent theory from his laboratory is that a weak magnetic field, such as that provided by TMS, can "split" the energy emitted from sub-atomic processes[14] occurring in neurons from which consciousness arises. This apparently creates a "second consciousness" in a person, and accounts for experiences, such as sense-of-presence, that are interpreted as paranormal (Booth et al. 2008). Take note, however, that this is a very complicated and speculative theory indeed.

CHAPTER 7

Criticisms of Tectonic Strain Theory and Transcranial Stimulation Methods, and Alternative Electromagnetic Theories

One of the notable aspects of Persinger's case study of the girl and her bedroom encounter with a supernatural baby is that she cannot be considered average, because she had suffered brain damage and she held an extreme religious interpretation for her experience. And yet a case study such as this is often broadly generalized to the population, and from it derives the common assumption that all reports of bedside haunting can be solved simply by turning off the clock radio, or advising sufferers to sleep on one's side to reduce the chance of sleep paralysis. Furthermore, the theory of temporal lobe lability and anomalous experience can be applied to any paranormal or theological encounter if the sufferer scores high on a temporal lobe lability questionnaire. In this sense the theory retains some of the problems leveled at other explanations for paranormal experiences that rely on the measurement of subtle individual differences. The fact is that it's terribly rare for the witness of a "there-and-then" paranormal case to possess a clinically diagnosed labile or epileptic state — even Maureen Puddy was never diagnosed in this way. For this reason, and despite two decades of complicated scientific research papers espousing the theories made popular by Michael Persinger, there still remains — right or wrong — a degree of hostility directed towards them. Here are some of those criticisms articulated.

Do Magnetic Fields Actually Influence the Brain?

Peter Hough and Moyshe Kalman support a paranormal interpretation of experiences such as alien abductions (Hough and Kalman 1997). Arguing against techniques such as transcranial magnetic stimulation (TMS), they present the opinion of a neuroscientist named Matthew Walker from the Epilepsy Research Group at the Institute of Neurology in England who uses laboratory-based magnetic field stimulation of the human brain that is over ten thousand times greater than the Earth's magnetic field. The implication is that these high levels of field are needed to perform neurological research, and are vastly greater than anything produced naturally. Hence in their opinion it is unlikely that geomagnetic forces induce the types of psychological states that create paranormal experiences. Hough and Kalman state that while Walker isn't a believer in UFOs, given a choice between Persinger's theory and UFOs, Walker "would back the UFOs."

The figure of *ten thousand times* likely comes from the fact that a typical small two centimeter magnet is ten thousand times stronger than the earth's field[1] (Campbell 2003). Wallace Campbell is a physicist and authority on geomagnetic fields, and is slightly less pessimistic than Walker about the effects of geomagnetic forces on the brain — after all, TMS is used as a clinical tool in contemporary medical research. Nevertheless, he urges some caution, stating that while it's not implausible that the brain could be influenced by anything ranging from local and small geomagnetic fluxes to geomagnetic storms, he doesn't believe the question of how brain processes are affected by external field stimulation has been answered satisfactorily.

The argument over the influence of geomagnetic forces on the brain is similar to that surrounding the association between extremely low frequency magnetic fields in and around the home and the greater incidence of miscarriages and diseases such as leukemia. The consensus is that although some studies have shown a positive correlations between the fields and medical disorders, they still contain quite fundamental flaws, and experts conclude that despite the attractive "logic" of the hypothesis, no evidence exists for such a relationship (Tenforde 1996). Similarly, there have many relationships demonstrated by Persinger and other scientists between periods of geomagnetic disturbance and variables such as psychopathological disturbance, epileptic seizures and even human mortality. These findings might appear logical, but remain only relationships.

To stress his point, Campbell points out that Persinger found a correlation coefficient of 0.60 between a high geomagnetic index and increased risk of death in laboratory rats bred to be prone to epileptic seizure. Now, while correlations such as this are important as early steps in understanding a phenomenon scientifically, bear in mind that a correlation does not necessarily mean one variable causes the other. In fact, quite large correlation coefficients can be manufactured from pairing all sorts of silly data. As an example, Campbell points out that a correlation of 0.49 can be found by matching the annual number of publications (between 1910 and 1967) of the English mathematician Sydney Chapman and the number of sunspots for any year. Now, it's far more logical to believe that this high correlation was due to Chapman's motivation for writing about the solar storms rather than the storms' invisible magnetic influence on his brain.

To be fair, Persinger would counter Walker's (and other skeptics') criticisms by suggesting that it's not the strength of the magnetic field that's important, but the field's characteristics. A very weak field, delivered in a particular pulsed form[2] as opposed to a continuous wave, can subtly influence brain activity. This is in spite of the fashionable belief that any differences between pulsed-type fields and continuous wave fields on biological material are "small and sometimes conflicting" (e.g., Postow and Swicord 1996).

Criticisms of Tectonic Strain Theory

Criticizing tectonic strain theory, the Canadian astronomer Chris Rutkowski argues that substantial — and perhaps unrealistic — energy levels are required for a luminous ball, one meter in diameter, to appear 100 meters from an observer and give off visible light of comparable power to a 60 watt lightbulb. This energy requirement is even greater if the fault that produces it is very deep — to get to the surface the radiation has to pass through a hostile Earth's crust, which is not a good energy conductor. Ad hoc theories like "natural circuits" and "energy tunnels" that help to transmit the radiation through rock have to be devised and accepted before the influence of tectonic strain over the human brain can be seriously considered — particularly since it is the weak seismic events that are most implicated as the cause of anomalous paranormal phenomena.

More fundamental problems with tectonic strain theory were also identified by Rutkowski almost thirty years ago (Rutkowski 1983). As we've discussed, Persinger and his colleagues report correlations between the Earth's fault-line activity and UFO reports. However, UFO reports themselves come in all shapes and sizes, from mere lights in the sky to intense close encounters involving alien entities, and the geophysical data with which these reports are correlated is very basic. Consequently, the relationships are weak, and rely on what is called "lag" to give them strength. That is, UFO reports don't necessarily have to coincide at the same time as earthquake activity for a relationship to be "discovered." Rather, if UFO reports appear in any number before or after the seismic activity then it is still taken as a meaningful relationship because the specific actions of the fault on emitted radiation is still not known, so mind-altering energy might be released and result in UFO reports up to six months prior, or six months succeeding, an earth tremor.

This type of analysis shares great similarity with — hence the problems of—*psi displacement*. Recall that in a psychic test there's a complicated interrelationship between Zener card runs and probability. A participant in a psychic trial might only pick five cards correctly out of 25 on a single run, which is chance. However, if the experimenter looks hard enough at the raw data they might find a success rate of 12 out of 25 when they systematically match the person's call two cards before any one trial — the displacement effect. Alternately, statistical significance might be achieved for the participant if the experimenter matches their call three cards before. Or four. In a similar way, matching UFO or ghost sightings, or alien abductions, with the Earth's geomagnetic changes are prone to this type of statistical manipulation.

Rutkowski argues that any resulting statistical relationship that incorporates sighting lag is ridiculous, since the theory doesn't require a UFO report to be associated with an earthquake epicenter in the same location. In other words, UFOs might have been witnessed in and around a small town during May, and a researcher might after the fact examine the geomagnetic data, finding out that a barely noticeable earthquake occurred in an adjacent district ... at the end of the previous February. The researcher might then argue that it took three months for the geomagnetic manifestation to surface as visible lightforms. Such a conclusion, while it might be perfectly valid, is still not strong science.

Lag time is not the only hindrance to an association between geomagnetism and paranormal phenomenon. The area surrounding the earthquake epicenter used to collect UFO reports can also be very large. Since there is no real understanding of how long it will take for the energy of an earthquake to manifest and distort human perception (if at all), or where that energy will "pop out" on the earth's surface, it seems reasonable to initially choose a liberal radius from which to pick UFO sightings. But this simply increases the likelihood of finding more UFO reports, and therefore it's perhaps not surprising that statistically significant correlations emerge from the data.

Yet another problem is deciding whether the visual manifestation of tectonic strain, such as a UFO sighting, should be most prevalent during periods of static low geomagnetism, static high geomagnetism or geomagnetic flux. If the first option is demonstrated by one researcher, and the third option by another, ad hoc justification can be made to "prove" a consistent relationship exist despite the inherent contradictions in the findings. This concern is acknowledged by sleep researcher Jorge Conesa (2000), who admits that the data for paranormal reports, temporal lobe signs and geomagnetic activity seem counterintuitive, since paranormal reports are prevalent during periods of abrupt geomagnetic flux and also on days of exceedingly low geomagnetic activity. If a change in magnetic field is so crucial for the induction of transient seizures in the temporal lobes, how can this account for reports of paranormal phenomena in the absence of fluctuating fields? To deal with this conundrum in a somewhat far-fetched manner, Conesa suggests that a sensitive person might experience high electromagnetic radiation in their workplace, but then go home where there is low radiation, and this creates an electromagnetic gradient which encourages temporal lobe lability.

Taking this approach one step further, it's possible that any interested researcher could trawl through geophysical data in a region of the Earth and subsequently present a set of research findings showing multiple "paranormal" experiences occurred during days of consistently high magnetic activity. Conesa's thesis could then be applied to this data. That is, paranormal activity is to be expected in the location since the high magnetic activity likely succeeded a period of low activity. This corresponds to a state of magnetic flux, albeit occurring over a longer period of time.

Staying with the correlational problems associated with tectonic strain theory, in 1993 Howard Wilkinson and Alan Gauld tried to match correlations Persinger had calculated in 1989 linking spontaneous psi events (such as extrasensory predictions of a "crisis") and fluctuations in the Earth's geomagnetic activity. They used the same geomagnetic activity and paranormal event data that Persinger used, but their results weren't statistically significant. They did, however, acknowledge that their criteria for paranormal case selection might have been a little different from Persinger's, which explained the different result. This nonetheless suggests that the relationships between geomagnetism and paranormal phenomena are fragile, and statistical significance can be achieved by adding a few cases here, or taking away a few there.

Wilkinson and Gauld then performed a very detailed analysis of spontaneous paranormal cases and geomagnetic data over a one hundred year period using their own criteria. While acknowledging the complexity of the data, one of the conclusions they came to is that increases in telepathic and clairvoyant experiences are not related to days of low relative geomagnetic activity (that is, relative to the days before and after) but perhaps low absolute geomagnetic activity. That is, slow increases and decreases in overall activity over a one hundred year period. Haunting and poltergeist experiences, on the other hand, appear to occur when the geomagnetic activity is generally high overall (Wilkinson and Gauld 1993). The findings are vulnerable to probabilistic and statistical artifacts, however, and leaves the reader unconvinced of a true underlying effect.

Criticisms of Transcranial Magnetic Stimulation

Regarding the wishy-washy reports of paranormal-like experiences reported using transcranial magnetic stimulation in the laboratory, Hough and Kalman again quote Matthew Walker, who argues that while brain stimulation might be able to induce basic behaviors such as "limb movements," "illusions of light," "fear" and "depersonalization," it has never been shown to induce a complex and prolonged hallucinations — something that contains all the facets of an alien abduction.

Rather annoyed that temporal lobe epilepsy has such a cure-all reputation for paranormal encounters, Hough and Kalman further describe how an abductee called Laura (the sister of Jayne from Chapter 4) consulted eleven different neurologists in the hope of explaining the ongoing paranormal problems affecting her and her family. When temporal lobe epilepsy was finally discounted, an explanation of sleep paralysis was finally applied to her case, although apparently some of her experiences occurred when she was (allegedly) wide awake.

Nonetheless, from the 1990s onwards Persinger's findings were getting a fair degree of press coverage from around the world, particularly in relation to the religious connotations of experiencing a sense-of-presence following a temporal lobe transient, or the apparent fact that Persinger could make "almost anyone feel as if they've been snatched by spacemen," as one Australian newspaper article declared (Phillips 2001). Not all the publicity was positive, however. In a 2003 article in the *Hamilton Spectator*, Canadian broadcaster Jay Ingram describes a claim by Persinger that the resurrection of Jesus might have been attributable to the combination of temporal lobe epilepsy and the consumption of a trance-inducing drug. Ingram related how he thought the suggestion was a "clever parody." However, since Persinger is a hard-core skeptic, Ingram had to assume the proposition was serious.

Then in 2005 a scientific article was published in the journal *Neuroscience Letters* by Pehr Granqvist — a Swedish researcher interested in religious experience and psychological theories of attachment. Granqvist and his colleagues attempted to replicate reports of hallucinated experiences using Persinger's method of transcranial magnetic stimulation (Granqvist, Fredrikson, Unge, Hagenfeldt, Valind, Larhammar and Larsson 2005). The types of sensations participants narrated during stimulation were measured using an instrument called the *EXIT* scale, detailing various somatosensory experiences. The Swedes also used a transcranial stimulating machine and computer program developed by Persinger's co-worker Stanley Koren, following consultation with Persinger himself.

Most importantly, they also measured the level of suggestibility in their participants, and ensured the experiment was double blind. This means that in any session participants might have randomly received either an actual magnetic stimulation or no stimulation, and the experimenters themselves did not know which condition the participants were receiving. Under these rigorous conditions, no statistically significant effect was found linking reports of strange sensations with the application of TMS.

The Swedes proposed that a participant's subjective experiences, measured using the *EXIT* scale, were very disparate and vague. For example, they might simply report a tingling sensation while hooked up to the equipment. Furthermore, such reports were more likely to be made by highly suggestible people, regardless of whether or not they'd received TMS. The conclusion reached was that people with a high level of openness to strange experiences had more of these experiences when placed in a sensory deprivation environment — just the type of situation discussed in Chapter 4. The fact that participants were attached to a transcranial stimulation helmet simply assisted with the interpretation of what the participant was experiencing. It didn't matter whether the helmet was turned on or not.[3]

Put another way, if you place an impressive looking transcranial stimulating helmet on your head and are bursting with expectation about what might happen to you (perhaps having seen a demonstration on television), you might seek out body sensations you normally wouldn't notice. This might be tingling in your foot that's just normal pins-and-needles, or pressure on your thigh which feels like a disembodied hand, but in reality just the tight clothing you're wearing. Suggestible people, who are highly absorbed and more aware of their bodily sensations, are just the type of people to be influenced by this type of experimental procedure.

Jay Ingram also weighs in on the debate about the legitimacy of TMS. Writing in the *Toronto Star*, he describes how he participated in one of Persinger's demonstrations, in which he sat in an armchair in a soundproof laboratory, his eyes covered by half-ping-pong balls and the transcranial helmet resting on his head. In the darkness, with the temporal lobes imperceptibly stimulated by the helmet, he sought access to the visions allegedly crafted by a temporal lobe seizure. All he got was a small, vague white figure in the distance, admitting that he was trying really hard to sense something (Ingram 2004). Granqvist and colleagues might propose that it was Ingram's lack of suggestibility that led to his somewhat unsatisfactory experiences under the "God-helmet."

Ingram further suggests the "extraordinary" experiences reported by skeptic Susan Blackmore while undergoing stimulation — and widely reported as evidence of the method's success — is a product of the suggestibility inherent to a TMS study. Ingram questions what Blackmore's extraordinary experiences actually amounted to, other than the fact that as a supporter of Persinger's theories of paranormal experience, she might be particularly prone to fulfilling her expectations?

Persinger and Koren (2005) responded to the Swedish group's accusation with the charge that Granqvist and colleagues didn't apply the appropriate magnetic field to their participants' brains. Had they done this, they would have been able to achieve supportive findings. More specifically, they argue that the average results achieved by the Swedish experimental participants seemed too close to the Swedish control participants, and the Canadians' own control groups. This implies that Granqvist's experimental group never received an appropriate level of TMS, explaining why they couldn't replicate the earlier studies. Persinger's group also claim the Swedes didn't use the correct computer to run the suitable software, and when Granqvist originally visited the Canadians' laboratory and asked advice on conducting a transcranial experiment, the Canadians thought they wanted to perform another type of study[4] and the advice they gave was not appropriate. Nevertheless, Persinger and Koren comment, through gritted teeth perhaps, "We congratulate our colleagues in Sweden for the courage to begin the steps to replicate [our] experiments."

In reply, Granqvist retorts that he and his group were personally told the computer they used would accept the required software for the experiment, and that Persinger started making excuses for the conflicting findings only after he found out what the Swedes were up to.

Since the Swedish results were published they have found favor among many waiting for an opportunity to attack Persinger's research findings. For example, the paranormal arch-skeptic Joe Nickell uses the Swedish results to cast doubt on Persinger and co-workers' theories, although his reasons are somewhat different from those of paranormalists (Nickell 2005). Nickell seems a little uncomfortable that in recent years Persinger has worked on projects with parapsychologists such as William Roll, rather than sticking with the more acceptable scientific materialism that Persinger has displayed in his main body of work.

To others, explaining paranormal experiences purely on the basis of electromagnetically-generated temporal lobe seizures is one of those scientific approaches which, in Jay Ingram's words, betrays "the rational scientist's need to explain absolutely everything, no matter how baroque the explanation" (Ingram 2003b). Yet the kerfuffle that took place following publication of Granqvist's unsuccessful replication study seems only to have been a blip in the continuum of TMS research. In recent years, Granqvist has returned to research on religious themes, and Persinger has continued — in a business-as-usual fashion — to use the TMS to study the effect of magnetic field on a variety of behavioral systems. These include memory (Mach and Persinger 2009), decision making and judgment (Ross, Koren and Persinger 2008) and in the alleviation of epileptic symptoms (e.g., Persinger, Hoang and Baker-Price 2009) — although he and his colleagues in this latter article do acknowledge that some biophysicists don't think the concept of TMS is sensible. Research and review articles have also been written that shore up support for the actions of weak, time-varying magnetic fields on brain function, a common criticism by skeptics of the TMS technique (e.g., Booth, Koren and Persinger 2008, Persinger, Saroka, Koren and St. Pierre 2010). For the moment all remains quiet, until the next replication study, perhaps?

Soft and Hard Electromagnetic Theory

Moving on from the epileptic basis of paranormal experience, it's worthwhile noting that human sensory systems are specifically tuned to pick up specific forms of stimuli in the external world, most notably the small band of electromagnetic radiation that is the visible spectrum of light. The presence of an "unseen" reality of energy outside this spectrum has led to speculation that paranormal entities like ghosts are actually concentrations of invisible electromagnetic radiation perceived through our conventional sensory systems (Maher 1999),[5] but only at certain times, or by the right people (sensitives), or by machinery such as cameras or infrared detectors used to measure the goings-on in a haunted house. These detectors most commonly show balls of normally invisible light called orbs, rather than actual ghostly shapes.

This proposal avoids the awkward assumption that the radiation directly induces changes in brain activity, leading to seizures and hallucinations. Some people simply perceive it, the way they would perceive any other conventional sensory stimuli. Evidence for these invisible sources of energy is sought in old houses, graveyards and ancient sites of human habitation using tools such as electromagnetic detectors, although one has to be careful with how any sensational findings are interpreted. Parapsychologist Lloyd Auerbach mentions how people using electromagnetic meters often become overexcited following a high reading on such a detector, only to discover they've been standing next to a microwave oven. He also claims he's found more bad wiring than ghosts using these devices (Kirby 2005).

James Houran would agree with regards to the visual recording of invisible electromagnetic energy. In one study he used different kinds of film (such as infrared) to record the "energies" in a reputedly haunted graveyard — the kind where ghost-hunters frequently take photos of orbs. He reported nothing of interest, other than a lot of unexposed film, and argues that contextual cues might allow such outcomes to be interpreted as paranormal (Houran 1997).

Notwithstanding these criticisms, there are two different approaches to the proposal that some special people (or any of us, at certain times of our

An orb photographed in the vicinity of the Avebury prehistoric site in Wiltshire, southwest England (exact date unknown). This picture combines two paranormal themes in one, the presence of orbs and the mysterious purpose of an ancient land-mark, the vicinity of which is home to crop-circles, UFOs and a variety of other para-normal phenomena. Unlike pictures of (seemingly identical) orbs taken in and around old houses, which certainly would be attributed a ghostly origin, these orbs within Avebury's standing stones — if not mundane anomalies on film — are considered by proponents to be expressions of the "energy" that abounds in these Neolithic sacred centers. Whether this "earth energy" is the same as the "human energy" in a haunted house is a question I certainly can't answer (Fortean Picture Library).

lives) can hear or see normally "invisible" energy through their regular sensory systems. These I will call *soft electromagnetic* and *hard electromagnetic* theories[6]. The term *soft* refers to the belief that the energy is, put simply, dumb. As a form of energy, it's no different from microwaves emanating from a microwave oven or infrared (heat) waves leaving your body. There a two subdivisions of this pro-posal. The more respectable of the two considers this invisible energy as natural, and when a sensitive person perceives this energy they experience nothing more than a fleeting image of something ambiguous. This image might then be confab-ulated into an illusion based on all the processes discussed in Chapter 3. The less respectable, more radical approach contends this energy is meaningful in the sense that it is truly anomalous and related perhaps to an actual, deceased individual, although it has no intelligent autonomy in its own right.

This idea is akin to the *veridical afterimage* theory of hauntings proposed by Edmund Gurney and Frederick Myers in the late 19th century, in which a dying person releases psychic "energy" into the surrounding environment (Maher 1999). This energy might then linger at that location to be perceived telepathically by a sensitive bystander. The impression might be of a person or persons living sometime in the past, "burnt into" the environment of a room or landscape. Witnesses see the apparition(s) walk through walls that once held a doorframe, long ago, or amble through the air in an old hallway missing its staircase. The ghost might even stand at the side of a road, where they might once have stood before they were killed. However, it's widely viewed that because they're nothing more than a form of persistent environmental energy, these ghosts cannot interact with a witness (in the way a television doesn't react to its viewer). Such apparitions are also frequently seen out of the corner of the witness's eye because people are more sensitive to picking up low levels of electromagnetic radiation (such as light) in the periphery of their visual field than in the central field (or fovea).

As to the configuration this energy takes, Janusz Slawinski proposes that a "flash" of electromagnetic radiation leaves the body at death and carries with it all the characteristics of the deceased person's personality and memory (Slawinski 1987). Consequently, the ghost that lingers on this plane is seen by those sensitive to the invisible electromagnetic spectrum, but is not necessarily in the shape of the human from which it originated. It may be that the observer perceives this "spectral energy," as Michaeleen Maher describes it, in its most basic form. They then confabulate the sensation into a more structured apparition (Maher 1999), using all the cognitive processes we've discussed when exploring the construction of visual illusions. How the ghost takes shape will be affected by such things as the percipient's psychometric sensibility, creative faculty and psychological defenses, according to Maher, and this might explain cases where more than one person simultaneously experiences the impression of a ghost, but describes it in very different ways. In one local case I examined, three witnesses reported a ghostly encounter in a house in Sydney, Australia. Walking into a room together, one witness saw the brief image of a man sitting in a lounge chair with his head in his hands, one saw what would best be described as a orb of light[7] that rapidly faded to nothing, and the third person just felt physically sick — different reactions to the same manifestation of allegedly invisible energy.

According to Maher, the way individuals respond differently to ghostly encounters explains the research findings from haunted houses where the correct location of a haunted site is consistently identified by sensitives, but the form of the ghost is variable. Again, this sound very much like our illusion hypothesis, with an ambiguous source of information that is now truly anomalous (as opposed to it being mundane and simply misinterpreted). Acknowledging the strong possibility that contextual cues influence people's choice of ghostly locations, perhaps some individuals are better than others at picking the correct location of an actual, paranormal ghost in a haunted house, inn or apartment. Yet when it comes to describing the apparition, the sensitive does no better than anyone else.

Awkwardly for the theory of ghosts as energy traces from dying individuals, there are plenty of case-studies where the apparition has characteristics entirely at odds with that of someone dying. One famous example comes from England in 1953. Harry Martindale was working in the cellar of a building in York when he saw a column of tired-looking Roman Legionnaires (with one riding a horse!) march in progression straight out of the room's wall. It transpired that the house had been built on an old Roman road, and the theory goes that this physical structure somehow held a holographic-like memory of a real event that had occurred over 1,500 years previously (Bord and Bord 1987). Assuming both Harry Martindale's apparitions, and the veridical afterimage of a dying person, are truly paranormal, it would need to be explained how the same ghostly "symptom" arises from two completely different foundations. Perhaps the energy release from a single death is equivalent to the collective stress discharged by a cohort of beaten Legionnaires? Would this account for seemingly analogous visual experiences? And what of animal ghosts, or apparitions of inanimate objects? How are these derived from the release of psychic energy? In the late 1990s the wife of a friend of mine, driving alone at night, was run off a quiet country road by a "ghost truck." This begs the question — was the truck driven by a ghost? If it was, then the vehicle must have been an inseparable accompaniment to the apparition. This sounds ridiculous, but how is it different from accepting that a ghost wears ghostly clothes — I've yet to hear of a naked ghost!

Discussion becomes even more convoluted, if that's possible, when considering whether "apparitional energy" possesses actual intelligence. This is the hard electromagnetic viewpoint, which theorizes that ghostly energy, despite being unstructured, has the capability of interacting with the witness because of the survival of unique and individual traits. Slawinski's ghosts are of this nature, and while on the topic of interactive energy, researcher and author Paul Devereux[8] speaks of visible energies such as earthlights behaving in seemingly intelligent ways.

Paraphysical advocates such as John Keel go further and discuss the separation of this world and other speculative worlds as represented by a curtain consisting of a "labyrinth of electromagnetic frequencies" behind which an intelligence exists, which he gives the eerie and impressive-sounding name of "the phenomenon" and elsewhere "ultraterrestrials." For eons, the phenomenon pops through "windows" to play havoc with the human race, taking the form of apparitions, UFO occupants or strange animals (e.g., Keel 1971).

While terribly interesting, it's not in the scope of this book to discuss how a person's psychic energy — as a burst of dumb or intelligent electromagnetism — can survive death and impregnate the walls of a house and haunt it, or how a truck or cat can be a ghost, or how extra-dimensional ultraterrestrials have tormented humans throughout history. Don't be disappointed, though, since the psychological theories we'll now turn to with regard to paranormal experience are just as fantastic — and fascinating — as any of these questions.

CHAPTER 8

Psychodynamic Approaches to Paranormal Experience: Psychoanalysis and the Birth Memories Hypothesis

For the stereotypical, scientific psychologist, this book ends here, because the previous chapters have outlined all the psychological tools required to explain paranormal belief and experience (albeit with the odd "weird bit" that might earn the disapproval of a skeptic).

Therefore, we should now be able to choose a case-study and examine the witness's story carefully, extracting as much information about them — their background and personal situation — as about the event itself. Having teased out the most important facts, and drawing on the wealth of theories available, it's almost certain that a standard, uncontroversial psychological explanation can be provided. This doesn't mean the explanation is any good — it might conveniently ignore some aspects of the case, or emphasize others unnecessarily. Alternately, it might be a very good fit for the evidence. Nevertheless, such an explanation is going to impress a lot of people because it sounds scientific, and that's why so much psychological language has filtered into everyday attempts at rationalizing paranormal experience.

Yet the psychology of paranormal experience doesn't end here. There are still whole branches of psychological theory that we haven't touched on yet that have a lot to offer in accounting for these experiences. Nonetheless, many ordinary psychologists treat these views with the same horror as they might astrology, or anything they consider "new age." It's a kind of psychology that simply isn't respectable. Still, these theories have been around since the beginning of psychology as a discipline and give a human perspective to paranormal encounters that's frequently missing in the drier scientific approach. This

181

means it doesn't necessarily treat people as stupid, or assume there's something wrong with them neurologically. They also assume that the psychological source of a person's paranormal experience is not something able to be entirely understood in a conventional scientific laboratory, so it has the added notion that the paranormal is potentially inexplicable.

Psychodynamics is an over-arching term for these psychological approaches which place great emphasis on the unconscious forces that influence human behavior. Central to the premise is the idea that, from birth, psychological energy is conserved in the same way that physical energy is conserved. When a match burns to black ash, the matter that makes up the stick of wood doesn't just disappear out of existence. Rather it is converted to heat and gases. Overall, energy is conserved and altered from one state to another. In the same manner, a person's life experiences are associated with psychological energy which can be outwardly expressed in a variety ways — typically healthy thoughts and behavior. However, at times the energy might be moved to, and stored in, the deep unconscious if the contents (thoughts and feelings) are too unpleasant to deal with. On account of this law of conservation of psychological energy, such repressed material cannot be wished away or destroyed. And for some unfortunate people, the energy may be inadvertently released and expressed in other forms, such as the psychological disorder of neurosis. The unconscious is therefore considered a dynamic entity, meaning that it is not a robotic, machine-like repository of forgotten information that many mainstream psychologists might think, but has its own autonomy and at times can make its hidden operations felt in waking consciousness.

Psychoanalysis and Psi

The premier expression of psychodynamics is psychoanalysis, a method of psychological enquiry developed by Sigmund Freud in the late 19th and early 20th century. The basic tenets are that certain universal events occur to everyone in early childhood, and these lead to the development of personality — the levels of which are known as the ego and superego. Childhood events of particular developmental importance are those associated with the child's relationships with its mother and father, and the control of basic drives such as hunger, thirst and sexuality — and the infantile awareness (or apprehension) of incest and masturbation (Ferenczi 1916). However, the memory of such primal ideas often cannot be sustained in waking consciousness as the child grows since this would undermine the stable and socialized adult.

As a consequence, the ideas are necessarily repressed to the extent that they are consciously forgotten, although they still reside deep in the dynamic unconscious. In adulthood, and for reasons that might include an abnormal relationship in childhood, inadequately repressed material might begin to leak into a patient's consciousness from an unconscious repository of ideas. The patient might bolster mental defenses to protect their psyche[1] from the emerging thoughts, but over time this will largely be unsuccessful. To Freud, the mental illnesses of neurosis and hysteria were indicators of childhood anxieties manifesting in adulthood. Defense mechanisms to guard the patient's ego from damage might be erected by the patient, for instance persisting with the unpleasant idea's repression, or projecting its content onto someone else. An example of projection might involve a person who feels moral anxiety about their own aggressive and sexual impulses obtaining relief from this self-knowledge by attributing the thoughts to a colleague, such that it is they who are seen to be overly aggressive and sexually charged (Hall 1959).

Sigmund Freud in 1901 when he was 45 years old. While Freudian psychoanalysis is limited to clarifying psi experiences in a therapy session, the more general psychodynamic approach—of which psychoanalysis is a part—has broader application to almost all forms of paranormal experience. This psychodynamic approach provides very different explanations to those offered by mainstream, scientific psychology (Mary Evans Picture Library).

In Freud's opinion, Freud was psychoanalysis, and psychoanalysis was Freud. Followers deviating from the key tenets were often expelled from the movement and barred from using the psychoanalytic title. Therefore, conventional psychoanalysts during Freud's life, and after his death, have always maintained a very defined set of fundamental beliefs and opinions with regard to the origin of mental illness. Regarding the paranormal, however, there is some variation in attitude. This is because Freud wrote the occasional, ambiguous article and letter (and at times held discussions) about his feelings towards telepathy. Some of his articles maintained that telepathic events represented the completely rational workings of the unconscious mind. In *Dreams and Telepathy* published in 1922, Freud considers the telepathic dream to be derived from an individual's unconscious desires. In this same year he received a letter in which the correspondent told of a dream where his second wife gave birth to twins. The next day the correspondent learned that his daughter to his first wife, in a distant city, had been the one giving birth to twins. As a precognitive case this story is hardly inspiring, and Freud has no problem explaining the dream in a more mechanistic and typically psychodynamic manner; the correspondent had somehow subliminally learned of his daughter's pregnancy and this snippet of forgotten information had assisted in the creation of a dream with a deeper meaning; the correspondent wished his daughter was his current wife (Eisenbud 1975).

Freud was also a member of the Society for Psychical Research and at times publicly narrated stories of psi he'd heard that had impressed him. In fact, he had conducted his own thought-transference experiments in the mid 1920s. When in this mood, Freud considered telepathy to be a legitimate phenomenon, although nothing more than an archaic ability manifesting on rare occasions in modern life. The awkward thing about such primitive psychic information is that the "sensed" material could itself be censored by the unconscious if it contained unpalatable material (Heywood 1974). As a consequence, the content of the telepathic impression might be difficult to interpret by the patient and their psychoanalyst.

The ambivalence Freud held towards psi might have been due to his fear of marginalizing psychoanalysis, which from its inception was open to attack from the scientific establishment (Totton 2003). While many mainstream psychologists would now accept the Freud was quite creative in developing a model of a dynamic unconscious, there has always been great resistance to many psychoanalytic concepts — a female's alleged penis envy has been much ridiculed over the decades, as has its male counterpart, womb envy.[2] Claims of theoretical unfalsifiability[3] have consistently been leveled at Freud's methods.

Such a concern would account for Freud's often staunch opposition to psi, and his desire to explain the telepathic experiences of patients in rational, materialistic terms (Inglis 1986). This approach would also be the official position of a vast majority of psychoanalysts today. Nevertheless, after Freud's death a handful of psychoanalysts, including Jule Eisenbud, felt comfortable speaking and writing about psi, particularly the psychic events they believed occurred during the therapy. To these practitioners, psychical events are real processes caused by a transference of thoughts between analyst and patient. Some even recognize this transference as a potential problem to the neutrality of the therapy session, whereby the psychoanalyst might unknowingly convey to the patient their own feelings and attitudes telepathically (Lazar 2001). From this point of view, it can be difficult for an analyst to be completely objective about their patient when this patient can, through psi, respond to the ideas and wishes hidden in the analyst's mind and throw them back in conversation or in the narratives of their dreams. As a consequence, much of the psychoanalytic writing on the paranormal deals strictly with telepathy and its potential impact on the analyst-patient relationship, not paranormal events in general (Ullman 2003).

However, according to Montague Ullman, psychic transference can at times be advantageous to therapy. For example, patients can make use of thought-transference to broadcast deep personal issues while at the same time "disclaim any responsibility," avoiding the potential embarrassment and stress of acknowledging their thoughts and desires. Apparently, this often involves their amorous feelings for the therapist!

From the psychoanalyst's perspective, psi-conditioned dreams can also derive from the wider relationships existing among the analyst and their many patients. For instance, a female client in therapy with Eisenbud experienced a dream in which she felt like a child when precluded from a discussion between two adults. Unknown to the client, Eisenbud had the previous day shared a good therapeutic experience with another patient (Eisenbud 1954). In Eisenbud's opinion, the patient's latent psychic ability allowed her to discover this event, and her subsequent jealousy was expressed in the form of a clairvoyant dream. However, Eisenbud was convinced of the rarity of anything more than such symbolic psi in therapeutic practice. When more meaningful examples of (allegedly) precognitive dreams do occur, in Eisenbud's opinion it is because the precognitive patient has been pushed to try and "out-do" the telepathic performances of other patients also competing for the analyst's attention.

Psychoanalytic Explanations For Psi Ability

It's all very well to accept telepathy or precognition as contributing to the contents of dreams, but how would a Freudian psychoanalyst explain psi ability?[4] Most accounts are a development of Freud's notion of telepathy as a primitive and superseded trait. Psychoanalysis being what it is, the early mother-child attachment, with all its fundamental peculiarities, is of particular fascination. The psychiatrist Jan Ehrenwald wrote in 1971 that telepathy is an "embryological matrix of communication" between the child and their mother that is eventually superseded by the faculty of speech. Since these telepathic proto-messages are so primitive, they cannot communicate straightforward ideas into the child's higher consciousness. Rather, they relay primitive, non-verbal "distress calls" or comfort messages including endearment or reassurance, the purpose of which is to alter the child's behavior.

However, as the child develops they begin to resent the mother's encroachment on their personal consciousness. This is because they are gradually learning to direct their own actions and develop their own ego. Consequently, barriers are set up to repulse external influences from other, stronger egos — particularly the mother's. Another very psychoanalytical reason for the discontinuation of natural telepathic communications involves the "Oedipus complex" ... the psychoanalytic theory that the infant wants to hide their thoughts of murdering the father to be with the mother! (Totton 2003). Ehrenwald argues that this repression of telepathic powers is mandatory in Western culture, and if the barriers aren't set up and the telepathic relationship is prolonged, it may result in a schizophrenic child of the symbiotic or autistic type[5] (Ehrenwald 1971).

When some adults experience flashes of telepathy in later years, unsurprisingly the content of the ideas is primitive, irrational, childlike and symbolic in form, and people are surprised by the reappearance of this forgotten talent. Whether the transfer of information is through physical processes of intonation, body language and pheromones (Totton 2003) or through some more mysterious paranormal process is not really of much concern to the psychoanalyst.

Writing in 1962, Herbert Strean and Marie Nelson further suggest that telepathic phenomena might be specific to patients with narcissistic disorder. In this illness, a distant developmental event in childhood has caused the adult patient to be "fixated at a pregenital and pre-oedipal level" — a time before any mental psi barriers have been erected. Hence the telepathic communications which might emerge between the analyst and analysand (the client being analysed in a psychoanalytic session) mimics the preverbal attachment between mother and child. Furthermore, since the patient's ego remains underdeveloped, the resulting content of the communication can be bitter and frustrated — recall the dream of Eisenbud's jealous patient. In a practical sense analysts are encouraged to recognize these possibilities, and deal with them using their psychoanalytic training

Psychoanalysis, Demons and Poltergeists

Beyond psi, there is little consideration in Freudian psychoanalysis for paranormal or supernatural events. If an individual claims to have encountered a paranormal being such as a ghost, their experiences would be treated as symptoms of an underlying psychoanalytic problem. In 1923 Freud touched on the occult when he analyzed an historical case of demonic possession, seeing the demon as a repressed impulse unpleasant to the ego. When recognized by the patient, the impulse was externalized as a defense mechanism to protect the psyche (Ivey 2002). When the reverse occurs, and good impulses are externalized, the patient thinks themselves the embodiment of evil. That is, they think they're possessed by demons.

In a different vein, the Hungarian psychoanalyst Géza Róheim argued in the 1930s that ogres and demons were representations of the patient's earlier discovery, in childhood, of their parents having sex — what psychoanalysts label the primal scene (Okami, Olmstead, Abramson and Pendleton 1998). South African psychologist Gavin Ivey urges caution, however, in assuming that "demons" are simply metaphors for unconscious constructs of the psyche (Ivey 2002). The danger is that such hidden mental processes, themselves metaphors, are discussed as though they are real things when in fact they are no more than labels for complicated, little understood processes. To replace "demon" with "the psyche" sounds more respectable, but doesn't necessarily help to explain what is happening to the patient anymore successfully.

This dilemma also applies to the treatment of poltergeists as a psycho-analytical problem derived from sexual dysfunction in young people, rather than the manifestation of a supernatural force.[6] As a supporter of the reality of apparitions, Michaeleen Maher laments the assumption that poltergeists are only a problem for hysterical young girls with psychoanalytic neuroses, a theory widely accepted because it makes use of impressive-sounding terms such as "focal person," "attenuation," and "recurrent spontaneous psychokinesis" (Maher 2000).

Psychoanalysis and Alien Abductions

In recent years, perhaps because of its widespread media appeal, alien abduction syndrome has come to the attention of some psychoanalysts. According to French psychologists Jean-Claude Maleval and Nathalie Charraud, the symptoms of slight physical injury seen in abductees (from bruises to light hemorrhaging), the abductees' universal rejection by society as abnormal, their relationship problems and the frequent incidents of missing time they report, suggest all the hallmarks of hysterical delirium (Maleval and Charraud 2003). Furthermore, when a supportive therapist comes along and treats one of these people for the after-effects of a legitimate kidnapping, the patient's fantasy symptoms turn into a "social fact." In reality, according to Maleval and Charraud, the abductee as a hysteric is actually displaying their primal fantasy for passive seduction. More bluntly, their desire to be raped. Thus these psychoanalysts demand recognition of neurotic symptoms in stories of alien medical examinations involving, among other things, insertion of instruments into the victim's vagina, or male anus (accompanied by the taking of sperm samples using an ejaculation machine).

When later encouraged by the therapist or hypnotist to believe they have been controlled by all-powerful alien beings, the hysteric is said to find themselves strangely satisfied, which explains why they are not as anxious as one might expect compared to people who really do experience kidnapping or abuse.[7] Maleval and Charraud argue that the façade of the abduction fantasy is a successful mask, or defense against, the more dangerous "real" — the psychodynamic source of desire (e.g., the primal incestuous urge). Apparently there's even some alluring narcissism in the defense mechanism of "abduction by aliens" in that the victim can feel they are special because they are in fact a human-alien hybrid, or are helping to create a super race, depending on the story encouraged by their clinical mentor.

Taking a slightly different psychoanalytic approach, the psychiatrist Stuart Twemlow believes alien abductions and near death experiences (NDEs) are, in their own unique way, an unconscious method of anxiety reduction (Twemlow 1994). An alien abduction is a form of projection, where all the unacceptable thoughts belonging to the psychotic abductee's fragmented psyche are projected onto an inanimate external world. This he calls *projective identification*. On the other hand, the NDE uses adaptive regression whereby the patient is in unconscious panic about their sense of self and being. They use the content of the NDE (however it is derived) to help reaffirm their continued, mortal existence ... since it's an absolute requirement of the process that they return to life. In addition, because of its traumatic subject matter, the abduction is a more dangerous psychodynamic event than an NDE. But why an abduction or NDE in the first place? To Twemlow, the difference in theme is a function of the early developmental experiences of the patient. Put simply, humans share cross-cultural similarities in their early life experiences, but also draw on the myths and legends from their surrounding society.

As you'll recall, this is yet another manifestation of the psychosocial hypothesis, whereby social stories assist a person's psychological requirements. We've seen the term *psychosocial* used to account for poltergeist infestations and fantasy prone personality, but it can also be applied more broadly to describe the human experience by examining the types of stories all people at all times tell one another. Specific content within the stories might differ among various peoples at different times and places, but some theorists argue that the origin of the content can occasionally be traced, and the farther back this origin is, the greater the number of cultures that will display this similarity. As an example, author and researcher Martin Kottmeyer argues that science fiction stories provide all the ingredients of an alien abduction narrative, yet the typical abduction scenario is not necessarily confined to individuals from a modern, very Western background. In another cultural setting an abduction might occur, but the typical grey alien — that hairless, small and slender entity with a grayish skin tone, degenerate facial features and large black eyes (Kottmeyer 2001) — might be replaced by some other creature or entity. While on the theme of the "grey," theology professor Christopher Partridge proposes that such a malevolent alien typology is derived straight from Christian demonology and the "grey" is a modern, technological demon (Partridge 2004). Therefore, perhaps we shouldn't be surprised if the "amoral, humanoid

The quintessential Grey by artist Debbie Lee, an overwhelmingly popular abducting alien from the last 30 years. If the skeptical view is taken that the entity is not literally real, or encountered in some other non-physical realm — and that some cases aren't outright hoaxes — one is left with the interesting question of where this depiction originated. One view, espoused by well-read commentators such as Martim Kottmeyer, is that the entity represents a more evolved human dependent on greater brain function (the larger head) and less dependent on more animalistic physiological traits (atrophied limbs and digestive systems, no hair, etc.), an idea toyed with by science fiction writers for over a century. Whether this portrayal enters the abductees (assumed) hallucinogenic visions through popular culture, or something deeper and more mystical (archetypal) is another matter. A conventional view would be that the psychosocial development of the Grey through the 1960s and 1970s is easy to trace, perhaps culminating with its "perfect" and now invariant appearance, pictured here, by the mid–1980s (Fortean Picture Library).

and demonic" creature which we see as the typical modern alien is also found in contact cases from various other Judeo-Christian cultures, and cultures linked to early Judeo-Christian doctrine.

Alternative Psychoanalytic Models

An alternate and certainly "heretical" branch of psychoanalysis was practiced by Wilhelm Reich. Reich started his psychoanalytic career in a conventional fashion in Vienna in the 1920s and held the respect of Freud himself. He was particularly interested in the libido and its role as a source of energy (Pietikainen 2002), and his studies combined sexuality, Marxism and mainstream psychoanalysis into a confusing thesis that won him few friends. He was widely, and some say unfairly, viewed as being crazy. He left Europe for the United States just before the Second World War and began investigating bions, an alleged energy which he believed infused all living and non-living matter. Reich called the energy that bions emitted orgone energy, and in the later years of his life got himself in trouble with the government for building and promoting the orgone accumulator. This was a large box made of alternating wood and steel said to amplify environmental orgone. When sitting inside it, the amplifier apparently allowed the blue rays of orgone energy to be seen (Self 1997). In Reich's opinion this accumulated orgone energy — the physical manifestation of libido — had therapeutic effects, so sitting in the box was good for the health. However, the authorities thought differently and cracked down on the sale and shipment of the device. Ending the story on a melancholy note, Reich died of a heart attack in 1957 while jailed in Lewisburg, Pennsylvania.

Reich's interest in orgone energy led to the creation of a therapy technique involving manipulation of the body (through methods including direct pressure and pinching of muscles) coupled with, when necessary, more standard psychoanalytical procedures such as dream analysis (Nelson 1976). Reich believed that malfunctions of both the psyche and the body (or soma) stem from dammed-up orgone energy requiring release (Briehl 1995). Unblocking the tension in the body helps remove the "armor" preventing the healthy flow of orgone. The trapped emotions associated with the orgone can then be freed, and physical and mental symptoms of disorder reduced. For example, a disorder such as neurosis is caused by energy trapped in chronically tense muscles, so a form of physiotherapy will help to alleviate the neurotic symptoms.

Although rare, Reichian therapists still exist and practice, and at times consider the causes of paranormal experiences. The psychotherapist Nick Totton was trained in Reichian practice, and was told by his teacher that all paranormal experiences were the distorted projections of people's inner body events painted onto the outside world. Apparently, people are well aware of their emotions and sexual drive but tend not to notice their subliminal body sensations. On occasion these somatic sensations are perceived but can't be explained so they are unconsciously projected out into the world to become some (mistaken) external reality (Totton 2003). When an increased appreciation of our internal milieu occurs through Reichian training, the practitioner opens themselves to a range of seemingly paranormal experiences. For instance, Totton mentions how, as he stood on a low bridge, he was aware the movement of water underneath as a "fizzing" sensations in his feet and legs. Thus his training in self-awareness of organ function, as Reich described it, can manifest as a variety of unusual skills. Therefore, from a Reichian perspective, events interpreted as paranormal emanate from physiological, rather than psychic, processes.

Although heretical, Reichian theory is nonetheless founded in psychoanalysis, so it's not surprising to learn that the loss of somatic awareness in adults apparently occurs at the moment of birth. Here, the child experiences an intense mixture of great physical pain, confused thoughts and unfathomable feelings. There's no possibility that their new mind can integrate such a vast array of material, so the only option is to repress much of it, resulting in a separation of one part of self from another. Totton's analogy is the umbilical cord. Just as the child is physically separated from their mother at birth through the cutting of the cord, the repression process severs the human from their deeper sense of self, leading to potential paranormal experiences in later life (Totton 2003).

Totton's description of birth as the origin of later paranormal encounters bears resemblance to a theory developed in the mid–1970s to explain alien abduction syndrome. This theory, which isn't psychoanalytic, nevertheless sees the syndrome not as a real kidnapping by extraterrestrial beings, or a hysterical neurosis, but as a memory of this very birthing process.

The Birth Memories Hypothesis

The best way to introduce the birth memories hypothesis is to first describe a rather celebrated study by a California State University English professor, Alvin Lawson, and a medical practitioner from Anaheim, William McCall. The year was 1977, and the researchers interviewed sixteen people to ensure that they were naive about UFOs and alien abduction. Being 1977, it was much easier to find uninformed participants than it would be today, since the concept of alien abduction was less well known back then, although a few famous cases were public knowledge.[8] Once recruited, the participants were placed under deep hypnosis and asked to respond to eight questions:

(1) Imagine you are in your favorite place, relaxed and comfortable, when you suddenly see a UFO. Describe what you see.

(2) Imagine you are aboard that UFO. How do you get aboard?

(3) Imagine you are inside that UFO. Describe what you see there.

(4) Imagine you are seeing some entities or beings on board that UFO. Describe them as completely as you can.

(5) You are undergoing some kind of physical examination. Describe what is happening to you.

(6) You are given some sort of message by the occupants of that UFO. What does the message say, and how was it made known to you?

(7) You are returned safely to where you were before you sighted the UFO. How did you get there, and how do you feel?

(8) Imagine it has been some time since you have had that UFO encounter. Is there anything which indicates that your personality or your physiological and/or psychological functions have been affected in any way by your UFO experience?

The participants' answers to each of the questions were then compared with the details contained in four "legitimate," multiple-witness abduction cases identified by Lawson and McCall. The initial objective of the *Hypnosis of Imaginary Abductees* study was to determine how the imagined narratives of experimental participants differed from "real" abductions stories. This was because Lawson and McCall, to a certain extent, believed in the abduction phenomenon and hoped to develop a useful method of distinguishing authentic abduction cases (containing unique details not present in the answers of experimental participants) from abduction cases that were hoaxes or fantasies (with details similar to those reported by participants imagining an abduction).

One of the motivations for the study was that Lawson and McCall were suspicions of the burgeoning use of hypnosis to draw out the experiences of alleged abductees. A few years earlier, they had genuinely believed a local account involving Brian Scott, known as the Garden Grove abduction. However, when they investigated further they found the account contained many elements of fantasy and potential hoax. Lawson and McCall were particularly concerned about abduction cases involving time-lapse, where the hypnosis session was many months or years after the paranormal event. Often the time-lapse abductees had no strong recollection of anything ever having happened to them, but as they lay in a relaxed state on the hypnotist's couch all sorts of scattered imagery entered their minds. They would repeat this to the hypnotist, who might subtly guide them towards a coherent abduction account created from all the bits and pieces they were imagining. Nevertheless, the subject themselves might question whether the story they begin to remember was real or purely imaginary. For example, an abductee named Alan Godfrey was himself unsure about the reliability of the abduction story he narrated under hypnosis, and he thought some of the content might have derived from stories he had read, rather than the actual incident itself (Randles and Hough 1997).

Examining the results of the *Hypnosis of Imaginary Abductees* study, Lawson and McCall were surprised to find that a strong similarity existed between participants' imaginary tales and the content of abductions cases they considered legitimate. For example, in common with the typical "authentic" abductee, the hypnotic participants spoke of entering a ship[9] and meeting aliens. They also received a medical examination. By 1981, Lawson had come to the conclusion that alien abductions are not objectively real after all, but simply a modern treatment of a narrative shared by all people which can be re-told under certain circumstances, including hypnosis.

To Lawson, the obvious shared experience was birth, and the typical alien abduction account is jam-packed with perinatal imagery (meaning the period before, and just after, birth). However, the idea that people can somehow draw on the unconscious memory of their own birth is not originally Lawson's. In essence, it's a more extreme treatment of the psychoanalytic hypothesis that early life experiences — including experiences in the womb — are crucial determinants of an adult's personality. It also owes a lot to the writings of Stanislaw Grof, who, in a 1975 book called *Realms of the Human Unconscious: Observations from LSD Research,* speculated that the hallucinatory imagery reported by LSD users was perinatal. The possibility that these very early birth memories affect adult behavior has since become a popular, albeit fringe, theory and a method of therapy. There's even a journal with articles dedicated to early influences on adult psychology, called the *Journal of Prenatal and Perinatal Psychology.*

Where Lawson was creative was his application of the existing theory of perinatal influence to abductions, teasing out similarities in both an abduction scenario and a birth event. These include (and there are a lot of similarities); loss of control, seeing bright lights, paralysis, being struck by a lightbeam, hearing metallic sounds, the abductee changing size, a big round room with a door in the middle, seeing starry skies, encountering absurd events and entities, a physical examination, reliving of the abductee's medical history, bodily dismemberment, miscellaneous womb imagery, amnesia, a loss of the sense of time, levitation by a tube of light or a tunnel, umbilical pain, relief after intense pain or threat, breathing problems, unpleasant tastes and odors, pressure on head and body and finally a life review on a screen.

Phew!

To support his theory, Lawson used the narratives of an abductee named Betty Andreasson[10] as evidence for birth imagery in the abduction process. In one of Betty's accounts, she was abducted into a "cylindrical room" where she sat on a chair enclosed in a clear plastic cover which was then filled with grey fluid. Despite the fluid, she was able to continue breathing through tubes entering her nostrils and mouth. A voice in her head told her to close her eyes, and she experienced a sweet substance in her mouth, a pleasant vibration and a sensation of relaxation and happiness, becoming at one with the "undulating fluid." Later, the fluid was drained and she was released ... an event analogous to being born?

Criticisms of the Birth Memories Hypothesis

As a rejoinder, Hilary Evans claims that in their 1977 study, Lawson and McCall's hypnotized participants may have received the content of their narrative directly from the hypnotist through telepathy, rather than reliving a birth memory, perhaps in a psychoanalytical way to please them. (Evans 1986). However, most critics aren't so kind to Lawson's theory. The birth memories

Alvin Lawson enthusiastically lectures to an audience at a UFO conference in Salzburg in 1982. Lawson is pointing to what appears to be a uterus on the projector screen, no doubt making the connection between aspects of the birthing process and characteristics of alien abduction syndrome. The notion that abduction reports represent memories of birth is open to ridicule and the theory has few supporters — skeptics, diehard believers or those in the middle ground. Nevertheless, the birth memories hypothesis makes an enjoyable and fascinating discussion topic, since the connections Lawson made between specific abduction cases and perinatal imagery are very creative (Mary Evans Picture Library).

hypothesis has always experienced great resistance from both supporters and skeptics of alien abductions. Supporters don't like it because it discounts the extraterrestrial nature of the experience. On the other hand, skeptics think the theory is just as ridiculous as believing real aliens kidnap people and take them into spaceships. The main scientific objection tendered by both groups regards infantile amnesia, whereby memories before approximately 2 ½ years of age are inherently unreliable (Crawley and Eacott 1999). The memories might be there, but difficult to retrieve (the Freudian approach), or simply prone to replacement, or never registered, or were quickly lost in the early years of life. Regardless of what the specifics are, they are certainly not available in adulthood (Howe and Courage 1993).

Nevertheless, an early memory, even one demonstrated as being present at birth (for example, a newborn's demonstrated preference for a story that had been read to them while they were in the womb compared with a novel story), will be in the form of a conditioned response or fragmentary association rather than a proper, adult-like autobiographical memory (Howe 2000). In fact, the standard scientific argument is that it is physiologically impossible for memories to be formed at, or before, birth. Memory researcher Yuko Munakata informs us that the hippocampus is an important structure for episodic memory, or memory of events in a person's everyday life. Encoding these events is based on the initial creation of hippocampal "representations" which are stored over the longer term as cortical representations elsewhere in the brain. These long term memories can later be retrieved and recollected when the hippocampus coordinates the coherent reactivation of the representations of these memories that are distributed in various parts of the higher brain (Fenker, Schott, Richardson-Klavehn, Heinze and Düzel 2005).

However, even if cortical representations could be recorded in early life, as the brain develops there is a considerable degree of cortical reorganization. As a consequence, the necessary association between hippocampus and cortex, which is the trigger for recall, no longer exists (Munakata 2004). More simply, as the brain grows and changes the hippocampus can't match its original representations of an early memory with those of the cortex. No emergent memory is therefore possible, which explains physiologically the phenomenon of infantile amnesia.

In response to these criticisms regarding early childhood memories, Lawson responded that an "emotional memory" center in the amygdala records the first few years of emotional life, and this includes pre-natal events, until the hippocampal-based declarative memory center kicks in and self-awareness arises. Yet while the amygdala is believed to mediate emotional memory in adults, its perinatal role (if any) has not been examined scientifically in any detail.

Richard Haines also criticizes the methodology of the original *Hypnosis of Imaginary Abductees* study (Haines 1980). Firstly, he argues that the veracity of the "legitimate" abduction cases — to which the imaginary narratives are compared — requires better confirmation. The four examples of alien kidnapping Lawson and McCall referred to aren't many, and we are left unsure as to how "real" they are. That is, did the witnesses really experience an anomalous event (whatever its cause)? If there is suspicion that at least some of the abductees' stories are confabulations, then the conclusions of the study are invalid — it's nothing more than a comparison of fabricated stories with imaginary stories. Secondly, while Haines acknowledges that the sixteen hypnotized subjects produced coherent UFO abduction narratives without prompting, comparison of the these narratives with the "legitimate" stories was not in terms of content but only the number of information bits they had in common. That is, five bits information in a section of an imaginary story corresponds to five bits of information in an authentic story.

Realistically, a more sophisticated analysis should have been performed, for example blind qualitative categorization of the narratives by more than one person reading and rating them. In the words of the parapsychologist D. Scott Rogo, similarities between the imaginary and abduction groups existed in Lawson's opinion only, and are nothing more than anecdotal parallels "taken grossly out of context" (Rogo 1980). In folklorist Eddie Bullard's opinion, the birth memories hypothesis is not convincing because it attempts to tie abductions with prenatal events using a grab-bag of isolated, abstract images and not the actual storylines, which contain important sequences and patterns of events that might not have a birth association after all (Bullard 1988).

Nevertheless, Lawson's claims of similarities between the content of the abduction story and birth imagery are at least worth considering. One of the most obvious resemblances he quotes is the fetal appearance of the infamous "Grey." This alien type came to dominate the abduction narrative in the late 1970s, at the time of Lawson and McCall's first study, and is most prevalent in the U.S. Nevertheless, it's difficult to account for abduction stories at earlier times, or from contemporary non–U.S. sources where, for example, the abducting aliens can be anything from shapeless blobs, to robots, to hairy dwarves.[11] It's also difficult to understand why the imagery is of an external representation of the fetus when surely the abductee themselves should be the one looking like a fetus. Lawson counters this argument by suggesting fetuses are known to actively touch their bodies in the womb, and might develop a representation of their "own body, placenta, and umbilical cord." The "Grey" is therefore a representation of the fetal self-image.

The same goes for the apparent propensity of the aliens to wear large belt buckles, medallions or other devices on their abdomens. These Lawson believes to be projected representations of the abductee's own navel area and umbilical cord (Lawson 2001b).

Therefore, to account for these anomalies it is necessary to complicate the hypothesis, re-working a simple, primitive memory of birth into a complex pseudo-psychodynamic story that transfers the symbolic aspects of the birth process to external agents such as an imaginary "Grey." Not surprisingly, Lawson uses terms such as "indirect" and "metaphorical" to explain the anomalies, one being the awkward fact that abduction accounts are mainly about entering the spacecraft (womb) when birth is, obviously, the other way around (Lawson 2001c). Thus reports of abductees entering or leaving the spacecraft suggest to Lawson a symbolic birth, not a real memory of birth.

Lawson also suggests that the abduction narrative is complicated by "fantasies, hallucinatory imagery and later memories, along with birth data" (Lawson 1984). Therefore, it doesn't matter if the abduction account can't exactly fit the perinatal experience since the abduction is entirely symbolic. While it makes certain sense that a primitive, non-declarative memory should be expressed in very remote and symbolic form, this will not satisfy the skeptic who demands a theory that can be falsified experimentally.

A follow-up study by Lawson in 1979 was an attempt to add experimental clout to the birth memories hypothesis (Lawson 1984) and used a natural-group design[12] that compared the narratives of hypnotized abductees who he discovered had undergone either a Caesarean birth or a natural vaginal birth. He concluded that the Caesarean participants gave accounts which, by and large, lacked tunnel imagery to explain how they entered or left their imaginary UFO. This is apparently because they had never actually experienced their mother's birth canal.

This study, however, suffers from the same problems plaguing the original 1977 research. Perceptual psychologist Stuart Appelle, in a detailed examination of alien abduction theories, makes the telling point that while there were eight Caesarean subjects (hardly a number conducive to statistical power), there were only two vaginal birth subjects. The unsatisfying number of participants, coupled with the lack of verification as to whether the Caesarean subjects were actually Caesarean subjects,[13] opens the conclusions to much criticism (Appelle 1996). Most tellingly, Appelle makes the point that one of the two vaginal subjects also didn't include tunnel imagery to explain how they departed the UFO after their abduction experience — that's 50 percent of the sample. The expression used by this participant to describe their return from the spacecraft was "instantaneous return," similar to expressions such as "I was zapped out" used by the other Caesarean subjects.

To be fair, Alvin Lawson perhaps would have been the first to claim that the results do not necessarily prove a birth memories–abduction relationship. Rather, he argued that the unique narratives from abductees match quite closely the details of their reported birth. For example, an abductee who'd had a breech birth left their "imaginary" UFO by sitting down over a trapdoor before sinking to the ground outside. Another who had been forceps-delivered told of a metal clamp holding him and twisting his back during the abduction. However, it is equally as likely that the participant's knowledge of their birth, perhaps told to him by their mother as a child or a teenager, would have inspired the content of the abduction imagery.

A final, fundamental question which requires answering is why birth memories should recur in adulthood at all. This is not to mean how or why perinatal memories are created in the first place, which is an important and difficult topic in its own right. Rather, the birth memories hypothesis should be able to explain why memories express themselves in certain adults in very specific ways, assuming such memories are legitimate, and stored as "rough, wordless blueprints" in the brain (Lawson 2001c).

Lawson (2001a) believes that birth memories are particularly ingrained because the process of birth is so traumatic. Fantasizing during a drug-induced hallucination, a hypnotic trance, fatigue, monotony, isolation or when simply daydreaming is therefore likely to uncover them and result in a spontaneous abduction experience (Lawson 1994). Alternately, abductees might be neurotics with a deep therapeutic need to spontaneously relive the birth experience which gave them the neurosis in the first place (Lawson 1984). Presumably, cultural conditioning determines the form of the superficial, "kidnapped-by-aliens" scenario. Post-fantasy suggestion, inspired by a therapist or the media, then molds the fragmented story into a shared and pervasive modern mythology.

CHAPTER 9

Advanced Psychodynamic Theories: The Projection of the Paranormal

While we're on the topic of alien abductions, it's worth examining other, fringe psychological theories developed to account for the phenomenon. It is perhaps different from other forms of paranormal experience in that it is contemporary[1], complex and threatening. Of course there are contemporary hauntings cases and recent tales of such things as spontaneous psychokinesis, but these deviate little from the cases and tales of 100 years ago. While there might exist the odd obscure report of astral travel or a science fiction story from the early 1900s that has elements in common with later alien abduction syndrome, there is undoubtedly a definitive modern flavor that sets the abduction phenomenon apart from other paranormal topics.

The syndrome's complexity is shared by a few other paranormal experiences, one example being stories of recurrent poltergeist activity that plague some people throughout their lives. Yet these don't quite share the intensity and threatening nature of abductions, with the implication that humans are helpless in the face of a seemingly omnipotent alien force. So far, we've examined theories that haven't taken the stories literally and attribute them to be, among other things, false memories, masochistic urges or symptoms of hysterical delirium. Probably the most controversial we've discussed is Alvin Lawson's birth memories hypothesis which, unlike other mainstream psychological theories, proposes that the abduction experience is not entirely irrelevant. In fact, Lawson even suggested that the birth trauma re-enacted in perinatal imagery might have a vague therapeutic value.

In this chapter we explore theories claiming that alien abduction and entity contact is psychologically meaningful to the abductee. That is, the ingredients and storyline of the experience derive from the abductee's deep unconscious, and for a purpose. One of these theories deals solely with alien abduction, and was developed by D. Scott Rogo following his examination of the Betty and Barney Hill case from the early 1960s. He then refined the theory as he gained access to more abduction accounts. A good starting point is therefore to briefly narrate four of these tales (leaving out quite a bit of detail), then discuss Rogo's unique perspective on each.

The Hill, Andreasson, Tujunga Canyon and Higdon Abductions

(1) In 1961 one of the most famous abductions occurred — the one that really kick-started the phenomenon and brought it to public attention. Betty and Barney Hill were driving one night in New Hampshire when at about 11 P.M. they witnessed a bright star-like object in the sky that seemed to be following them. Eventually, the light stopped and hovered close by, and Barney got out of the car to get a better look with his binoculars. He saw through the lens a flying saucer with occupants inside who were watching him. Understandably fearful, Barney rushed back to the car, but in the process of leaving the scene he heard a strange beeping sound. Arriving home, the Hills discovered they had taken two hours longer in their journey than expected — an early account of missing time. Over the next few years, Betty experienced strange dreams, and Barney was beset with unusual anxieties and illnesses. In 1964, both Betty and Barney were hypnotized by a psychiatrist Benjamin Simon and gave independent accounts of being taken on board a spacecraft by small beings with large heads,[2] separated and forced to undertake a medical examination. Betty was subjected to a pregnancy test which made use of a needle inserted into her navel, and Barney had sperm and skin samples removed. Following her examination, Betty was shown a map of the star system from which the aliens originated before the couple were returned to their car. In 1966, their experiences were published in a book by John Fuller called *The Interrupted Journey* and the story became a prototype for later roadside abduction accounts.

(2) Arguably the model for a home abduction derived from the 1967 experience of Betty Andreasson, a resident of Massachusetts, investigated by UFO researcher Ray Fowler. Betty was in the kitchen of her home — her seven children and parents were also in the house — when she saw a light hovering outside. A strange sensation settled over the house, and her father looked out to see with some shock a group of strange humanoid creatures approaching. He remembered nothing more, but under hypnosis in 1977 Betty recalled being taken outside the house (after floating through the solid kitchen door) and entering the visitors' spacecraft. Here she received a physical examination, in one place involving the removal of a small implant from her nose. She was then placed in a flotation tank[3] before being taken to a strange alien environment where she witnessed the fiery destruction and rebirth of a phoenix-like bird. Returning home and put to bed, Betty was made to forget what had happened to her (Fowler 1980).

(3) In 1953, Sara Shaw and Jan Whitley lived together in a small cabin in the Tujunga Canyons district of Los Angeles. Many years later, under hypnosis, Sara recalled being floated out of their cabin one evening and into a UFO occupied by small aliens. Jan was also floated out of the cabin, but fought against the abduction unlike Sara — who apparently remained indifferent to the experience. As might be expected of such a typical (although historically very early) bedroom abduction scenario, separate examinations followed. Sara's examination was performed by male entities, while female entities stood behind and watched. She was then given a tour of the ship and told of a cure for cancer (Druffel and Rogo 1989).

(4) The final story is my favorite. Carl Higdon was hunting alone in the forests of Wyoming in 1974 when, as he shot at some elk, he actually saw the bullet that had been fired from his rifle slow down and drop to the ground. As he walked over to pick up the bullet he heard a noise behind him, and turned to see a tall man-like being dressed in a black suit watching him. The entity identified itself as "Ausso" and asked Higdon to come with him, and the hunter complied. Higdon soon found himself strapped to a chair inside a type of cubicle within a spacecraft, and the craft left earth on a long journey to a different world dominated by a tower. Next to the tower Higdon saw a number of humans of different ages — one older man with four youngsters. They were dressed normally and talked among themselves. Ausso then took Higdon inside the tower and made him stand for a number of minutes in a room while he was examined by a shield-like device. Following the examination, Ausso explained that Higdon "was not what they needed" and would be taken back to his own world. Somehow he was returned to the forest, and in a dazed state managed to radio for help. He was taken to hospital and recovered after a few days.

From Rogo's perspective, the popular account of what happened to these people is really only half the story. It's just as important to know about the abductee themselves, to see if any personal issues can shed light on their experiences. After Rogo read Fuller's book on the Hills' kidnapping, he came to the conclusion that issues affecting the couple's lives were symbolically represented in the content of the abduction (Rogo 1983). The event itself was a deep psychological fantasy — the "missing time" was only discovered by investigators and the hypnotic recollections were distorted reconstructions of Betty's anxiety dreams. This anxiety apparently centered on the fact that Barney was a black postal worker and Betty was a socially prominent white woman, and the year was 1961. A degree of tension, perhaps unconscious, was felt by both of them over the way their community viewed the marriage. Hence Rogo was not surprised that the impersonal aliens in the spacecraft separated the couple, gave Betty a pregnancy test to make sure she wasn't pregnant, and symbolically castrated Barney.

In time, Rogo adapted his thesis as he became aware of abduction cases with multiple (and unmarried) witnesses. This suggested to him that the phenomenon might actually possess some objective reality after all. Nevertheless, he felt the symbolism in storyline still was too great to ignore. For example, the Betty Andreasson abduction[4] was partly confirmed by her father and oldest daughter, yet aspects of her life at the time were seemingly shaped the story of the encounter. Rogo suspected that Betty must have been highly anxious at the time of her abduction since she was a mother of seven children and at the time her alcoholic husband had been admitted to hospital following a serious car accident. She was also a very strong Christian, and Rogo saw her experiences as a reaffirmation of her faith during difficult times. The removal of implanted objects during the medical examination, the time spent in the liquid-filled vessel and the witnessed death and rebirth of the phoenix represents the breaking apart, cleansing and reconstruction of her faith. On one occasion while speaking to the aliens Betty was also asked for food, but not the food she was preparing in the kitchen. They wanted only burnt food — "knowledge tried by fire." Betty finally got the message and brought them a Bible. As Rogo makes clear, this is not what one would expect from your "average" extraterrestrial encounter!

With regards Sara Shaw, Rogo interviewed her in depth and came to the conclusion that her family and sexual history was a determining factor in the abduction. Her dominant mother had given her antiquated views about sexual relations, and to please her Sara had moved in with Jan to avoid male contact. Apparently, this isolated life was unfulfilling, and she eventually moved back to society following counseling. Rogo suspects that the abduction was symbolic of this decision. The impersonal (male) aliens entered her bedroom took her to their craft and separated her from Jan. She was not stressed by this, even as the male alien abductors undressed her as the female ones looked on passively. Rogo (1983) writes that the events are a reconstruction of messages emanating from Sara's unconscious psyche, informing her that her current way of life was unrewarding and that she needed to separate from Jan and "enter into normal social and sexual relationships with men."[5]

Rogo explanation of the Higdon encounter also has a sexual nature. After reading the report by Leo Sprinkle, a psychologist and one of the original investigators of the Higdon case, Rogo came to a startling conclusion. In the report he learned that Higdon had undergone a vasectomy some years before the encounter and had wondered aloud to Sprinkle whether that was why he wasn't considered "any good" to Ausso the alien. This is despite the fact that in the original version of the story, Ausso told Higdon he wasn't "what they needed." Rogo concluded from Higdon's "Freudian slip" (so to speak) that the whole episode was symbolic of his belief that the vasectomy had made him inadequate. Therefore, the bullet fired from the (phallic) rifle also lost it potency. The tower is phallic, and the man he sees there is his own self, surrounded by his four children. They ignore him, and then Ausso reminds him how he is not needed. Rogo concluded that the abduction was, in symbolic form, a representation of Higdon's fears of worthlessness and impotency now that he was unable to have more children.

Therefore, in Rogo's opinion, an "alien abduction" is a visionary journey, experienced by countless people throughout history, in which the abductee undergoes symbolic trial by ordeal in order to gain as-yet unrecognized knowledge about themselves (Rogo 1980). Rogo claimed that abductions are "merely an elaborate stage setting used to camouflage the fact that the victim — far from being abducted by outer space beings, is being forced to confront some secret aspect of his own self!"

Even the abductee themselves might suspect a deep purpose to their experience. John Hodges, while speaking to investigator Ann Druffel about an abduction he experienced in 1971, is quoted as saying that he thought "the entire thing was a fantastic, beautiful theatre.... A display solely for my benefit to convey something that right now is unbeknownst to me" (Rogo 1980).

The proposition that an abduction is the consequence of an unconscious and tension-relieving action identifies Rogo's hypothesis as psychodynamic. However, it imparts more respectability to the event compared with the psychoanalyst's belief that abductions are merely representations of primitive, impulsive urges or trauma-related defense mechanisms. Yet Rogo's confidence in the physical reality of the event pushes the hypothesis outside the realms of even fringe psychological theories. An alien abduction is not simply a subjective, personal experience brought about by base tensions welling up within the abductee. The abductee must also possess unusual psychical abilities, and perhaps have a demonstrated history of recurrent poltergeist-like activity. Some external "intelligence" notices this (dramatically called the Phenomenon — the same word used by John Keel for his "ultraterrestrials"), alongside a life crisis the individual must be suffering, and generates the encounter — perhaps as a way to help them. And, in common with Keel's Phenomenon, it is apparently linked not to outer space, but to something intrinsically related to this world and the people in it. Rogo uses the term "universal unconscious," in that the Phenomenon is aware of thoughts, feelings and actions, and becomes involve where, for whatever reason, it thinks it is appropriate.

Explaining abduction cases with multiple witnesses, Rogo proposes that the abductee is the focus of a projected, symbolic kidnapping that can, because of the ubiquitous authority of the Phenomenon, be witnessed by others who might by accident become actors in the abductee's staged play.

Thought-Forms

Remaining on the psychological fringe for a moment, it is fun pondering whether the human mind might be entirely responsible for the projected abduction. Perhaps there's no need to attribute encounters with weird-looking aliens to some transcendental cosmic intelligence — even if other witnesses can see them too. Now, most mainstream psychologists would not begrudge using the term "projection" when applied to a person who might project or externalize hidden personal qualities onto others, and therefore react to that person in a way that satisfies some unconscious dynamic. However, they would surely blanch at the proposal that the projection takes the form of something physically real.

Nevertheless, the idea that the human mind has the capability of generating a genuine, consensus experience can be found in the occult[6] and mystical literature going back many decades. Theosophists Annie Besant and Charles Leadbeater wrote a book about thought-forms called, not surprisingly, *Thought Forms*. These authors claim that ideas cause vibrations[7] which radiate from the thinker's body and, if strong enough, set off a pattern of sympathetic vibration in a receiver's mind which reconstitutes the same idea — an explanation for psi. Apparently the vibrations emanate from various levels of "mental matter" which, it goes without saying, are hard to depict in a scientific, reductionist manner. Nevertheless, depending on the idea they derive from, the energy of the vibration can be thrown off and externalized, as the thinker's own body form (an apparition), a material object, or something with its own autonomy, constructing itself from the qualities inherent in the environment that surrounds it (Besant and Leadbeater 1905).

However, the most famous case of a "real" thought-form would probably be that created by the mystic Alexandra David-Neel, who, in a book about her travels through India and the Himalayas, described how she created a *tulpa* (thought-form) while practicing Buddhism in Tibet in the early part of the 20th century. In seclusion, and meditating for months on end, David-Neel concentrated her mind on the image of a short, fat and jolly monk. Gradually the image took on a fixed quality and became a guest in her apartment. When she later left the apartment to go on a tour, her monk followed, at times showing autonomous behavior. He was even able to be physically felt on occasions. Over the next few weeks, the features of the tulpa changed, the monk becoming a leaner and somewhat malevolent character. David-Neel believed this modification was due to the hallucination escaping her control — it was apparently also seen by other people in her traveling party. Eventually, she was forced to spend six months willing it out of existence. However, Evans (1984) cautions against taking this story too literally. Not only is it written as a climax to her otherwise very serious book (giving the impression of an anachronistic literary device to satisfy the reader), but credible reports involving the creation of a tulpa are exceedingly rare. There are simply too few reported examples of such a creation despite intense interest in the concept.

One such example of tulpa creation occurred in the early part of the 20th century when the occultist Dion Fortune[8] lay in bed dozing and thinking badly of a friend who had slighted her. The idea of going berserk in anger was appealing, and she immediately thought of Fenris, the wolf of Norse mythology. A sensation suddenly occurred in her chest, and she felt presence of a wolf near her face. Fortune's *tulpa* apparently derived from emotional brooding over the incident, coupled with the correct invocation and a state between sleeping and wakefulness where there was the greatest chance that of extrusion of the "etheric double" (Wilson 1971).

As the story goes, the thought-form escaped her room, and was seen by others in the house or appeared as a character in their dreams that night. To reabsorb her unfortunate creation, Fortune was told by an advisor to forgive her friend, which she decided to do. With this the wolf reappeared to her and was literally drawn back into her body.

Other, far less dramatic cases of thought-forms have been reported over the years and appear in various popular book and magazine sources. The prototypical example would be the hazy materialization of an object such as a clock or a vase of flowers — generated when like-minded individuals come together under guidance in a séance room and concentrate on materializing an apport. These creations are very much the exception, however, and the skeptic could easily argue that the group members are privy to a shared illusion or hallucination. It goes without saying that there's not even a half-formed theory to explain how conscious or subconscious desires can manifest as physical reality. As an advance on Annie Besant's writings, one could conjecture a type of non-material field (akin to subjective mental processes) which is anchored by material reality, in the same way that opposing electric charges at two different positions in space are "real" while the field created by them is theoretical — although it still has a very real effect on charged particles caught in its domain of influence.

Admittedly this is a very weak analogy, but one shouldn't dismiss out of hand the less controversial possibility that complicated paranormal events, such as abductions, are psychological manifestations of unconscious tension. Rogo's treatment of abduction cases from the '60s and '70s is rather creative, and the hypothesis intuitively fits the components of these cases. Without resorting to extreme theories of cosmic intelligence, it still seems as valuable as any other psychodynamic explanation. However, like all psychodynamic approaches, it doesn't possess predictive power, since the explanation for an abduction (or any other type of paranormal encounter) can only be made after the experience has occurred, and the investigator creatively ties in the components of the case with the personal history of the experient. This might have some unconventional therapeutic worth, but would not be considered scientific from the viewpoint of any mainstream psychologist.

Rogo died in 1990, and it's intriguing to think what he would have made of a famous Australian abduction that occurred outside Melbourne in 1993, complete with independent eyewitness testimony. Let's examine this case to understand how easy it is, in an after-the-fact fashion, to interpret it in terms of the Rogo hypothesis.

The Kelly Cahill Abduction

At dusk in the August of 1993, Kelly Cahill (a pseudonym) and her husband Andrew were driving to a friend's house in the Dandenong Ranges, which are a set of low hills on the eastern outskirts of Melbourne. The journey took approximately 90 minutes, and on the drive up Kelly saw, for a brief moment, a UFO in a field adjacent to the road. She plucked up the courage to tell her husband, Andrew, but since he didn't believe in UFOs, he dismissed the sighting curtly. They spent the evening with their friends and left the hills after midnight for the journey home. On the way back, both Kelly and Andrew saw the orange lights of another UFO hovering beside a quiet stretch of road. Abruptly it disappeared, but on rounding the next bend they saw an even bigger craft in a nearby field. This is where Kelly's conscious recollection of the events ended, and further details of the encounter emerged through fragments of memory and dream material.

In the pieced-together story, Andrew stopped their car and the couple left the vehicle to approach the object. Kelly even remembered to take her handbag. Readers will recall this desire for a closer look was shared by Barney Hill before his abduction. By the time Kelly had reached the field, a second car had apparently pulled up about 100 meters away, and the three occupants of this vehicle also witnessed the UFO. The lone occupant of a motorbike was also present, some distance behind. Once in the field, Kelly saw dark entities approaching, two meters tall with glowing red eyes. Similar beings were heading for the three occupants of the second car. Two of these occupants allegedly have recollections of a subsequent abduction, although the memories aren't visual but auditory. Interestingly, they also regard their experiences as voluntary and not necessarily unpleasant.

In contrast, Kelly's interaction with the beings was not enjoyable. Their red, fly-like eyes suggested to Kelly that they lacked souls. In the book she published about the abduction, called *Encounter* (Cahill 1996), Kelly recounts how she cried out, "They're evil! They're going to kill us." She was consequently winded and knocked to the ground. Presumably, the entities did this to stop her screaming, although a skeptic might point out that the electric fence in the field, offhandedly mentioned by Kelly in her book, was responsible. There then occurred a complex series of abduction events which included periods of blackout, conversations with the evil being(s), nausea, fear and anger. All the abductees from the various vehicles were eventually released, but when Kelly arrived home she became ill and noticed she and her husband had unaccountable "missing time."

Physical traces were discovered on her body in the coming weeks, and over the next few months Kelly experienced lucid dreams. The most significant dream occurred immediately after the encounter, and appeared to be a narration of the events inside the UFO. Subsequent dreams involved the same type of unpleasant dark entity that occupied the UFO, but this time entering her bedroom. The suggestion was that the beings were still deeply interested in Kelly for some nefarious reason.

As a roadside abduction story the Kelly Cahill case certainly is pretty straightforward, apart from the unusual aspect of multiple witnesses and its aura of evil. Nevertheless, this abridged version leaves out significant details about Kelly's personal situation which, if one were to take Rogo's abduction hypothesis seriously, might explain why the abduction occurred.

Of this personal background, perhaps the most important is the relationship tensions that apparently existed between Kelly and her husband, in particular those associated with their religious beliefs. Such anxieties were highlighted in a interview published on the internet between Kelly and a Christian commentator in which Kelly's background was discussed in great detail. It transpires that Kelly had embraced Pentecostal Christianity six years prior to the 1993 encounter, and frequently attended church and Bible study classes. Andrew, her husband, was Muslim. Therefore, elements of both the Betty and Barney Hill relationship, and Betty Andreasson's religiosity, could be liberally applied to this abduction case.

Eventually, it seems Kelly became disillusioned with the church, yet was still "living her life entirely for God"—she wanted communion with God so as "to get closer to him and become perfect." It's been written that for three weeks in July of 1993, not long before the abduction, Kelly "holed herself up" in a room of her house praying and studying the Bible while Andrew supported her and looked after their children—he respected the fervor of her divine search, even if it wasn't compatible with his own religious background.

Towards the end of her three week quest, Kelly was blown away by a sample of God's power when she asked, "I want You here! I want Your pure presence." What Rogo would have thought of this unusual need, coupled with the "spiritual and psychological ramifications" on her marriage, is anyone's guess. Perhaps he would have predicted an abduction, which in fact took place little over a month later. Symbolic elements in the encounter that seem related to her spiritual tension are abundant. For example, Kelly writes that the black entities she met in the field emanated an evil energy which was the antithesis of the "God energy" she had earlier experienced in her room. She felt they "mocked" God. In a further interesting development, we learn that when she first saw the original orange UFO on the drive up to her friend's house, Kelly prayed, "Father.... Wait for me. I'll be back down this way in a few hours" (Chalker 1996).

It's curious that she was motivated enough to say a prayer after witnessing an ambiguous light display in a paddock on the side of the road. It might suggest that the coming event was not unexpected.

The association between the earlier prayer, and the UFO entities later encountered, is made explicit in a conversation Kelly overheard that night at the height of the abduction. As the story goes, after she was knocked over by the mysterious force, somewhere near Andrew asked with high emotion; "Why did you hit Kelly?" The reply from one of the entities was, "I wouldn't harm her. She's my daughter." The tone was interpreted by Kelly as sarcastic, and Australian UFO researcher Bill Chalker makes the reasonable assumption that the retort was in response to Kelly's earlier prayer to "God the Father." Perhaps it was to be expected because the alien was a projection of Kelly's own unconscious tension?

In fact, Kelly herself acknowledged that she was responsible for the event, and the people around her were simply unfortunate bystanders. She writes in her book that she got angry during the episode and screamed, "How dare you do this to these innocent people?" because she felt responsible for bringing it on them. It was her fault.

From the perspective of the Rogo hypothesis, the Hill abduction was intrinsically related to their racially-mixed marriage and its wider acceptance. Betty Andreasson's benign communications with alien beings endorsed her religious faith and was essentially positive. In the Cahill abduction it could be argued that Kelly's unconscious need to transcend the ordinary and escape her sheltered life determined the theme of the encounter. "I look at people living nice Christian lives in churches," she said in her interview with the Christian commentator, "and it makes me happy because they see only the beauty and the goodness of what they have." Rogo might have written that Kelly needed to see the bad to endorse the good, hence the oppressive nature of the abduction.

Kelly's dreams also fit nicely into the psychodynamic mold. Immediately following the abduction she dreamt she was near the UFO and one of the dark entities was pulling her husband away. Kelly tackled the female entity and it fell to the ground, turning human. Nearby, an old lady screamed "Mur-

A depiction of the moment Kelly Cahill and her husband were abducted by unpleasant aliens on a quiet stretch of road outside of Melbourne, Australia, in 1993 (artist Michael Buhler). The red dragon on the spare wheel cover is an artistic reference to the claim that independent witnesses, also present at the abduction, recalled this motif in separate interviews — adding an aura of respectability to the case as a rare, multiple witnessed event. The account has elements in common with previous U.S. abductions, such as the famous Betty and Barney Hill case and Betty Andreasson's many alien contacts. Consequently, an interpretation of the Cahill incident using D. Scott Rogo's psychodynamic theory of alien abduction is easy to perform, albeit one of many psychological explanations that could be offered (Mary Evans Picture Library).

derer! Murderer!" Kelly was confused by this accusation, since she believed she hadn't murdered anyone. An interpretation would be that the female entity dragging her husband away was a representation of Kelly herself, and in "murdering" the entity she was symbolically destroying her marriage.

Later in the dream Kelly was led by another dark entity into a room with a table. She felt she knew the creature, and this meeting is symbolic of the struggle between her ego (herself) and her unconscious (the entity). On the table was a Bible, in fact one of Kelly's own that had disappeared weeks before. She was told by the entity that the Bible would have to be left behind. She chose the Bible and the dream ended. The very next day the lost book was found by her husband in the car. Recall that Betty Andreasson once gave her alien visitors a Bible, in essence spreading her faith to otherworldly beings. Applying the Rogo hypothesis, Kelly Cahill's encounter rather seems to be about forcing a decision about her life's direction, and in taking her Bible back she was retaining her faith. Nevertheless, such a choice, while perhaps "safer" than relinquishing her strong beliefs, might not be enough to alleviate the source of her anxiety. In addition to her recurrent bedroom visitors, Kelly suffered an alleged plague of parapsychological events in her home, and her marriage was ruined.[9]

One of the features of a Rogorian interpretation of the Cahill abduction is that the traumatic events necessarily place the abductee on a path of self-realization and recovery, and that it's up to the abductee to understand — presumably unconsciously — the message contained within the abduction storyline. After all, neither Betty or Barney Hill, Sara Shaw, Betty Andreasson, Charlie Higdon or Kelly Cahill consciously recognized that their abduction was, according to the theory, an artificial event designed purely for personal enlightenment. Yet if that's the case, why bother having them at all? As the abduction was generated by the unconscious, to be understood unconsciously, does this posit two types of unconscious that are independent of each other. How can that be tested and where does it end? Can there be a third, a fourth and a fifth type of unconscious?

Furthermore, if the abduction is created by some unknown and unknowable force called "the Phenomenon," then the force doesn't seem to do a terribly good job improving people's lives, for something that is so powerful. It seems Rogorian abductees just end up more confused and miserable. Indeed, it appears that the abductee's unconscious is doing no more than releasing its pent up frustrations like a kettle letting off steam, and doesn't care whether the reasons for the frustration are cognized by the unfortunate abductee's ego. However, even this explanation doesn't make sense of why the content has to follow the typical abduction pattern; with UFOs, aliens and all the associated extraterrestrial trappings. Taking abduction stories and teasing them apart in an ad hoc manner for psychodynamic analysis, while enticing and easy to do (just take the example of the Cahill abduction), ultimately doesn't help us to explain abductions — and to predict who is vulnerable to them and when they might undergo them.

Near Death Experiences and Abductions as Spiritual Journeys

While on the topic of abductions, psychologist Kenneth Ring has noted certain similarities between the experiences of the abductee and those reporting near death experiences (NDEs) (Ring 1989). Recall from the Introduction, a person undergoing an NDE typically senses a separation from their physical body, a feeling of peace and wellbeing, a movement through a space sometimes describe as a tunnel (though not necessarily frightening), a brilliant encompassing light within which they feel unconditional love and acceptance, "beings of light" or other spiritual entities, a life review and a request to return to the body — often with some reluctance.

Ring points out that these experiences are almost always hyper-real, in that they are not like a typical dream or daydream. They seem to take place in an imaginal, supersensible realm that feels like "here and now" reality yet is also infinite in its scope and occupants. Abduction often possess this quality, and although some storyline elements are similar, such as meeting alien-like beings, there is generally a difference in the emotions associated with the two journeys. NDEs are mostly positive, whereas abductions are mostly negative ... at least since the Hill's experience in 1961.

Ring argues that an NDE resembles a shamanic journey.[10] In such a journey, a member of a traditional, tribal (pre-agrarian) clan or culture, because of an individual peculiarity or motivation, is singled out for training in otherworldly contact. The person becomes a shaman, although psychologist Stanley Krippner reminds us that the expression "shaman" is purely a social construct — a simplistic, artificial, modern and Western label for a very complex phenomenon (Krippner 2002).

Nevertheless, shaman remains a term of convenience to describe the complex process of spiritual journeying. As currently accepted, the emerging shaman prepares themselves through rites such as fasting, isolation and drug ingestion before undertaking their trance-induced astral travel. During this travel, they participate in a number of otherworldly ordeals. Whether they enter a higher plane or lower (underworld) plane the shaman learns timeless mysteries and secrets which, once they've returned to their body, are useful to the tribe. These could include healing and wisdom (Eliade 1972). In this other world, the shaman is often guided by one or more entities. Thus there are certain parallels with a shamanic journey and altered states of consciousness such as an NDE, and perhaps some UFO abduction cases.

Another of the features of NDEs and abductions noted by Ring include the "awakening" of psychic abilities. This is an expected outcome of a shamanic journey, but perhaps less expected from someone returning from death or an alien spacecraft. Near death experients sometimes claim that extraordinary events happen to them after the journey, such as wristwatches running fast when they wear them, or lights dimming in their presence (Bonenfant 2000). However (and this is little known), they also frequently report these events before the NDE, suggesting they are marked in some way to be prone to the phenomenon.

At times, abductees also report poltergeist activity and healing abilities, along with heightened empathic concern (meaning they show empathy) and a sense that they have become separated intellectually and emotionally from other, normal people after their encounter. During an abduction, the abductee's guide[11] is frequently accompanied by grey clones, and the medical-style examination is seen by Kenneth Ring as equivalent of the "dismemberment" ceremony—a breaking down and rebirthing of the individual. Abductees also frequently receive esoteric or exceptional knowledge, such as the cure for cancer to be found in the Tujunga Canyons case, the details of which are often forgotten by the time they return to their homes.

Eddie Bullard believes there's more value in studying the complicated themes shared between abductions and supernatural contact than, say, fretting over the occasional similarity Alvin Lawson identified between abductions and birth-memories. These transcendental themes include "reproductive dependency," "deceit and illusion," "ordeal and transformation," "prophecy and hidden knowledge" and "a subterranean or ruined otherworld." In a similar way to the connection made long ago by Jacques Vallee in his book *Passport to Magonia* (1969), Bullard links these components of a typical abduction with storylines from traditional fairy kidnapping narratives, in which fairies take humans as sexual partners or steal human children, often leaving withered-looking changelings in their place (Bullard 1988). They might kidnap and employ midwives to deliver their babies, and their subterranean world might look rich and wonderful on outward appearance, but if the spell that holds it together is broken it appears as it really is—a land that is poor and inhabited by an ugly race of fairy-folk.

As a consequence of these rigid narrative similarities, Bullard sees abduction stories as more than mere folklore, because urban myths are very flexible in their content and often merge with one another at different times and places (Bullard 1991). For example, there's a well known fable about a madman on the loose with a hook in place of a hand, terrorizing teenagers in lovers' lanes. Sometimes this story is told on its own, with plenty of local variation, but sometimes it combines with the tale of the "murdered boyfriend," in which a teenaged couple's car breaks down in an isolated spot, and the boyfriend goes to get help while the girlfriend hides in the locked vehicle. During the night she hears strange noises, including something resembling raindrops on the roof. She is rescued the next morning, and discovers the corpse of her boyfriend hanging over the car, dripping blood! Sometimes the murderer is unknown, but often it is the hooked madman. According to Bullard, such alteration of content is not found in abduction lore, since the accounts retain too much similarity across time and place. In that case, he suggests, abductions are potentially based on something underlying reality.

Returning to the concept of a spiritual journey, the demeanor of the cosmic entities might differ between good ancestors (met during an NDE), amoral fairies or evil alien abductors. However, to Ring this is irrelevant because the purpose of the NDE or abduction is the same. It's all about transcendental education, whether the disguise is as a sage, trickster or demon.

The proposal from proponents of this school of mystical psychology is that humans have some pre-programmed predisposition to embark on a spiritual journey of otherworldly discovery. How that journey is interpreted is dependent on the individual and their cultural background. Why such a need is so important to humans, and hardwired in the unconscious, is a question more difficult to answer.

CHAPTER 10

Transpersonal Psychology

As you might have gleaned, psychodynamic explanations for paranormal experience differ in terms of the potency, and maturity, of the human unconscious. There's also variation as to how "real" the alleged paranormal events actually are. Accordingly, in conventional psychoanalysis the anxieties of an infantile psyche can manifest as a neurosis with all the trappings of paranormality — be it an illusionary psychical event or imaginary encounter with a demonic being. While a few psychoanalysts support the objective reality of paranormal events, such as thought-transference, they still see the cause as rooted in a primitive unconscious. Alternately, the birth memories hypothesis attributes abduction syndrome to the re-emergence of emotion-laden birth memories normally hidden from our self-awareness. Built-up tension is released, thus the hypothesis can be included in the psychodynamic category. However, the memories are based around a singular event more archaic than the repressed sexual experiences of an infant. Therefore, there is no consideration of the unconscious psyche as being anything but primitive.

While D. Scott Rogo's hypothesis is limited to alien abduction syndrome, it nevertheless attributes more autonomy to the unconscious than would be found in mainstream psychoanalysis. Yet his proposition that a controlling intelligence decides upon, then initiates, the abduction experience would make even the most open-minded psychologists uneasy.

To stay within the outer (but still acceptable) limits of psychology, it is tempting to suggest that there is no need to postulate external agents, but rather accept that the deep psyche is more sophisticated than most would credit. Not only is it a storehouse of veiled material and imagery, it also has its own dynamic reasons for unleashing this content in the form of a play with its conscious self as the principle actor. Some theorists, such as Kenneth Ring, see evidence for this dramatic production in the similarities among NDE, abductions and other entity experiences.

However, there is another psychological framework within which such

214

disparate phenomena as UFO, monster and ghost encounters can be placed, and which explains them in terms of profoundly complex unconscious processes.

Analytical Psychology

Carl Jung was a student and friend of Freud until a serious difference of opinion saw his expulsion from the psychoanalytic movement. Rather than being a deviant psychoanalyst, however, there is an argument that some of Jung's major ideas were formulated before he joined the movement, and his traumatic break nevertheless allowed him to develop his own theories with greater independence (Eisold 2002). Jung's movement became known as analytical psychology, to distinguish it from psychoanalysis.

Providing a simplistic overview, Jung's troubles with Freud began with their very different approach to dream imagery. In the early 1900s, Freud was tempted with the possibility that the symbols described in a patient's dreams were not gained from personal experience, yet he ultimately refuted this proposition and accepted that they were derived from "infantile, sexual urges" instead. Jung also acknowledged the importance of infantile material in dream imagery, but also considered the mythological associations between dream content and the stories told by all cultures across all times. It was this occult pursuit that set him on a different track from conventional psychoanalysis.[1] Nor was Jung quite as worried as Freud about discussing paranormal topics, and appreciated that people had them — and were frightened by them. Naturally, as a psychodynamic theorist Jung believed that a patient's paranormal experience might derive from the workings of their unconscious; however, they might be (surprisingly) far more happy with a supernatural explanation for their encounter. To tell them that what they'd witnessed was an insight into their own psyche was likely to cause considerable confusion and fear (Jung 1963/1989).

Archetypes

Jung's famous conclusion was that humans possess predispositions to apprehend common life events in a universally similar way. These ways of apprehension are most popularly known as *archetypes*, although other labels such as *dominants*, *imagos* and *primordial images* are sometimes used. The number of archetypes is not fixed, since they are not "things" residing in the mind. Nevertheless, the themes of some archetypes have been comprehended and given snappy labels such as *the Mother*, *the Hero* and *the Wise Old Man*. To take the first example, the unanimous experience of a mother, and what that means to be a mother, is unconsciously and universally understood by just about everyone. So too is the tale of the hero, who battles adversity to ultimately triumph over it. Other archetypes are less obvious, but just as important. One is the *Self*, which represents the "transcendence of opposites." This could imply the unification of an individual's conscious and unconscious, or their feminine and masculine sides (given the archetypal labels of *Anima* and *Animus* respectively). There is also the archetype of the *Shadow*, which does not necessarily represent evil, but rather the general concept of an "opposite."

Archetypal Symbols

The notion that archetypes can, at times, be apprehended by people makes the most sense when discussing the role of symbols. These symbols exist externally to the psyche and have an intimate and ancient connection with archetypes (Gordon 1985). Perhaps the associations were formed in antiquity, and therefore transcend cultural barriers. As such, the symbols possess an archetypal meaning distinct from their literal meaning. David Rosen and colleagues from the University of Houston claimed to have identified 40 of these archetypal symbols, including the representation of a window (meaning *Possibility*), a triangle (meaning *Synthesis*) and a diamond-shape (meaning *Self*). My favorite is the symbol of a cave, which has the archetypal significance of *Unconscious* (Rosen, Smith and Huston 1991).

Numbers can also pos-

A thoughtful Carl Jung in 1940. Jung's theories are particularly applicable to intense paranormal experiences, especially encounters with non-human entities. They retain popularity with enthusiasts because mainstream psychological theories do not provide a purpose for such encounters, other than being random hallucinations brought on by various brain disorders, either chronic or acute. The often profound nature of the experience is of no consequence. Analytical psychology provides an encounter with meaningfulness and therapeutic significance, although the scientific nature of such an explanation is tenuous (Mary Evans Picture Library).

sess symbolism, since they are imbued with an almost mystical quality. Perhaps this because Jung felt they were discovered, rather than created by humans (Jung 1959), hence the symbols reside in a mysterious order of existence. Being physical, they bridge the real with the imaginal.

It's also important to realize that a particular symbol isn't fixed to any single archetype, so to Jung a symbol for *Self* could variously be in the form of a child, Christ or Buddha, an egg, a hermaphroditic figure, or a jewel, flower or a chalice (that is, "treasures hard to obtain"). Geometric figures such as a circle, wheel or square, or anything divided into four equal parts (such as a circle with a cross in it) are also symbolic of the *Self* (Fordham 1953). These geometric shapes are called *mandalas*, after a Sanskrit word meaning "magic circle." A simple circle represents "unity," a circle cut in two represents "the divided self," but dividing the circle into two again (to make four parts) resolves — in Jung's opinion — the "unspeakable conflict posited by duality" and restores unity (Henderson 1973). The three steps to this process (single, dual and quaternity) is the trinity, which is an important way to achieve the quaternity. Confusing, isn't it?

Now, one doesn't have to get too mystical when discussing archetypes. Some theorists discuss the concept from the scientifically respectable perspective of evolutionary biology (Nunn 1997). That is, humans apparently possess — and transmit genetically — predispositions to certain forms (symbols) that have a common meaning and are universally interpreted as such (Huston 1999). Thus the Sun has been experienced by everyone, at all times, and is symbolic of a state of understanding (it's importance to life on Earth) that can't be comprehended in just a handful of words. Humans therefore have this deeper, wordless comprehension of complex material hardwired into their brain, in the same way they genetically inherit the blueprint for hands and feet, and the ability to love and hate. Indeed, the limbic system has been identified by supporters of this theory to be the source of the archetypes, and the universality of the experience (particularly religious experience) is said to derived from the fact that everyone has this vital functional system (Joseph 2001). Moreover, the proximity of the limbic system to the inferior temporal lobes, where neurons respond to specific neural imagery — such as geometric shapes — links the visual, symbolic process to the emotional (mystical/archetypal) one. While academic arguments could rage about the details of such a proposition, it couldn't be accused of being completely unscientific.

The Collective Unconscious

Nevertheless, this gentle genetic approach to mental inheritance doesn't satisfy all. To be a little more adventurous might mean accepting that individuals possess a personal unconscious based on their own life experience, yet have access to a collective unconscious[2] of universal psychic predispositions that aren't derived from everyday experience. The collective unconscious is where the archetypes reside, so to speak (Weitz 1976). To a certain extent, this definition could be thought of as a fancy re-wording of the "hardwired" theory — that is, the collective unconscious is pre-programmed in the brains of all people, in the same way that people are pre-programmed with the plans to grow hands and feet which are very similar to everyone else's hands and feet.

Nevertheless, an alternative interpretation of the "collective unconscious" label is that each human's psyche can be thought of as an individual iceberg floating in a cold sea ... or at least that what it seems when viewed from a boat on the ocean surface. The part of the iceberg that's visible consists of the individual's consciousness and personal unconscious. Around this iceberg float other, individual icebergs, but a quick look under the water will show that all these separate icebergs are in fact connected to form one big block of ice with multiple bits sticking up and piercing the surface of the sea. This underwater connection among all individuals represents the collective unconscious. In this model, humans aren't born with a download of the collective unconscious program that they carry around with them through life based on some reductionist psychological proposition. Rather, they have permanent access to a deeper transcendental pool of collective information at all times through their lives, although they remain blissfully unaware of this because they hardly ever access it, and if they do they assume the content they meet is from an external source — like a ghost — rather than from some unknowable place within their psyche. This is Jung's proposition about the paranormal, made in his 1963 work.

Jung, and most Jungians, arguably take this radical approach. In fact, one doesn't have to be a strict Jungian to dabble in the idea of a fundamental interconnectedness among people. Such a pursuit might be termed *transpersonal psychology*, to distinguish it from analytical psychology proper.[3] The transpersonal approach is often applied to the interpretation of dream material — the dream being a state where the individual is more open to receiving information from the deeper psyche. A symbol might appear in a dream that has a universal association with an archetype, but when discussing the symbol with the dreamer it might be found that the archetype it represents is of particular significance to their private concerns. In this sense, the interpretation might be based on a problem rooted in childhood, hence differs little from conventional psychoanalysis. The analyst Renaldo Maduro gives an example of a female patient who dreamed she found two rats in a garbage can, white and one black. The white one ran away, but the black one stayed and could not be killed — it just kept getting bigger. Finally, in the dream the patient accepts the black rat and it transforms into a grey mouse.

Maduro suggests this is indicative of the patient's relationship with her mother. On the surface the relationship seems almost too strong and positive, and in many respects the negative aspects (e.g., the relationship's exhausting nature) are denied. The black rat therefore represents the *Shadow*— the negative aspects — that cannot be dismissed so easily. When the patient's destructive feelings are acknowledged, the rat turns into a less threatening grey mouse, symbolizing the unification of opposites (black and white) (Maduro 1987). Thus it transpires a person can gain a better understanding of themselves from an implicit recognition of archetypes that confront them. The role played by the *Self* and *Shadow* are obvious, but the appearance of other archetypal symbols might also be advantageous if they embody an underrepresented aspect of the personality. A very rational, empirical man, for instance, might be confronted with feminine imagery in a dream which holds a message to compensate for his asymmetrical nature (Mansfield, Rhine-Feather and Hall 1998). Such a case indicates the purposiveness of the psyche. In other words, it isn't the mechanistic repository of information that it is often assumed to be in mainstream psychology.

Alternately, a dream image might have wider archetypal implications to humankind as a whole. In 1913 Jung himself had a dream of a "monstrous flood covering all the northern and low-lying lands between the North Sea and the Alps." In the dream, he saw thousands drowning and then end of civilization. The flood waters then turned to blood (Jung and Jaffe, 1989). Jung feared the onset of psychosis, but later interpreted the dream as a prediction of the ensuing Great War.

Synchronicity

Another Jungian proposal which deviates significantly from the safety of scientific psychology, and psychoanalysis, is synchronicity. To Jung, a synchronous event occurs when a mental process — a thought or a dream — is simultaneously accompanied by a physical event. Jung tells of an incident during a therapy session as a patient narrated the contents of their dream. In this dream, she was given a golden scarab beetle, symbolizing rebirth. At the very moment of speaking about this dream beetle, a real beetle flew into the closed window behind Jung. It was a rose-chafer beetle, the closest species to a golden scarab that can dwell in Europe, and its appearance at that moment was considered unusual. To Jung, this was a manifestation of synchronicity.

Synchronicity is quite a confusing concept because there is no implication that the mental event causes the physical event through a transference of energy (the way, in an opposite sense, physically stubbing your toe on a rock is commonly believed to cause the mental event of pain). Rather, synchronous events occur together in an acausal way. However, what makes the two events not simply coincidental is that they are meaningfully coincidental (in a very subjective, personal way). One of the ways to grapple how this could happen is to consider psychic[4] content and physical matter as two different aspects of the same underlying reality. The iceberg analogy helps to explain this. One iceberg is a thought, another some distance away is a physical event. They might share an associated, archetypal meaning, for example the thought-iceberg is a dream of a snake and the event-iceberg is an actual snake appearing in the garden the day after the dream. Both events seem coincidental but unrelated episodes, since they appear causally unconnected above the water. Way below, however, they belong to the same fundamental ground-of-being. They are simultaneous expressions of the same archetype (the snake and healing), but one event is not actually caused by the other.

Jung himself was at times hesitant about the implications of synchronicity. In a letter to psychiatrist Michael Fordham in 1957 he wondered how "even inanimate objects are capable of behaving as if they were acquainted with my thoughts?" (Donati 2004). Such "paranoid speculation," he believed, was best not made public, despite his intense interest in the possibilities it entailed.

Synchronicity, Quantum Physics, Ghosts and Psi

In developing a theory of synchronicity, Jung collaborated with the Nobel prize-winning physicist Wolfgang Pauli. Pauli had been a patient of Jung's in the 1930s, but is far more famous for his research in quantum physics, or the behavior of material particles at the most minute, sub-atomic scale. At such a small scale, things begin to possess discrete properties rather than continuous variation, in the way that different people have widely different weights or heights (Davies and Brown 1986). For example, when whizzing around an atom, electrons release energy in quantities called photons. They don't release a half-photon worth of energy, or a quarter-photon worth, or six-fifteenths worth. Just a photon-worth. That's a fact of nature.

Theoretical calculations during the early part of the 20th century about the behavior of particles inside the atom allowed understanding of how atoms are structured, and how chemical bonding occurs. These are ideas that are now simply taken for granted, so the notion that quantum theory is some new innovation is not accurate. Its discoveries have been incorporated into the discipline of physics since at least the 1920s, and have been demonstrated time and time again empirically so they can't really be questioned as completely imaginary or theoretical. However, the complication arises when considering the predictability of events at the quantum level. It's not really possible to predict how a sub-atomic particle such as an electron will behave, or, in stronger terms, the laws of nature simply don't allow for the ability to predict a sub-atomic event on a case-by-case basis. Oversimplified, if you held an electron in your hand and knew it could either travel left or right when you release it from your grip, you could never be certain what it would do until after you had let it go. Overall, you could confidently predict that half the time the electron will travel left, and half the time the electron will travel right. Predicting what will happen is fundamentally guesswork — guesswork that's woven into the fabric of reality.

Physicist Werner Heisenberg developed the uncertainty principle to explain how we could potentially locate the electron leaving your hand, or measure its motion, but never both simultaneously. That's not a problem with measurement technique. It's just that the electron doesn't have both properties fixed at the same time in the way a car can be located on a road and its speed measured simultaneously. Electrons are therefore fundamentally different from cars. In fact, at times they can behave like a field (recall the concept of electric or magnetic field), being everywhere at once but nowhere in particular. At other times it can behave like a particle with a location or a motion. This is termed the wave-particle property of the electron (or any other sub-atomic particle). How you wish to observe the particle will automatically resolve how the particle will behave.

The argument then raged as to what was really going on. Albert Einstein, for example, stressed that a sub-atomic particle such as an electron actually has all the normal qualities of macro-reality, such as simultaneous location and motion. However, the measurement of both properties at the same time is complicated by the smallness of their scale. Therefore, Heisenberg's uncertainty principle could be refuted by performing a simple experiment. Imagine a single particle is blown apart into two smaller particles traveling in opposite directions. I could measure the location of one particle on my side of the room, and you could measure the motion of the other particle on your side of the room. Put my location finding together with your motion finding, and this should give information about what either particle is doing and where they are simultaneously (assuming that the two particles are doing identical things, just in the opposite direction).

The renowned physicist Neils Bohr, on the other hand, was fixed on the idea of something fundamentally different — that nature is ultimately uncertain. Using the example above, any measurement of your particle will influence the state of my particle, no matter how far they are separated. For example, if you find your particle is traveling at 50 mph, you're actually not discovering what mine is doing independently of yours, on the other side of the room. You are *determining* what mine is doing! This type of communication (which is not strictly communication in the sense that we know) is termed *nonlocality*, meaning that two particles can influence each other instantaneously despite being in different places — something that seems logically absurd.

In the 1960s, the Irish physicist John Bell proposed a practical test that would determine whether our two sub-atomic particles actually possess a reality separate from the observer — the way we assume the objects around us possess quantities independent of our being present. In a very simplistic sense, if our two particles are blown apart and initially have identical properties, and we can somehow force a property[5] onto my particle in some way (for example, the path that it follows on my side of the room), logically we wouldn't expect your particle to know of the change and alter its own property in sympathy. However, by the 1980s actual experiments were performed which suggested that this was actually happening, and that Bohr's quantum theory was most appropriate.

Terms such as "spooky" are sometimes bandied around to emphasize the weirdness of two things seemingly communicating at impossible speeds, but it's probably less spooky than complicated. Imagine that your particle and my particle each possess a multitude of initial states. When you measure your particle to be traveling at 50 mph, you're contributing to the collapse of all possible speed states of my particle into one speed state ... 50 mph. Before your decision is made, both particles are tied up in some funny, wave-like state of "nothing-in-particular." This is a far more nebulous concept than the idea of your particle "telling" my particle what it is doing. And if you don't quite understand this, don't worry. The famous mathematician Richard Feynman once remarked, "I think I can safely say that nobody understands quantum mechanics" (Hey and Walters 2003).

Quantum Theory and the Paranormal

It is this theoretical complexity, the spookiness of nonlocality and the awkward, wave-particle nature of matter that lends quantum physics (rightly or wrongly) to theories of the paranormal. The most obvious would be a model for psi. If nonlocality can be demonstrated, why can't other forms of "impossible" communication, such as telepathy, occur within the framework of natural laws? One quite complicated proposal is based around the concept of sub-atomic particle pairs — known as "bosonic couples"— that are separated and travel in opposite directions like our earlier example. Each particle (an electron) possesses the fundamental property of spin, and this must be conserved in the system. For example, if one particle has a spin of +1, the other will have a spin of -1. These spins add up to zero, no matter where the two particles end up. Now, when one person physically interacts with another person, or a small inanimate object, there are be lots of these bosonic couples naturally floating around which separate at the moment of contact. Ultimately, one half of the pair stays in the first person, and the other half travels the second person or object. So far, so good.

The theory goes that these electrons might conceivably end up in parts of the brain associated with memory, and become part of the biochemical processes in those regions. Then, when the first person recalls a memory the properties of the electrons residing there will be affected, and because of the spin conservation law, the electrons in the second person, or object, are immediately altered to keep the combined properties at zero. It is suggested that this quantum process can result in hallucinated imagery in the second person (telepathy), or perhaps mild examples of psychokinesis in the inanimate object (William 1986).

The results of a controversial psychokinetic experiment by Frenchman René Peoc'h have also been explained using a quantum framework. In this study, chicks "imprinted" their behavior to a robot arm that moved in random motions in their cage. The chicks were subsequently restricted to an area of that cage, and it turned out that the robotic arm spent a lot more time near the chicks than it should have if it were acting in a truly arbitrary fashion. Mathematician Chris Clarke entertains the possibility of an entangled system in which the robot arm can be in one of countless states of position and velocity, and these possibilities interact with the combined consciousness of the chicks (and their desire for the arm to be within a comfort distance). The result is a collapse of possible states to only those where the arm is more likely to circulate within this comfort zone (Clarke 2008).

Another use of quantum physics is seen in Maher's (1999) proposal of a *quantum ghost* that has wave and particle properties. The wave aspect represents "the aggregate of all deceased personalities," and the particle aspect indicates a ghostly manifestation at a location. Consequently, quantum ghosts aren't constrained by location but are everywhere, anywhere, or "no place in particular" — a bit like a wave. The ghost itself would only display its particle nature when actually observed by a witness, meaning the witness and the ghost form a type of quantum relationship.

Returning to analytical psychology, associations between synchronicity and quantum physics are also seized upon, although a difference between the concept of "meaningful coincidence" as it applies to humans and the acausal nonlocality theorized by quantum physics has been identified (Donati 2004). A typical synchronous event has personal meaning, which is lacking in quantum particle experiments. Thus some of the awkward parapsychological findings by J.B. Rhine, such as the realization that psi ability was not affected by distance between the sender and receiver (suggesting no "energy" transmission was involved), was identified by Jung as simply acausality in operation. However, typical ESP and psychokinetic findings do not represent the profoundly meaningful acausality of archetypal expression (true synchronicity), but rather the unrelated acausal manifestation of natural laws of which quantum mechanics is simply a part (Mansfield et al. 1998).

Criticisms of Synchronicity and the Role of Quantum Physics

Naturally, few mainstream psychologists are comfortable with the concept of Jungian synchronicity, and account for seemingly acausal experiences using a more rational alterative—*apophenia*. Apophenia is a label describing the spontaneous perception of relationships and meanings in unrelated phenomena (Brugger 2001), and is a feature of schizotypy, which is characterized by loose cognitive associations. Consequently, skeptics can argue that Jung's experiences of synchronicity were a product of schizotypy, and by implication the expression of an underlyng mental illness.

Skeptics also argue that coincidental events happen regularly, so not every strange coincident has to be explained as synchronicity. In fact, we should expect coincidences to occur with enough trials, since by chance alone coincidences must occur by law of large numbers. The typical example would be precognitive dreams, where everyone on earth has multiple dreams (trials) a night, and there are lots of people, so there are potentially billions of dreams. If a few come true, that's not surprising (Hines 1988). However, psychologist Lance Storm from the University of Adelaide argues this doesn't take into account the personal meaningfulness that some coincidences possess, which set them apart from the coincidences predicted by the law (Storm 1999). For example, some dreams stand apart from others in their vividness and seeming purpose, and these are the ones identified by the dreamer as special and are frequently perceived as precognitive.

More telling is the concern real quantum physicists have with their discipline being used as a theoretical basis for paranormal events such as psi (Rae 1995). Firstly, these physicists argue that nonlocality isn't about transfer of information between separated, fundamental particles at all, and an observer of one particle (let's call it a photon) can't predict the orientation of the other photon until the two results are brought together and compared, in which case the correlation emerges. This can be thought of as an almost "there and then" effect, so perhaps the result is less a case of "nonlocality" than "indeterminacy of a result until that result is required." This is fundamentally different from the processes involved in a clairvoyant task, where an observer believes they know what the "target" is at some distant location and write it down or tell an observer what it is, and then find out at some later time they were very accurate in their description. It's difficult to imagine the target (whether a building, bridge, flower or painting) was in a state of quantum indeterminacy until the observer is taken to the location and their observation forces the appropriate description to manifest.

A second criticism is directed towards the quantum model of psychokinesis. Alistair Rae argues that the role of the mind (another term for the observer) is as a measuring apparatus only. The state of any sub-atomic particle is simply resolved by the observation (if you call that simple), it is not determined by the observation. According to a quantum framework, the mind cannot be said to do anything to matter, such as psychokinetic metal bending (e.g., spoons).[6]

The Projection of Archetypes

We've discussed in the previous chapter the idea that psychological projection can be as simple and uncontroversial as a person transferring their deep psychological requirements onto an external object or event. To a certain extent this was the position taken by Carl Jung and expanded in his book *Flying Saucers: A Modern Myth of Things Seen in the Sky*, published in 1959. To Jung, a paranormal object such as a flying saucer might actually exist in physical space and originate from another planet. Alternately, the UFO rumor might be a vast collection of misinterpretations — illusions and the like. However, these were not his area of expertise or concern. Rather, the witness will project onto this fortuitous disc-like (or cigar) shape hanging in the sky (whether real or illusionary) an archetypal significance[7] (termed a *subjective psychic prefiguration*) because of a vital psychic need they have. For example, the symbol for the *Self*, of God and *Perfection*, is spherical or disc-like. A person with a fractured *Self* would therefore be deeply affected by the shape of a UFO (real or illusionary). At the time Jung's book was written, there was still a good deal of respectability in the view that UFOs were actual spacecraft from other planets, so it was not unreasonable of Jung to take this cautious approach.[8] On the other hand, he didn't rule out the experience as being completely hallucinatory in the sense that an archetype "invaded the conscious mind with illusions and visions." Nor did he dismiss the possibility that a real physical event, and a purely mental experience, were a synchronistic, meaningful coincidence.

In contrast, a more extreme treatment of projection from some Jungian theorists is that an autonomous object, such as a real flying saucer, is an unnecessary complication. Perhaps this is because the elusive nature of UFOs — still

In 1966, 15-year-old Stephen Pratt photographed these UFOs over Conisbrough, in Yorkshire, England. The famous picture has had many supporters over the years, although one skeptical explanation is that young Stephen simply painted flying saucers on his bedroom window and took a photograph of them, with the town skyline prominent in the background. However, from the viewpoint of analytical psychology any controversy over the validity of this picture, or any other flying saucer sighting, is incidental to what the picture represents — the concept of an archetypal symbol of the *Self* externally projected for the purpose of realization, leading to potential psychic growth in the witness (Fortean Picture Library).

unresolved since Jung's 1959 book — has reduced the imperative to recognize them as true external objects in the realization of the archetype. Consequently, in the fashion of a thought-form, the hovering object is now not independent of the witness, but rather a psychological projection with the purpose of making known to the observer the deep personal crisis that their conscious self is neglecting. Indeed, Wolfgang Pauli observed in a letter to Jung's wife that a failure to attend to a psychological factor could provoke it into taking a parapsychic form, so as to gain recognition and attention through synchronistic events, "depressive states" or "incomprehensible emotions" (Van Erkelens 1991).

This theory resembles the Rogo hypothesis, with a thought-form replacing the cosmic intelligence. Where it differs is in the role of the collective unconscious. The material the producer of a thought-form can draw from is not limited to personal memories and recollections. Hilary Evans believes that people have within them the ability to "fabricate narratives of imagined experience" to a surprising degree — much more that they'd ever realize (Evans 1984).

That is, humans have access to material from the collective unconscious to fashion their paranormal experiences. The producer, according to Patrick Harpur, is partly autonomous, bridging the personal with the transpersonal. It is equivalent to the soul, which links the real (us) with the deeper spirit (Harpur 1994). Therefore, when we see a UFO the perception is partly derived from our personal unconscious and partly derived from something deeper (the collective unconscious). We take from our vision the message of the symbol. When we see a Bigfoot it is a projection partly from us, and partly from something deeper, and we take a different message from the symbol, depending on its archetypal significance.

While on the topic of a dynamic unconscious seeking attention, another complicated and "out there" theory of unconscious projection (although by no means Jungian) is proposed by Albert Budden (Budden 1995). He claims that the unconscious uses any ingredients it can, from nearby electromagnetic fields to memories of science fiction stories, to project the theater of an abduction, hence establish and maintain its own external social identity. It makes one feel rather sorry for the unconscious, if this is what is has to resort to in order to achieve recognition!

Alien Abduction and Archetypal Projections

Occasionally, attempts have been made to apply Jung's ideas on archetypes of the collective unconscious to the wealth of spontaneous cases found in the paranormal literature. For example, in their book *The Unidentified* (1975), Jerome Clark[9] and Loren Coleman discuss the Jungian overtones in a very early occupant contact case from the modern UFO era.

On July 23, 1947, in Bauru, Brazil, a surveyor named Jose Higgins was working outdoors with some colleagues when a 150-foot wide UFO landed nearby. The workmates fled, but Higgins stayed to watch as three seven-foot tall humanoids disembarked from the craft. Their sex was indeterminate, their legs were unusually long, they had no hair and their eyes were huge and round. They were dressed in transparent suits that were inflated "like rubber bags," and metal boxes were attached to their backs. Despite the description, Higgins found them strangely beautiful. Surrounded by the beings, Higgins felt they were trying to take him with them. One pointed a metal tube in his direction. Another poked eight circular holes in the ground with a stick. Of these holes, one was larger than the others and placed in the middle. The large circle, Higgins believed, was called "Alamo" while one of the smaller holes was "Orque." Luckily for Higgins, he was able to escape the beings because the entities seemed debilitated by the bright sunlight. He hid in a bush and watched them as they frolicked near their craft for half an hour before departing.

This encounter is rather crude by modern standards, and would be laughed off today as a ridiculous hoax. Accepting that *something* happened, Clark and Coleman look past the superficial events to expose the underlying Jungian themes. They argue the symbolism in the case is beyond the personal experience of Jose Higgins, hence must have been drawn from a transpersonal realm.

Firstly, the beings arrive in a round object which, like any other typical UFO, symbolizes the unification of the self. Therefore, from a Jungian perspective Higgins is about to receive a visionary lesson about the psychic duality affecting not just himself but humankind as a whole. There are three beings, a number traditionally representing the solution to duality; three is the action of unity upon duality. The sexless nature of the beings in another symbol of unity between the male conscious and female unconscious. The symbolism of the encounter becomes more complicated when the three beings surround him to become four. Adding one to three allows the "pure" spirit a corporeal form. However, the entities, representing unconsciousness, are unable to confront the bright sunlight of waking consciousness to complete the "quaternity," and Higgins is certainly reluctant to assist them by hanging around to be kidnapped. Perhaps that's why the UFO gives off a dull metal sheen and not the brilliant shimmer which traditionally represents wholeness. And rather than see the eight holes in the ground as seven planets surrounding some far off star, Clark and Coleman see it as a mandala, where all dualities are joined around a centre, with the seven small circles representing the seven stages of the universe[10] with the potential of being united with the center, again an act of psychic unification.

One of the spaceship entities points to one of the smaller planets, the seventh, to indicate that it is Higgins' masculine, rational consciousness that is obstructing the unification process (recalling that Higgins was a "mathematical" surveyor). The beings also frolic in a very fairy-like way to differentiate themselves (the unconscious) from the rational consciousness. Thus the "show" of the close encounter is an allegory of psychic health, and might take the form of a "flying saucer" for two reasons. Firstly so as to be taken more seriously by a society skeptical about superstitions such as gods and fairies, and secondly as a playful message that the significance the vision imparts is completely opposite to technology associated with an advanced, nuts-and-bolts spacecraft from a distant planet.

Further Archetypal Projections

Archetypes have meaning without fixed form, so it's not possible to build a typography of paranormal events and match them universally with archetypal references. To make things more difficult, the paranormal object or event might actually possess a legitimate reality; however, it might be "interpreted" archetypally in a completely different way. Alternately, the object or event might be hallucinatory projections created for the specific purpose of an archetypal interpretation. UFO entities, fairies, ghosts, hairy hominids, weird monsters, mystery cats[11] and black dogs may therefore be entities created from the same transcendental but simultaneously personal realm. The form the entity takes simply depends on circumstance.

Thankfully, some patterns might still be identifiable to make the interpretation of the experience comprehensible. According to Jung in his book *On the Nature of the Psyche*, because of their numinous (divine) character and spiritual connotations, it's not surprising that the archetypes often appear spirit-like in dreams, or as seemingly real but translucent ghosts. The message they bring might also be intimated from the form they take. We've already noticed the symbolic connection between a UFO shape and *Self.* The appearance of the alien being might also have archetypal significance. In dreams, Jung visualized a "leathery brown dwarf" guarding the entrance to the unconscious, which he interpreted as a primitive shadow for his ego. Connections might be made between Jung's guardian and the diminutive aliens (be they "Greys" or hairy dwarves) of popular lore, and such a typology of entities has been around even longer in science fiction stories. In "The Time Machine" (1895), H.G. Wells writes about a race of future beings derived from humankind who are small — about four feet high — frail and delicate, with large eyes, small mouths with thin lips, tiny ears and chins that are pointy.

Admittedly, the beings possessed hair (which I conveniently excluded), making them somewhat different from the typical "Grey" alien. Nevertheless, H.G. Wells was trying to imagine how people would look in future years when shaped by forces such as technology — hence the bodily atrophy. In this sense, the entity possesses a meaning that is not outwardly obvious but archetypal. And once imagined (for example, by a science fiction writer), the symbol enters the collective image-bank to be accessed by anyone when they require help expressing the form of the archetype (Evans 1984). For example, French sociologist Bertrand Meheust discovered that the aliens actually encountered by an illiterate Argentinean peasant in the 1970s had great similarities to the beings described in an obscure 1920s French science fiction story called *Hodomur, Man of Infinity.* The peasant wasn't expected to know of these fictional characters, and assuming it wasn't coincidence, the implication is that the similarity of the two descriptions is due to access of some kind of shared storehouse of narrative material.

In the same dream containing the "leathery brown dwarf," Jung and the dwarf combined killed a beautiful blond youth called Siegfried (the hero), and in this Jung saw a personal message about the dangers of hero worship. In Jung's later life this type of being, called a *Nordic* by alien enthusiasts, was very popular with contactees. The difference is that Jung's entities, including the Nordic, came (for the most part) in dreams, and were interpreted archetypally. The contactees saw them as real, utopian "space-brothers" and perhaps missed entirely their deep psychological significance as "technological angels" (Kottmeyer 2006) — a term first coined by Jung himself. We've already discussed how the "Grey" has elsewhere been interpreted as a technological demon.

Of course, not every encounter with the form of an archetype has to possess a UFO or alien flavor. The big hairy wildman be it Yeti, Bigfoot, or the Australian Yowie, might symbolize humans stripped of their civilized traits. They represent people liberated from society and returned to the elements — in the view of Clarke and Coleman, the symbol "contains hints of tremendous power, of total freedom from rules and restraint."

This striptease-like behavior of the unconscious will threaten the ego, which has to enact all sorts of defense mechanisms — from taboos and magic rituals to logic and reason — to prevent itself "collapsing" into the unconscious. Yet if something like stress does create cracks in the ego through which unconscious influence leaks, perhaps the patient will actually approve of the potential for unification with a safer, "primal paradise" and "golden age" in order to forget the hardships of the real world. Jung wrote his legacy at a time before the darker form of alien abduction emerged, when the contactees were still more prevalent than the abductees. Since this time, it perhaps might be suggested that the unconscious has not had much success using benevolent space brother symbolism, and turned to a more threatening theme to gain the attention of the ego!

The events of an near death experience might also embody the unification process, as could the more extensive "visionary rumor" experienced by groups of people in modern Western society — typically expressed as a mass UFO sighting. These visions may arise due to a fundamental mechanism acting on the collective mind which represents redemption and wholeness, but replaces the earlier, now unfashionable configuration of alleged superstition (sky-fairy battles and Marian visions) with more modern and respectable technology. The UFO is a vision seen in dreams and in the sky and unites "irreconcilable opposites," according to Jung in 1959. Consequently, they are well suited "to compensate the split-mindedness of our age."

Not all archetypal experiences, however, necessarily lead to the possibility of self-unification. In an earlier chapter, I mentioned how two very common haunting apparitions were the young Edwardian-era girl and the older man in the dark suit. From the perspective of analytical psychology, it might suggest these are symbols of the Anima and Animus, respectively. Alternatively, in a haunting case told to me, a young man who worked as a barman in a hotel was frightened of entering the downstairs storage area because he had previously seen a ghost there. The ghost was dark and human, but no features could be discerned. Naturally, the assumption made by those who heard the story was that the hotel was haunted. It wasn't a very old building, and had no known history of traumatic occurrences, so it was suggested that the ghost derived from something that happened in a former building on the site (if ever one existed). What tended to be overlooked was the fact that the witness saw the same ghost at other places apart from the hotel. Put simply, it followed him around. Such a personal manifestation (no one else had ever seen it) has all the trappings of the *Shadow*. To understand why this archetype might have been haunting him, and not others, would presumably require a session on the analyst's couch, from which a clearer picture of the barman's psychological requirements would be discovered.

Why Might the Archetypes Manifest? An Example

The average person isn't Carl Jung and hasn't the depth of knowledge and insight to interpret their visionary experiences (whether in dreams or real life) as holding personal significance. To the analytical psychologist, this would explain the heterogeneity of paranormal events — the same weird and wonderful things continue to occur to people because the motivations for them are universal. With this in mind, here is my best explanation — from an analytical psychology viewpoint — of how the barman's putative psychodynamic problems might have caused him to be haunted by a ghost at work and at home, using the concept of *ideas* as a starting point.

Any idea a person has possesses an opposite. For instance, the idea of performing a good service for a friend is countered by the idea of doing them harm. Like poles on a battery, these opposites give rise to psychic energy. One idea, that of serving another person selflessly, might be chosen by the individual and will be awarded the associated psychic energy. Perhaps the energy will used to complete a chore for the friend. However, as we know from psychodynamic theory the opposite, bad idea doesn't simply disappear. It is still an essential part of the psychic circuit, but generally does not interfere with the practice of the good idea. However, there are occasions when the choice of which idea to pursue is not so easy for the individual. Under these circumstances the two opposite ideas are far more evenly balanced, and although one idea is ultimately chosen (for example, the "good") the opposite will demand attention.

The best thing the individual could do is to acknowledge the bad idea as, at the very least, existing. If they studiously deny it as being possible to even think of, it will be pushed deep into the unconscious where it might touch on the archetypal realm of the collective unconscious. There it might constellate around the most appropriate archetype, the obvious choice in this example being the *Shadow*. The individual—our barman in this example—might then find themselves literally haunted by a dark shape in their dreams, which could grow in stature and frequency. They might even see it as the dark, projected ghost which follows them around at work, or anywhere else they travel. The idea demands acknowledgement. If this was the case for our barman, I hope he got the message.

The Experience Is Paramount

Obviously, the very essence of transpersonal psychology is unempirical, thus earns the disapproval of many mainstream psychologists. Deeming ideas to be like poles on a battery and giving rise to psychic energy is nothing more than a shaky analogy, and as we've seen, concepts such as synchronicity and the collective unconscious are discounted by mainstream psychologists as logically impossible, if not completely ridiculous. Nevertheless, analytical psychology doesn't pretend to be strictly scientific. Jung saw intuitive knowledge (such as recognition of the archetypes) as irrational in the sense that it was beyond reason, rather than contrary to reason (Reiner 2004). This honesty, coupled with its complex framework, has achieved a quiet respectability even with regards to its specific claims about paranormality. A further, privileged aspect of analytical psychology is that its focus is not about proving the "existence" or otherwise of paranormal experience. The anomalous event might be true and independent of the observer, or generated in some unknown fashion from the observer. The event might even be a hallucinatory episode quite explainable in neurophysiological terms. Whatever the source, the analytical psychologist is more interested in what that event means to the observer. That is, how they interpret it. This neatly removes the analyst from providing a justification for the existence of real ghosts, real aliens and real monsters, which is left to the pen of the more radical theorist.

A Final Remark on Transpersonal Psychology

If you think the idea of an alien, fairy, ghost, para-ape, swamp monster, mystery cat or black dog being a projection of the deep psyche is as radical as you can get, you haven't gone far enough. Some theorists enjoy toying with the idea that the projection is intrinsic to being human because a person, for whatever reason, is only aware of the here-and-now of their physical life. Charles Tart calls this perspective *mind embodied*, which is a useful working tool for everyday life and associated with realization of information entering the physical senses (Tart 1998). However, mind embodied is not the same as awareness of the whole mind, which spans the physical and transpersonal realms. *Whole mind* implies that the true individual is actually spread over a multiverse (lots of universes, or dimensions) which is an idea that might share rough similarity with a number of different religious perspectives, for example the concept in Eastern thought of *manas* (or mind, akin to mind embodied) and *atman* (or self, perhaps comparable to whole mind) (Tuske 1999).

From this perspective, when a person "realizes whole mind" and recognizes themselves in greater dimensional space, they might interpret the being(s) they encounter as independent entities — as aliens or strange beasts. However, the alien or strange beast is another, non-physical aspect of their own selves. The goal of life is to "realize self," to realize who the alien or beast is. It is about unifying the fragmented components of this dispersed, quasi-mystical personality. As Jung wrote, "You are neither and both male and female, neither and both ego and shadow, neither and both good and bad, neither and both conscious and unconscious, neither and both an individual and the whole of creation."

However (and this is the ominous bit!), once there is this realization there are no oppositions. Without the opposites there is no energy (think of the battery analogy), and you cease to act. Of course, you no longer need to act, since you are dead. Death is the ultimate unification of self, and perhaps the near death experience is a mere glimmer of this inevitable potential.

Notes

Introduction

1. Charles Tart (1998) calls this attitude scientism, whereby science is the vessel within which all knowledge is organized, as opposed to just another arrangement of knowledge within a wider framework.

2. There is some controversy as to whether differences exist between free and supported arm movements.

3. For example, there's a case from 1950s Western Australia where rains of stones pelted the roof of Alan Donaldson's house, and then followed him inside — as though there was no roof. It appears the stone shower followed him around, implying he was the agent of the infestation (Pinkney 2003).

4. An example would be the Enfield Poltergeist from 1970s London, where the most likely agent was an 11 year old called Janet — although her mother, Peggy, was also implicated. The release of psychological stress through psychokinesis was proposed as an explanation; however, there were also incidents of trickery reported, so it's one of those typical, messy poltergeist cases.

5. An equivalent "hellish" experience was reported by a smaller group of survivors, which understandably doesn't receive as much attention as the Heavenly experiences mentioned here.

6. As opposed to the more mystical view that mental and physical processes are "constructions placed upon reality," and one doesn't create the other (Carpenter 2004).

7. There's nothing easy about defining a ghostly experience. Hilary Evans makes the interesting point that the distinction between ghostly phenomena and, say, flying saucer phenomena is not supported by evidence (Evans 1984). It is simply a pervasive assumption. Thus when a witness reports seeing a ghost here is no reason not to suppose they might have seen another person's alien, and vice versa. Similarly, a ghost sighting might be a mistaken crisis apparition.

8. UFO researchers Jacques Vallee and Eric Davis give the phenomenon an alternative label of unidentified aerial phenomena, or UAP, to avoid the extraterrestrial assumption since religious and supernatural events are also seen in the sky (Vallee and Davis 2003).

9. The witness had been meditating in the bush for spiritual reasons before his encounter.

10. To be fair, few psychological theories can explain data to a high degree of efficiency, or adequately predict an event or behavior. These include theories that have nothing to do with the paranormal.

Chapter 1

1. Although psi is really a descriptive label because it doesn't necessarily imply anything paranormal — nothing is assumed about underlying causes of a psi event (Bem and Honorton 1994).

2. There's the strong possibility the story is a hoax; more recent research has suggested the second will was a forgery (Roach 2005).

3. Caroline Watt, in a presidential address for the 48th Annual Convention of the Parapsychological Association (Watt 2005), suggests more systematic research needs to be performed to determine what variables in the ganzfeld make it a psi-conducive technique — for example, do closed eyelids work as well as eye shields to assist in psi transmission?

4. The author recalls one Zener card trial he conducted in a classroom setting where the outright score of the participant was 4/25, but 18/25 when re-analyzed in terms of a one-ahead displacement effect. Ironically, the re-analysis was only performed as a lesson to show how the displacement effect was calculated.

5. Usually a minimum of 95 percent. This definition of significance is a bit simplistic, but since I'm not writing a statistics textbook it will suffice.

6. A response to what Honorton deemed a flawed meta-analysis study by Ray Hyman in 1985. Hyman in turn was not happy with Honorton's processes. In 1986 they issued a joint statement acknowledging the statistical significance of the overall ganzfeld findings, but differed as to whether this significance was proof of psi.

7. Continuing this theme, nothing should be theoretically detected because, according to the psychologist Michael Persinger, it is highly unlikely that sufficient amounts of energy can be generated by the brain that can travel any effective distance.

8. This means the same, significant findings can be shown anywhere, at anytime, rather than being a "one-off." However, Parker (1991) makes the salient point that many mainstream psychological findings lack repeatability, which is conveniently ignored by critics of the repeatability of parapsychological outcomes.

9. A chemist, biologist and writer who helped expose the alleged fraud in Samual Soal's parapsychological findings.

10. As we will see in a later chapter, some investigators take the scientific research method to alleged haunted houses.

11. A theory remarkably similar to Tyrell's early views on the psychical "ghost" discussed earlier in the chapter.

12. Which, somewhat surprisingly, they admit occurred on other occasions, although under "relaxed" experimental conditions.

13. The same way visible light passing through a small slit is shown to form alternating bright and dark bands on a piece of paper. This is assumed to be evidence for the wave nature of light (as opposed to it being a particle, which can also be demonstrated in a different kind of experiment).

14. Termed a *transmission model* by William Braud, psychologist and director of the Institute of Transpersonal Psychology. This distinguishes it from the other, more complicated psi models — termed *reorganization* and *correspondence*, which don't involve the spread of information from one person to the other.

Chapter 2

1. A description of which is available in any introductory psychology textbook or on the Web.

2. In practice these apparently simple learning paradigms are quite difficult to achieve consistently.

3. A term used to avoid the assumption that the animal is self-aware of its own learning processes. It avoids the impression that the pigeon consciously makes associations in some kind of intelligent fashion — it is not the pigeon's mind, but the pigeon's nervous system, that performs the learning.

4. Although specific types of superstitious beliefs or behaviors such as those associated with gambling addiction are studied in great detail, although they are not necessarily identified as superstitious — it is not the purpose of such studies to examine the entire field of superstition.

5. Implying that there's a contrast between a dumb "sheep" follower versus an intelligent, independent "goat" thinker.

6. A controversial test in mainstream psychology because many psychologists question its validity, and are wary of the mysticism associated with the writings of Carl Jung. We'll examine Jung's theories toward the end of this book.

7. People with anhedonia lack the ability to experience pleasure.

8. Widely known as *instruments*. This name gives sheets of paper more of a scientific respectability.

9. Understandably, questionnaire construction is a little bit more complicated than this.

10. Entities such as Yetis, the Loch Ness Monster and aliens.

11. That is, the creature in theory must have arrived from somewhere ... whether from ancestors in the dinosaur era or outer space, or something equally as fantastic.

12. This view treats all dream material as equivalent, which is not necessarily the case. Some dreams are far more vivid than others and are held by the dreamer to be of vast importance. It is these dreams that are alleged to be the prophetic ones (Storm 1999).

13. Michael Thalbourne (2010) cautions that no one really knows what makes a "happy schizotype" happy — there are plenty of personality variables that might interact with the schizotype trait to allow a person to be theoretically psychopathological, yet seemingly well-adjusted compared with other schizotypes.

14. These authors define character, on the other hand, as a personality dimension that's prone to environment and social learning. Character can mature and change throughout life, whereas temperament is quite rigid in its expression.

15. A perspective not shared by researchers such as Maher (2000), who argues for a ghostly source of poltergeist experiences.

Chapter 3

1. Someone who "sees" the supernatural realm.

2. Maher (1999) points out that there are eight striking similarities between apparitions and human auras, which suggests to her that the phenomena are very closely related. From a different perspective, theosophical writings of the late 19th and early 20th centuries (much influenced by Eastern mysticism) actually categorized the different hues of a person's thoughts as "vibrations," and these might now be labeled a manifesting aura. Some examples of the many colors include grey-green, indicating deceit, and brownish-green with speckles of scarlet, signifying jealousy (Besant and Leadbeater 1905).

3. I've never accepted these stories as necessarily true, nevertheless I've certainly heard more than I'd expect from independent eyewitnesses, given the dramatic nature of the experience.

4. This contradicts the assertion by Bozzano that their ghostly form is contemporary to the age ... but we are dealing with ghosts, so anything is possible!

5. A terrifying mythical apparition — see Simon Sherwood's 2000 article titled "Black Dog Apparitions" for one man's encounter with a black dog (*Journal of the American Society for Psychical Research*, 94/3–4, 151–164).

6. There's a correlation between boundary deficit and transliminality, among other personality and neurological factors, so there might be a deeper structure from which these related personality variables emerge (Palmer et al. 2006).

7. The most well-known is the 1970s collaboration between the somewhat eccentric inventor William O'Neill and his benefactor, George Meek, in developing the Spiricom machine. In one case, the spirit of a deceased man called Doc Nick would talk through the machine at a special frequency, which provided the energy to allow the vocal cords of the deceased doctor's astral body to be made audible. This story is narrated in John Fuller's book *The Ghost of 29 Megacycles*.

8. Using the jargon of the field, a spirit is someone who has "transitioned" to the other side, since there's no such thing as actual death.

9. The Andrews family, of Andover in Hampshire, England, communicated via rappings with what they considered a spirit. The case was investigated, and rappings recorded, by Barrie Colvin himself.

10. As an aside, Haines (1980) notes that the majority of UFO sightings are from 1 to 60 minutes, not on the order of seconds, so the skeptical assumption of UFO reports that the witness sees something briefly and then confabulates it might be erroneous after all.

11. Kuhlmann at one time worked at the Minnesota "School for the feeble-minded and colony for epileptics," a name you'd expect no school to possess today. He was a well published psychologist in his day.

12. From a skeptical point of view, the stimulus might be no more tangible than a ray of light. In 1980, a landed UFO was claimed to have been seen by U.S. Air Force personnel in Rendlesham Forest on the English east coast. Later, stories of occupant contact were published. Skeptics propose the initial stimulus was a lighthouse on the coast, a number of miles away, and memory confabulation occurred over the intervening years to create a famous case. Supporters claim these lights can't possibly have been the source of the incident.

13. "Men in Black" and "Bogus Social Workers" are two examples. Hough and Kalman (1997) have an intriguing review of the Bogus Social Workers phenomenon.

14. Which can transform, for some witnesses, into "a metallic cigar with windows through which extraterrestrial occupants can be seen," according to Hillary Evans (1982).

15. A Yowie is the Australian equivalent of Bigfoot.

16. This doesn't explain how two people from a group of four see the same ghostly figure at roughly the same time and without communicating to each other, and immediately after describe it independently to their companions who didn't see it. Collective delusion assisted by telepathy seems a bit too convoluted an explanation for this occurrence.

Chapter 4

1. The Pleiades is a star group popular with proponents of the extraterrestrial hypothesis as the origin of a variety of alien types.

2. They do not mention that abductees are often repeaters, meaning they report a lifetime of abductions.

3. Newman and Baumeister (1996b) retort that masochism is a more extreme and "multipronged" assault on self-identity than these listed behaviors.

4. This involves the breaking up of the single self into alternative identities.

5. Milliamps, a measure of electric current.

6. Parra does acknowledge that the data is only from questionnaires, and that there's some uncertainty as to whether the participants' answers were in response to the questions the researchers were asking.

7. It could be argued that driving is primarily a visuo-spatial task, not a linguistic one,

and since self-awareness has been linked to linguistic skills, it's perhaps not surprising that an unconscious part of our brain is in charge of negotiating a car or other vehicle along a road.

8. This is more correctly labeled *isolated sleep paralysis*, which implies the disorder is not present in conjunction with other sleep disorders such as narcolepsy, a condition where the patient can fall asleep, in broad daylight, when apparently wide awake.

9. The idea that a deeper, older part of the brain — conveniently labeled "the limbic system" — deals with subjective and physical aspects of emotion, and an overlying cortical region controls our thinking, has captured psychological discussion because it is a convenient metaphor for "emotion" versus "cognition," and "unconscious" versus "conscious" respectively (Servan-Schreiber, Perlstein, Cohen and Mintun 1998). The problem with this distinction is that the limbic system is a more fluid concept; some structures anatomically defined as "limbic" appear to play a very cognitive role. The hippocampus, with its function of consolidating memory, is a typical example. Nevertheless, amygdaloid and parahippocampal regions do seem to have a functional role in the subjective experience of anxiety and fear, and the physical correlates of emotion, such as visceral (gut) sensations, can be induced by direct activation of limbic areas. For the purpose of this discussion, we'll stick to the handy label of limbic moderating the expression of emotion.

10. While acknowledging neurological possibilities such as sleep paralysis, the authors Peter Hough and Moyshe Kalman maintain a paranormal perspective of the abduction reports by Jayne and others.

11. Further research might define the transition between a state of extreme fatigue to immediate REM sleep as the defining feature, which resolves this contradiction.

12. The problem exists in reverse, too. Blackmore (1998) refers to a highly controversial Roper Poll developed by abduction proponents Budd Hopkins, David Jacobs and Ron Westrum that concluded 3.7 million Americans have been abducted by aliens. This conclusion is based on some of the 5947 participants answering positively to questions such as having seen a UFO, a ghost, having had an out-of-body experience, having seen unusual lights in a room and having woken up paralyzed. The authors assumed these participants were abductees, although as Blackmore points out, the self-reports are more indicative of a sleep paralysis episode. Jacobs writes in his book *The Threat* that ghost encounters are screen memories for aliens — that is the aliens disguise themselves as spirits. This surely would upset ghost hunters.

Chapter 5

1. Also known as *general clonic-tonic* because of the associated body stiffening.

2. Called *petit mal* or absence seizures.

3. Temporal lobe epilepsy can also be a sid e-effect of organic disease such as brain tumors of the temporal lobes.

4. The assumption that every mental state (symptom) is associated with a neural state (e.g., measured by EEG) is known as the *supervenience thesis*, and is very popular in mainstream psychology — and counteracts duality theory discussed previously. Correlations can certainly be shown between mental and neural activity, but there is no definitive causal relationship (Monaco, Mula and Cavanna 2005). Some researchers have even demonstrated significant relationships between subjective paranormal experiences and temporal lobe symptoms, but not between paranormal experience and EEG patterns. This is probably because EEG is simply too gross a measure to detect deep brain dysfunction (Palmer and Neppe 2003).

5. From the Greek *rhin* meaning nose, hence rhinoceros (with a big horn sticking out of the nose area).

6. We have a few basic tastes and can smell many different smells, and combined the sensation is called "flavor." This combination of the individual taste and smell components of a food or drink (and other potential associations) occurs in regions of the temporal lobes.

7. The axons of nerve cells in the region suffered from demyelination, or a decay of the insulating sheath that surrounds them that facilitates action potential transmission.

8. A theory that was made popular by psychologist Julian Jaynes in his 1976 book *The Origins of Consciousness in the Breakdown of the Bicameral Mind.* He argued that consciousness (or better still, self-awareness) is intrinsically related to language; if we know no language, we can't be self-aware. Nevertheless, this theory has been criticized by academics in many different fields, not just psychology.

9. Or damage caused by brain injury such as shearing or strain of callosum-anterior commissure.

10. The assumption here is that the "sense" might be coupled with a visual hallucination, making it more "real" to the perceiver.

11. Regions within the amygdala are believed to mediate the emotional processes associated with social bonding (e.g., Trezza and Campolongo 2009).

12. An entirely different concept from "seeing an aura," or the colorful outline that some people report around other people that we discussed earlier in the book.

13. To understand qualia, think of what it means to experience the color red as red, or an apple as tasting just like an apple — it's experiential "stuff of life" we take for granted.

14. William James took an interest in the psychology of religious experience in the early part of the 20th century, and even then warned against a method of reductionist materialism that "finishes up Saint Paul by calling his vision on the road to Damascus a discharging lesion of the occipital lobe, he being an epileptic" (Devinsky and Lai 2008). To a certain extent this warning has not been heeded in contemporary psychological literature.

15. As Grahame Hancock does, in his fascinating book *Supernatural.* From a different perspective, David Luke has written a comprehensive review article in *The Journal of Parapsychology* summarizing the frequently significant role psychoactive drugs play in facilitating psi — largely in a laboratory settings (e.g., card-reading). From this viewpoint, drug action isn't purely hallucinatory.

16. A report which argues for the physical reality of the alien odor stimuli, not the temporal lobe epilepsy hypothesis.

17. Persinger suggests that visceral hallucinations associated with the alimentary canal (the anatomical term for the long, variable tube comprising the mouth, throat, stomach, small intestine, large intestine and anus) explain the frequency of reports of aliens taking an interest in a victim's anus — the infamous "anal probing" much beloved of abduction skeptics who enjoy joking about the phenomenon.

Chapter 6

1. This study used very strong fields which aren't naturally occurring and are not of a level used in the research we'll discuss.

2. It's not just Earth energies alone that might exert such an influence. Edwin May controversially proposes that psi events are best when the Milky Way is hidden, and worst when it is overhead. The theory states that some mysterious variety of radiation emanates from the center of the Galaxy which disrupts the practice of anomalous cognition.

3. There are a number of different pairs of magnetic poles, north and south, so it's actually a bit more complicated than this, but the concept is more than adequate for this discussion.

4. Nanotesla, a unit of measure for weak, natural magnetic fields.

5. Hence they're very long and considered to possess extremely low frequency.

6. A statement nevertheless criticized by the editor of the journal to which this paper was submitted on account of the lack of evidence.

7. With regard to lack of sleep, the same could be said for parents of newborn children, but I haven't heard of any increased propensity to see ghosts in these people. Maybe they're too tired to worry?

8. A technique first performed in the 1960s by Gertrude Schmeidler (see Maher 1999).

9. A marginal interaction was found for the variable of belief, in that ghost-believers might be more prone to this suggestion than non-believers.

10. Michael Jawer, writing in the *Journal of the Society for Psychical Research*, suggests that people sensitive to apparitions might be more prone to conditions such as allergies or migraines — which might be intrinsically related to the manifestation of their experience. He identifies "sensitivity" as being an actual neurobiological phenomenon linked, among other things, to personality factors.

11. Many ghost researchers see high levels of magnetism as evidence of a real apparition, rather than a natural reason for a ghostly experience.

12. Braithwaite and colleagues mention that magnetic field anomalies in buildings might not necessarily be time based, but location based too (e.g., changes across rooms, or perhaps from inside to outside the building). The influence of magnetic fields on behavior might therefore be difficult to measure, and research results inconsistent among studies. Such an admission, while logical, weakens the theory considerably since it implies unfalsifiability.

13. Consisting of complex, frequency-modulated fields.

14. Represented by electrons moving from one energy state to another.

Chapter 7

1. Near the equator, the earth's field is 30,000 gamma (a unit of measure equivalent to the nT) and the two centimeter magnet is 1×10^8 gamma, a degree of difference of 10,000.

2. That is, the field is experienced not as a continuous influence but as small bursts lasting only microseconds, and up to 1000 of these bursts occur every second.

3. These researchers also concede that, technically-speaking, the transcranial fields weren't strong enough to induce a current in the brain in the first place.

4. Obviously not a study that might be critical of transcranial magnetic stimulation.

5. One conventional sensory system might even be your skin. A study by Lysenko and Barilo, published in the *Journal of the Society for Psychical Research*, mentions the possibility of "dermo-optic" perception; that is, the ability of human skin to transduce a light signal that falls on it into a change in alpha activity in the brain. Perhaps the perception of a ghost originates from the skin?

6. This is my terminology, as far as I'm aware, so they haven't any official endorsement as labels for the described events.

7. A singular experience, since one tends to hear of ghostly orbs appearing in photographs of houses, or graveyards, but they aren't actually seen by the photographer, or anyone in the vicinity of the photograph being taken.

8. A pioneer in the field of earthlights research.

Chapter 8

1. Variously meaning the unconscious, mind, and in some contexts soul.

2. Womb envy encompasses more than jealousy of the biological womb. It refers to a more widespread resentment, by males, of certain female abilities (Berke 1997).

3. If I told you that you had a repressed, unconscious desire which emerged for some strange reason as nose-picking behavior (I caught you doing it once), you might retort, "No I don't. Prove it." To which I reply craftily, "See, you're denying it. The idea must be repressed. I just did prove it." There's no objective measure of repression, and no evidence could be presented proving me wrong (unfalsifiability). The scientific method requires the possibility that a hypothesis can be proven wrong.

4. They're not really explaining psi at all, just describing a process by which it (in some unknown way) manifests.

5. That is, they lack the concept of themselves as an individual.

6. Recall the person-centered model of poltergeists proposed by Teguis and Flynn.

7. Although not strictly psychoanalytic, Newman and Baumeister's description of alien abductions as escape-from-self is worth considering here.

8. Notable examples are the Betty and Barney Hill case, the Charlie Hickson case and the Travis Walton case, all of which are discussed in this book.

9. Lawson distinguishes the witnessing of UFOs from abduction cases, since he argues the "ships" reported in the latter narratives are often only seen as a bright light, or not seen at all, and the abductee can only assume a UFO was responsible for their ordeal.

10. We'll examine Betty's abduction in more detail in Chapter 9.

11. A popular entity in South American cases.

12. These are designs which attempt to resemble as closely as possible a true experiment. In this case, Lawson used an experimental (Caesarean) and a control (vaginal) birth group. However, unlike a true experiment the subjects could not be randomly assigned to either group; in this example they had to be either Caesarean or natural.

13. Lawson himself states, "We were unable to verify whether subjects were in fact Cesareans; thus our data are anecdotally based."

Chapter 9

1. Arguably not as popular as it was in the mid–1980s to mid–1990s, when the topic was more novel than it is today.

2. Somewhat different in form from the infamous "Grey" which achieved fame from the mid–1980s onward. For example, the Hills' aliens had eyes with pupils rather than the dark orbs of the modern alien variant. In fact, Barney claimed later that the beings staring at him from the UFO looked like "red-headed Irishmen" (Bowen 1969).

3. See Chapter 8 for Alvin Lawson's interpretation of this incident.

4. Apparently, she'd had numerous abductions throughout her life, both before and after the one reported.

5. Ann Druffel investigated the Tujunga incident with the help of, among others, William McCall — best remembered as the research partner of Alvin Lawson. Druffel worked closely with Rogo on this case and others but takes a slightly different view — that the abducting aliens aren't space beings but rather a type of entity known variously as fairy, or jinn, that have historically tormented humankind and are using the guise of UFO occupants to perpetuate their annoying behavior. This perspective is similar to John Keel's "ultraterrestrial" theory, and the "dimensional" approach of UFO researcher Jacques Vallee.

6. Occult in this context simply means "hidden," as in hidden magical knowledge that is passed down by adepts to others initiated in the tradition. There is no necessary connotation with anything evil, although it is possible that occultists could perform practices or rites for ostensibly evil purposes.

7. Previously referred to as a source of aura-hues.

8. Violet Firth, a teacher who became a psychoanalyst and well-versed occultist and who wrote a popular book called *Psychic Self-Defense* (1930), in part explaining how to protect oneself from the malignant, harmful thoughts of other people that can drain a victim of their vitality.

9. Evans (1984) describes a case from 1964 in which a woman and her mother-in-law witnessed the surreal scene of a UFO crew repairing their craft. The woman seemed very honest, but the event very unlikely. Research subsequently showed her to be in personal, spiritual turmoil, and she converted to Mormonism within the year. While not as dramatic as the Cahill case, the presence of an independent witness, and the spiritual nature of her tension, suggests this case shares a lot with the later Australian abduction.

10. Named after the Siberian tribe who were studied by anthropologists in the early 20th century and who still performed these types of practices.

11. Sometimes known to the abductee as the "elder." Betty Andreasson used "watchers" to describe some of her alien captors.

Chapter 10

1. Jung's work involves outwardly "non-occult" pursuits also, such as the development of the personality constructs of introversion and extraversion. Yet even these concepts have a paranormal association — as we've seen extraverts are considered to be more receptive of psi events than introverts.

2. The notion of a collective unconscious was not discovered by Jung. The poet Yeats (1865–1939), for example, wrote of the manifestation of the dynamic subconscious and understood the power of symbols on human behavior (e.g., Hollis 1973). Similar concepts also exist in older Western and Eastern mystic traditions.

3. Although analytical psychology is often called transpersonal psychology, I've used the latter term to encompass all transpersonal theories, not necessarily Jungian.

4. Here meaning from the psyche, rather than related to psi.

5. Called polarity.

6. Quite a lot of empirical evidence has apparently shown that matter, and natural states (e.g., random number generators) are influenced by human thought — although much of this evidence is empirical and the theory is vague as to how or why it happens, so it doesn't influence the skeptics' viewpoint.

7. As we might expect, Alvin Lawson (1984) believed the disc shape of a UFO contained birth associations, since the ovum attached to the uterine wall has an embryonic disc like a circular plate (the human) inside it. Drawing on Jung, he further suggests this represents an awareness of the initial "integral, whole, or individual," which matches Jung's concept of the mandala as "unity, wholeness, and individuation."

8. "Either psychic projections throw back a radar echo," Jung writes skeptically, "or the appearance of real objects affords an opportunity for mythological projections." From this passage it seems he can't be accused of pushing the notion of thought-forms.

9. Jerome Clark apparently lost enthusiasm with the ideas put forward in this Jung-inspired UFO book, and became more open to the extraterrestrial hypothesis (Bullard 1992). Thus one mustn't be fooled into thinking that transpersonal psychology is the necessary final resting place of a well-traveled paranormal researcher.

10. Seven is an important number because seven objects (the Sun, Moon, Mercury, Venus, Mars, Jupiter and Saturn) were visible in the sky to ancient people, and these behaved differently from the background heavens.

11. My black cat encounter was likely to be a real, out-of-place panther, since I don't seem to have been struck by any symbolic message (although perhaps I did, and it was all unconscious!).

Bibliography

Alcock, J.E. (1981). *Parapsychology: Science or magic?* Oxford, U.K.: Pergammon Press.

Alvarado, C.S., and N.L. Zingrone (1995). Characteristics of hauntings with and without apparitions: An analysis of published cases. *Journal of the Society for Psychical Research*, 60 (841), 385–397.

Anonymous (1995). Hidden hallucinations. *Psychology Today*, 28 (4), 18–21.

Anonymous (2005). Falling apart: Dissociation and its disorders. *Harvard Mental Health Letter*, 21 (7), 1–4.

Antoniello, D., B.M. Kluger, D.H. Sahlein, and K.M. Heilman (2010). Phantom limb after stroke: An underreported phenomenon. *Cortex: A Journal Devoted to the Study of the Nervous System and Behavior*, 46 (9), 1114–1122.

Appelle, S. (1995/1996). The abduction experience: A critical evaluation of theory and evidence. *Journal of UFO Studies*, 6, 29–78.

Arndt, J., and J. Greenberg (1996). Fantastic accounts can take many forms: False memory construction? Yes. Escape from self? We don't think so. *Psychological Inquiry*, 7 (2), 127–132.

Awadalla, A., G. Al-Fayez, M. Harville, H. Arikawa, M.E. Tomeo, D.I. Templer, and R. Underwood (2004). Comparative prevalence of isolated sleep paralysis in Kuwaiti, Sudanese, and American college students. *Psychological Reports*, 95 (1), 317–322.

Balanovski, E., and J.G. Taylor (1978). Can electromagnetism account for extra-sensory phenomena? *Nature*, 276 (5683), 64–67.

Banaji, M.R., and J.F. Kihlstrom (1996). The ordinary nature of alien abduction memories. *Psychological Inquiry*, 7 (2), 132–135.

Bancaud, J., F. Brunet-Bourgin, P. Cahauvel, and E. Halgren (1994). Anatomical origin of déjà vu and vivid "memories" in human temporal lobe epilepsy. *Brain*, 117 (1), 71–90.

Banks, J. (2001). Rorschach audio: Ghost voices and perceptual creativity. *Leonardo Musical Journal*, 11, 77–83.

Bartholomew, R.E., K. Basterfield, and G.S. Howard (1991). UFO abductees and contactees: Psychopathology or fantasy proneness? *Professional Psychology: Research and Practice*, 22 (3), 215–222.

Bem, D.J., and C. Honorton (1994). Does psi exist? Replicable evidence for an anomalous process of information transfer. *Psychological Bulletin*, 115 (1), 4–18.

Bensley, D.A. (2003). Can minds leave bodies? A cognitive science perspective. *Skeptical Inquirer*, 27, 34–39.

Berke, J.H. (1997). Womb envy. *Journal of Melanie Klein and Object Relations*, 15 (3), 443–466.

Besant, A., and C.W. Leadbeater (1905). *Thought forms*. London: The Theosophical Publishing House.

Bien, C.G., F.O. Benninger, H. Urbach, J. Schramm, M. Kurthen, and C.E. Elger (2000). Localizing value of epileptic visual auras. *Brain*, 123 (2), 244.

Blackmore, S. (1998). Abduction by aliens or sleep paralysis? *The Skeptical Inquirer*, 22 (3), 23–28.

Blackmore, S., and R. Moore (1994). Seeing things: Visual recognition and belief in the paranormal. *European Journal of Parapsychology*, 10, 91–103.

Blanke, O., T. Landis, and M. Seeck (2000). Electrical cortical stimulation of the human prefrontal cortex evokes complex visual hallucinations. *Epilepsy and Behavior*, 1, 356–361.

Blanke, O., S. Ortigue, T. Landis, and M. Seeck (2002). Stimulating illusory own-body perceptions. *Nature*, 419, 269–270.

Blumenfeld, H., G.I. Varghese, M.J. Purcaro, J.E. Motelow, M. Enev, K.A. McNally, A.R. Levin, L.J. Hirsch, R. Tikofsky, I.G. Zubal, A.L. Paige, and S.S. Spencer (2009). Cortical and subcortical networks in human secondarily generalized tonic-clonic seizures. *Brain: A Journal of Neurology*, 132 (4), 999–1012.

Bonenfant, R.J. (2000). A near-death experience followed by the visitation of an "angel-like" being. *Journal of Near-Death Studies*, 19 (2), 103–113.

Booker, R. (2002). Sleep deprivation. *British Medical Journal*, 325 (7359), 318.

Booth J.N., S.A. Koren and M.A. Persinger (2008). Increased theta activity in quantitative electroencephalographic (QEEG) measurements during exposure to complex weak magnetic fields. *Electromagnetic Biology and Medicine*, 27 (4), 426–36.

Bord, J., and C. Bord (1987). *Modern mysteries of Britain: 100 years of strange events*. London: Grafton Books.

Bowen, C. (1969). *The humanoids*. London: Neville Spearman.

Bower, G.H., M.B. Karlin, and A. Dueck (1975). Comprehension and memory of pictures. *Memory and Cognition*, 3, 216–220.

Braithwaite, J.J. (2005). Using digital magnetometry to quantify anomalous magnetic fields associated with spontaneous strange experiences: The magnetic anomaly detection system (MADS). *Journal of Parapsychology*, 69 (1), 151–171.

Braithwaite, J.J., K. Perez-Aquino, and M. Townsend (2004). In search of magnetic anomalies associated with haunt-type experiences: Pulses and patterns in dual time-synchronized measurements. *Journal of Parapsychology*, 68 (2), 255–288.

Braithwaite, J.J., and M. Townsend (2005). Research note: Sleeping with the entity — a quantitative magnetic investigation of an English castle's reputedly "haunted" bedroom. *European Journal of Parapsychology*, 20 (1), 65–78.

Braithwaite, J.J., and M. Townsend (2008). Sleeping with the entity; part II — temporally complex distortions in the magnetic field from human movement in a bed located in an English castle's reputedly haunted bedroom. *European Journal of Parapsychology*, 23 (1), 90–126.

Braud, W.G. (1994). The role of mind in the physical world: A psychologist's view. *European Journal of Parapsychology*, 10, 66–77.

Briehl, W. (1995). Wilhelm Reich. *Psychoanalytic Pioneers*, 1/1, 430–439.

Broughton, R.S. (1992). Psi-missing displacement effect in old data. *Journal of Parapsychology*, 56 (1), 31–38.

Brown, A.S. (2003). A review of the déjà vu experience. *Psychological Bulletin*, 129 (3), 394–413.

Bruck, M., and S. Ceci (2007). The suggestibility of young children. In T.J. Lawson (ed.), *Scientific Perspectives on Pseudoscience and the Paranormal* (24–33). Upper Saddle River, N.J.: Pearson.

Brugger, P. (2001). From haunted brain to haunted science: A cognitive neuroscience view of paranormal and pseudoscientific thought. In J. Houran and R. Lange (eds.), *Hauntings and poltergeists: Multidisciplinary perspectives.* Jefferson, NC: McFarland.

Brugger, P., and A.T. Baumann (1994). Repetition avoidance in response to imaginary questions: The effect of respondents' belief in ESP. *Psychological Reports,* 75, 883–893.

Brugger, P., A. Gamma, R. Muri, M. Schafer, and K.I. Taylor (1993). Functional hemispheric asymmetry and belief in ESP. *Perceptual and Motor Skills,* 77, 1299–1308.

Brugger, P., and R.E. Graves (1997). Testing vs. believing hypotheses: Magical ideation in the judgment of contingencies. *Cognitive Neuropsychiatry,* 2 (4), 251–272.

Budden, A. (1995). *UFOs, psychic close encounters: The electromagnetic indictment.* London: Blandford.

Bullard, T.E. (1988). Folklore scholarship and UFO reality. *International UFO Reporter,* 13 (4), 9–13.

Bullard, T.E. (1991). Why abduction reports are not urban legends. *International UFO Reporter,* 16 (6), 15–24.

Bullard, T.E. (1992). Folkloric dimensions of the UFO phenomenon. *Journal of UFO Studies,* 3, 1–57.

Burgess, C.A., I. Kirsch, H. Shane, K.L. Niederauer, S.M. Graham, and A. Bacon (1998). Facilitated communication as an ideomotor response. *Psychological Science,* 9, 71–74.

Butler, T. (2002). Electronic voice phenomena: A tool for validating personal survival. *Journal of Religion and Psychical Research,* 25 (4), 215–227.

Cahill, K. (1996). *Encounter.* Sydney: Harper-Collins.

Cammaroto, S., G. D'Aleo, C. Smorto, and P. Bramanti (2008). Charles Bonnet syndrome. *Functional Neurology,* 23 (3), 123–128.

Campbell, W.H. (2003). *Introduction to geomagnetic fields* (2nd ed.). Cambridge, U.K.: Cambridge University Press.

Carlson, N.R. (2005). *Foundations of physiological psychology* (6th ed.). Boston: Pearson.

Carpenter, J.C. (2004). First sight: Part one, a model of psi and the mind. *Journal of Parapsychology,* 68 (2), 217–254.

Carpenter, J.C. (2008). Relations between ESP and memory in light of the first sight model of psi. *Journal of Parapsychology,* 72 (1), 47–76.

Carter, C. (2010). "Heads I lose, tails you win," or, how Richard Wiseman nullifies positive results, and what to do about it: A response to Wiseman's (2010) critique of parapsychology. *Journal of the Society for Psychical Research,* 74, 156–167.

Case, T., J. Fitness, D.R. Cairns, and R.J. Stevenson (2004). Coping with uncertainty: Superstitious strategies and secondary control. *Journal of Applied Social Psychology,* 34 (4), 848–871.

Castillo, R.J. (2003). Trance, functional psychosis, and culture. *Psychiatry,* 66 (1), 9–21.

Chalker, B. (1996). *The Oz files.* Potts Point, Sydney: Duffy and Snellgrove.

Chen, C., Y-H. Shih, D-J. Yen, J-F. Lirng, Y-C. Guo, H-Y. Yu, and C-H. Yiu (2003). Olfactory auras in patients with temporal lobe epilepsy. *Epilepsia,* 44 (2), 257–260.

Chequers, J., S. Joseph, and D. Diduca (1997). Belief in extraterrestrial life, UFO-related beliefs, and schizotypal personality. *Personality and Individual Differences,* 23 (3), 519–521.

Cherry, C. (2003). Explicability, psychoanalysis and the paranormal. In N. Totton (ed.), *Psychoanalysis and the Paranormal: Lands of Darkness,* 73–104. London: Karnac.

Cheyne, J.A. (2002). Situational factors affecting sleep paralysis and associated hallucinations: Position and timing effects. *Journal of Sleep Research,* 11, 169–177.

Cheyne, J.A., and T.A. Girard (2004). Spatial characteristics of hallucinations associated with sleep paralysis. *Cognitive Neuropsychiatry,* 9 (4), 281–300.

Cheyne, J.A., and T.A. Girard (2007). Paranoid delusions and threatening hallucinations: A prospective study of sleep paralysis experiences. *Consciousness and Cognition,* 16 (4), 959–974.

Cheyne, J.A., I.R. Newby-Clarke, and S.D. Rueffer (1999). Relations among hypnagogic and hypnopompic experiences associated with sleep paralysis. *Journal of Sleep Research*, 8, 313–317.

Christiansen, M.P. (2004). Exploratory validation of Persinger's model of vectoral cerebral hemisphericity for grief apparitions. *Dissertation Abstracts International Section B: The Sciences and Engineering*, 65 (3-B), 1540.

Clarke, C. (2008). A new quantum theoretical framework for parapsychology. *European Journal of Parapsychology*, 23 (1), 3–30.

Clarke, D. (1991). Belief in the paranormal: A New Zealand survey. *Journal of the Society for Psychical Research*, 57 (823), 412–425.

Clarke, J., and L. Coleman (1975). *The Unidentified: Notes Towards Solving the UFO Mystery*. New York: Warner Paperback Library.

Colvin, B. (2010). The acoustic properties of unexplained rapping sounds. *The Journal of the Society for Psychical Research*, 73 (2), 65–93.

Comparelli, A., A. De Carolis, G.D. Kotzalidis, A. Masillo, S. Ferracuti, and J. Conesa (2000). Geomagnetic, cross-cultural and occupational faces of sleep paralysis: An ecological perspective. *Sleep and Hypnosis*, 2 (3), 105–111.

Comparelli, A., A. De Carolis, G.D. Kotzalidis, A. Masillo, S. Ferracuti, and R. Tatarelli (2010). A woman lost in the cemetery: A case of time-limited amnesia. *Neurocase*, 16 (1), 23–30.

Cook, C.M., and M.A. Persinger (1997). Experimental induction of the "sensed presence" in normal subjects and an exceptional subject. *Perceptual and Motor Skills*, 85 (2), 683–693.

Corliss, W.R. (1983). *Handbook of Unusual Natural Phenomena*. Garden City, N.Y.: Anchor Press/Doubleday.

Cosh, C. (1996). Superstition or science? *Alberta Report/Newsmagazine*, 23 (14) 3/18/96.

Craft, M. (1996). *Alien impact*. New York: St. Martin's Press.

Crandall, J.E. (1985). Effects of favorable and unfavorable conditions on the psi-missing displacement effect. *Journal of the American Society for Psychical Research*, 79 (1), 27–38.

Crandall, J.E., and D.D. Hite (1983). Psi-missing and displacement: Evidence for improperly focused psi? *Journal of the American Society for Psychical Research*, 77 (3), 209–228.

Crawley, R.A., and M.J. Eacott (1999). Memory for early life events: Consistency of retrieval of memories over a one-year interval. *Memory*, 7 (4), 439–460.

Crawley, S.E., C.C. French, and S.A. Yesson (2002). Evidence for transliminality from a subliminal card-guessing task. *Perception*, 31, 887–892.

Cummings, J.L. (1997). Neuropsychiatric manifestations of right hemisphere lesions. *Brain and Language*, 57, 22–37.

Cutnell, J.D., K.W. and Johnson (2006). *Essentials of physics*. Hoboken, N.J.: Wiley.

Dagnall, N.A., G. Munley, A. Parker and K. Drinkwater (2010). Paranormal belief, schizotypy and transliminality. *Journal of Parapsychology*, 74, 117–143.

Davies, P.C.W., and J.R. Brown (1986). *The ghost in the atom: A discussion of the mysteries of quantum physics*. New York: Cambridge University Press.

Dear, B.F., and A.L. Jinks (2005). Perceptual and memory capabilities of witnesses to anomalous visual phenomena. *Australian Journal of Parapsychology*, 5 (1), 97–118.

Delanoy, D.L. (2001). Anomalous psychophysiological responses to remote cognition: The DMILS studies. *European Journal of Parapsychology*, 16, 30–41.

Del Prete, G., and P.E. Tressoldi (2005). Anomalous cognition in hypnagogic state with OBE induction: An experimental study. *Journal of Parapsychology*, 69 (2), 329–339.

De Santis, M.V., and R.H. Haude (1993). Effect of verbal interpretation on recall and recognition of ambiguous pictorial stimuli. *Perceptual and Motor Skills*, 76, 719–722.

Devereux, P. (2005). Koestler's legacy. *Fortean Times*, 201, 32–39.

Devinsky, O., S. Khan, and K. Alper (1998). Olfactory reference syndrome in a patient with partial epilepsy. *Neuropsychiatry, Neuropsychology and Behavioral Neurology*, 11 (2), 103–105.

Devinsky, O., and G. Lai (2008). Spirituality and religion in epilepsy. *Epilepsy and Behavior*, 12 (4), 636–643.

Diaz-Vivela, L., and C.J. Alvarez-Gonzalez (2004). Differences in paranormal beliefs across fields of study from a Spanish adaptation of Tobacyk's RPBS (Revised Paranormal Belief Scale). *Journal of Parapsychology*, 68, 405–421.

Dodds, E.R. (1934). Why I do not believe in survival. *Proceedings of the Society for Psychical Research*, 42, 147–172.

Donati, M. (2004). Beyond synchronicity: The worldview of Carl Gustav Jung and Wolfgang Pauli. *Journal of Analytical Psychology*, 49, 707–728.

Dorahy, M.J., C. Shannon, L. Seagar, M. Corr, K. Stewart, D. Hanna, C. Mulholland, and W. Middleton (2009). Auditory hallucinations in dissociative identity disorder and schizophrenia with and without a childhood trauma history: Similarities and differences. *Journal of Nervous and Mental Disease*, 197, 892–898.

Druffel, A., and D.S. Rogo (1989). *The Tujunga Canyon contacts*. New York: New American Library.

Dudley, T.R. (1999). Effect of restriction of working memory on reported paranormal belief. *Psychological Reports*, 84 (1), 313–316.

Dunne, B.J., and R.G. Jahn (2003). Information and uncertainty in remote perception research. *Journal of Scientific Exploration*, 17 (2), 207–241.

Easton, R.D., and R.E. Shor (1975). Information processing analysis of the Chevreul pendulum illusion. *Journal of Experimental Psychology: Human Perception and Performance*, 1 (3), 231–236.

Easton, R.D., and R.E. Shor, (1976). An experimental analysis of the Chevreul pendulum illusion. *Journal of General Psychology*, 95, 111–125.

Ebon, M. (1966). Telepathy and precognition in dreams. In M. Ebon (ed.) (1978). *The Signet Handbook of Parapsychology* (393–408). New York: Lombard Associates.

Edge, H. (1985). The dualist tradition in parapsychology. *European Journal of Parapsychology*, 6 (1), 81–93.

Ehrenwald, J. (1971). Mother-child symbiosis: Cradle of ESP. In M. Ebon (ed.) (1978). *The Signet Handbook of Parapsychology* (66–78). New York: Lombard Associates.

Ehrlichman, H., J.S. Antrobus, and M.S. Wiener (1985). EEG asymmetry and sleep mentation during REM and NREM. *Brain and Cognition*, 4 (4), 477–485.

Einstein, D.A., and R.G. Menzies (2004). The presence of magical thinking in obsessive compulsive disorder. *Behavior Research and Therapy*, 42 (5), 539–550.

Eisenbud, J. (1954). Behavioral correspondences to normally unpredictable future events. *Psychoanalytic Quarterly*, 23, 35–389.

Eisenbud, J. (1975). Psychiatric insights into psi. In M. Ebon (ed.) (1978). *The Signet Handbook of Parapsychology* (54–65). New York: Lombard Associates.

Eisold, K.E. (2002). Jung, Jungians, and psychoanalysis. *Psychoanalytic Psychology*, 19 (3), 501–524.

Eliade, M. (1972). *Shamanism: Archaic techniques of ecstasy*. Princeton, N.J.: Princeton University Press.

Enns, A. (2005). Voices of the dead: Transmission/translation/transgression. *Culture, Theory and Critique*, 46 (1), 11–27.

Epstein, S. (1991). Cognitive-experiential self-theory: implications for developmental psychology. In M.R. Gunnar, A.L. Stroufe, L.A. Alan (eds.), *Self-processes and development* (79–123). Hillsdale, NJ: Lawrence Erlbaum Associates.

Evans, H. (1984). *Visions, apparitions, alien visitors: A comparative study of the entity enigma*. London: Thorsons.

Fangmeier, T., M. Knauff, C.C. Ruff, and V. Sloutsky (2006). fMRI Evidence for a three-stage model of deductive reasoning. *Journal of Cognitive Neuroscience*, 18 (3), 320–334.

Fenker, D.B., B.H. Schott, A. Richardson-Klavehn, H-J. Heinze, and E. Düzel (2005). Recapitulating emotional context: Activity of amygdala, hippocampus and fusiform cortex during recollection and familiarity. *European Journal of Neuroscience*, 21 (7), 1993–1999.

Ferenczi, S. (1916). On onanism. In *Sex in psycho-analysis; Contributions to psycho-analysis* (157–163) (translated by E. Jones). Boston: Richard G. Badger, Gorham Press.

Festinger, L. (1962). Cognitive dissonance. *Scientific American*, 207 (4), 93–107.

Fordham, F. (1953). *An introduction to Jung's psychology*. Oxford: Penguin.

Fosse, R., R. Stickgold, and A. Hobson (2004). Thinking and hallucinating: Reciprocal changes in sleep. *Psychophysiology*, 41, 298–305.

Fowler, R.E. (1980). *The Andreasson Affair*. New York: Bantam Books.

Fox, J., and C. Williams (2000). Paranormal belief, experience and the Keirsey temperament sorter. *Psychological Reports*, 86, 1104–1106.

Frankel, R.B., and R.P. Liburdy (1996). Biological effects of static magnetic fields. In C. Polk and E. Postow (eds.), *Biological effects of electromagnetic fields* (2nd ed.) (149–184). Boca Raton: CRC Press.

Freedman, D.J., H.U. Grunebaum, F.A. Stare, and M. Greenblatt (1962). Imagery in sensory deprivation. In L.J. West (ed.), *Hallucinations* (108–117). Oxford: Grune and Stratton.

Fukuda, K., R.D. Ogilvie, and T. Takeuchi (2000). Recognition of sleep paralysis among normal adults in Canada and in Japan. *Psychiatry and Clinical Neurosciences*, 54, 292–293.

Furuya, H., K. Ikezoe, H. Shigeto, Y. Ohyagi, H. Arahata, E. Araki, and N. Fujii (2009). Sleep- and non–sleep-related hallucinations — relationship to ghost tales and their classifications. *Dreaming*, 19 (4), 232–238.

Gallagher, C., V.K. Kumar, and R.J. Pekala (1994). The anomalous experiences inventory: Reliability and validity. *Journal of Parapsychology*, 58, 402–428.

Gangdev, P. (2004). Relevance of sleep paralysis and hypnagogic hallucinations to psychiatry. *Australasian Psychiatry*, 12 (1), 77–80.

Girard, T.A., and J.A. Cheyne (2004). Individual differences in lateralization of hallucinations associated with sleep paralysis. *Brain and Cognition*, 9 (1), 93–111.

Gonzales, W.D., J.A. Joselyn, Y. Kamide, H.W. Kroehl, G. Rostoker, B.T. Tsurutani, and V.M. Vasyliunas (1994). What is a geomagnetic storm? *Journal of Geophysical Research*, 99, 5771–5792.

Gordon, R. (1985). Losing and finding: The location of archetypal experience. *The Journal of Analytical Psychology*, 30 (2), 117–133.

Gordon, S. (1992). *The Paranormal*. London: Caxton.

Granqvist, P., M. Fredrikson, P. Unge, A. Hagenfeldt, S. Valind, D. Larhammar, and M. Larsson (2005). Sensed presence and mystical experiences are predicted by suggestibility, not by the application of transcranial weak complex magnetic fields. *Neuroscience Letters*, 379, 1–6.

Grimmer, M.R., and K.D. White (1990). The structure of paranormal beliefs among Australian psychology students. *Journal of Psychology*, 124 (4), 357–370.

Guedj, E., S. Aubert, A. McGonigal, O. Mundler, and F. Bartolomei (2010). Déjà-vu in temporal lobe epilepsy: Metabolic pattern of cortical involvement in patients with normal brain MRI. *Neuropsychologia*, 48 (7), 2174–2181.

Haines, R.F. (1980). *Observing UFOs: An investigative handbook*. Chicago: Nelson-Hall.

Hall, C.S. (1959). *A primer of Freudian psychology*. New York: Mentor Books.

Halligan, P.W., J.C. Marshall, and V.S. Ramachandran (1994). Ghosts in the machine: A case description of visual and haptic hallucinations after right hemisphere stroke. *Cognitive Neuropsychology*, 11 (4), 459–477.

Hancock, G. (2005). *Supernatural: Meeting with the ancient teachers of mankind.* London: Century.

Hansel, C.E.M. (1989). *The search for psychic power: ESP and parapsychology revisited.* Buffalo, N.Y.: Prometheus.

Haraldsson, E., and L.R. Gissurarson (1987). Does geomagnetic activity affect extrasensory perception? *Personality and Individual Differences*, 8 (5), 745–747.

Hardcastle, V.G. (1999). Multiplex vs. multiple selves: Distinguishing dissociative disorders. *Monist*, 82 (4), 645–658.

Harpur, P. (1994). *Daimonic reality: A field guide to the other world.* London: Viking Arkana.

Hartman, S.E. (1999). Another view of the paranormal belief scale. *Journal of Parapsychology*, 63 (2), 131–141.

Henderson, J.L. (1973). The picture method in Jungian psychotherapy. *Art Psychotherapy*, 1 (2), 135–140.

Hergovich, A. (2003). Field dependence, suggestibility and belief in paranormal phenomena. *Personality and Individual Differences*, 34, 195–209.

Hergovich, A. (2004). The effect of pseudo-psychic demonstrations as dependent on belief in paranormal phenomena and suggestibility. *Personality and Individual Differences*, 36 (2), 365–380.

Hergovich, A., R. Schott, and M. Arendasy (2005). Paranormal belief and religiosity. *Journal of Parapsychology*, 69, 293–303.

Hershenson, M., and R.N. Haber (1965). The role of meaning in the perception of briefly exposed words. *Canadian Journal of Psychology*, 19 (1), 42–46.

Hey, A.J.G., and P. Walters (2003). *The New Quantum Universe.* Cambridge, U.K: Cambridge University Press.

Heywood, R. (1974). *Beyond the reach of sense.* New York: E.P. Dutton.

Hines, T. (1988). *Pseudoscience and the paranormal: A critical examination of the evidence.* Buffalo, N.Y.: Prometheus.

Hobson, J.A., E.F. Pace-Schott, and R. Stickgold (1998). To dream or not to dream? Relevant data from new neuroimaging and electrophysiological studies. *Current Opinion in Neurobiology*, 8 (2), 239–244.

Holden, K.J., and C.C. French (2002). Alien abduction experiences: Some clues from neuropsychology and neuropsychiatry. *Cognitive Neuropsychiatry*, 7 (3), 163–178.

Hollingworth, H.L. (1911). The psychology of drowsiness: An introspective and analytical study. *The American Journal of Psychology*, 22 (1), 99–111.

Hollis, J.R. (1973). Convergent patterns in Yeats and Jung. *Psychological Perspectives*, 4 (1), 60–68.

Holroyd, S. (1980). *Alien intelligence.* London: Abacus.

Hough, P., and M. Kalman (1997). *The truth about alien abductions.* London: Blandford.

Houran, J. (1997). Predicting anomalous effects on film: An empirical test. *Perceptual and Motor Skills*, 84 (2), 691–694.

Houran, J. (1997). Tolerance of ambiguity and the perception of UFOs. *Perceptual and Motor Skills*, 85, 973–974.

Houran, J. (2000). Toward a psychology of "entity encounter experiences." *Journal of the Society for Psychical Research*, 64, 141–158.

Houran, J., D.D. Ashe, and M.A. Thalbourne (2003). Encounter experiences in the context of mental boundaries and bilaterality. *Journal of the Society for Psychical Research*, 67 (873), 260–280.

Houran, J., V.K. Kumar, M.A. Thalbourne, and N.E. Lavertue (2002). Haunted by somatic tendencies: Spirit infestation as psychogenic illness. *Mental Health, Religion and Culture*, 5 (2), 119–133.

Houran, J., M.A. Thalbourne, and D.D. Ashe (2000). Testing a psycho-anthropological view of paranormal belief and experience. *North American Journal of Psychology*, 2 (1), 127–138.

Houtkooper, J.M. (2003). An ESP experiment with natural and simulated sferics: Displacement scores and psychological variables. *European Journal of Parapsychology*, 18, 49–64.

Howe, M.L. (2000). Memory development from birth to 2 years of age. In M.L. Howe (ed.), *The fate of early memories: developmental science and the retention of childhood experiences* (19–33). Washington, D.C.: American Psychological Association.

Howe, M.L., and M.L. Courage (1993). On resolving the enigma of infantile amnesia. *Psychological Bulletin*, 113 (2), 305–326.

Hufford, D. (1982). *The terror that comes in the night*. Philadelphia: University of Pennsylvania Press.

Huston, H. (1999). The evolutionary significance of archetypal dreams. In D.H. Rosen and M.C. Luebbert (eds.), *Evolution of the Psyche* (188–195). Westport, CT: Greenwood.

Hyman, R. (1985). The ganzfeld psi experiment: A critical appraisal. *Journal of Parapsychology*, 49 (1), 3–49.

Hyman, R. (2010). Meta-analysis that conceals more than it reveals: Comment on Storm et al. (2010). *Psychological Bulletin*, 136 (4), 486–490.

Hynek, J.A. (1966). Are flying saucers real? *The Saturday Evening Post* (12/17/1966), 17–21.

Inglis, B. (1986). *The paranormal: An encyclopedia of psychic phenomena*. London: Paladin.

Ingram, J. (2003a). Did Jesus suffer from epilepsy? Scientist theorizes over resurrection. *Hamilton Spectator*, 11/4/2003.

Ingram, J. (2003b). Resurrection skeptic goes to baroque extremes. *Toronto Star*, 04/13/2003.

Ingram, J. (2004). Close encounters of the magnetic kind. *Toronto Star*, 12/26/2004.

Irwin, H. (1986). Personality and psi performance: directions of current research. *Parapsychology Review*, 17 (5), 1–5.

Irwin, H.J. (1991). Reasoning skills of paranormal believers. *Journal of Parapsychology*, 55, 281–300.

Irwin, H.J. (1993). Belief in the paranormal: A review of the empirical literature. *Journal of the American Society for Psychical Research*, 87 (1), 1–39.

Irwin, H.J., and M.J. Green (1998). Schizotypal processes and belief in the paranormal: A multidimensional study. *European Journal of Parapsychology*, 14, 1–15.

Irwin, H.J., M.J. Green (1999). Schizotypal processes and belief in the paranormal: A multidimensional study. *European Journal of Parapsychology*, 14, 1–15.

Ivey, G. (2002). Diabolical discourses: Demonic possession and evil in modern psychopathology. *South African Journal of Psychology*, 32 (4), 54–59.

Jacome, D.E. (1999). Volitional monocular lilliputian visual hallucinations and synesthesia. *European Journal of Neurology*, 41, 54–56.

Jawer, M. (2006). Environmental sensitivity: A link with apparitional experience? *Journal of the Society for Psychical Research*, 70 (882), 25–47.

Johnston, J.C., H.P. DeGroot, and N.P. Spanos (1994). The structure of paranormal belief: A factor-analytic approach. *Imagination Cognition and Personality*. 14 (2), 165–174.

Johnston, M.J.S. (1989). Review of magnetic and electric field effects near active faults and volcanoes in the U.S.A. *Physics of the Earth and Planetary Interiors*, 57, 47–63.

Joseph, R. (2001). The limbic system and the soul: Evolution and the neuroanatomy of religious experience. *Zygon*, 36 (1), 105–136.

Jung, C.G. (1959). A visionary rumour. *Journal of Analytical Psychology*, 4 (1), 5–19.

Jung, C.G. (1960). *Collected Works*. Vol. 8. *The structure and dynamics of the psyche*. Oxford: Pantheon.

Jung, C.G. (1960). *Synchronicity, an acausal connecting principle.* Oxford: Pantheon.

Jung, C.G., and A. Jaffe (1961/1989). *Memories, dreams, reflections.* New York: Vintage Books.

Jung, C.G., and A. Jaffe (ed.) (1963/1989). *Memories, dreams, reflections.* New York: Random House.

Kamogawa, M., H. Ofuruton, and Y-H. Ohtsuki (2005). Earthquake light: 1995 Kobe earthquake in Japan. *Atmospheric Research,* 76, 438–444.

Kasper, B.S., E.M. Kasper, E. Pauli, and H. Stefan (2010). Phenomenology of hallucinations, illusions, and delusions as part of seizure semiology. *Epilepsy and Behavior,* 18 (1–2), 13–23.

Keel, J. (1971/1975). *Our haunted planet.* London: Futura.

Keel, J. (1975/1976). *Strange creatures from time and space.* London: Sphere Books.

Kennedy, J.E. (2001). Why is PSI so elusive? A review and proposed model. *The Journal of Parapsychology,* 65 (3), 219–246.

Kennedy, J.E. (2005). Personality and motivations to believe, misbelieve, and disbelieve in paranormal phenomena. *Journal of Parapsychology,* 69 (2), 263–292.

Kerckhoff, A.C., K.W. Back, and N. Miller (1965). Sociometric patterns in hysterical contagion. *Sociometry,* 28 (1), 2–15.

Keschner, M., M.B., Binder, and I. Strauss (1938). Localized tactile hallucinations indicate tumor of the opposite parietal lobe. Mental symptoms associated with brain tumors. *Journal of the American Medical Association,* 110, 714–718.

King, L.A., C.M., Burton, J.A. Hicks, and S.M. Drigotas (2007). Ghosts, UFOs, and magic: Positive affect and the experiential system. *Journal of Personality and Social Psychology,* 92, 905–919.

Kirby, C. (2005). Ghost hunters utilize latest technology; paranormal research has become a popular pursuit. *San Francisco Chronicle,* 31 October 2005.

Klass, P. (1997). A field guide to UFOs. *Astronomy,* 25 (9), 31–35.

Knight, R.T., M.F. Grabowecky, and D. Scabini (1995). Role of human prefrontal cortex in attention control. *Advances in Neurology,* 66, 21–34.

Koch, C., and F. Crick (2001). The zombie within. *Nature,* 411 (6840), 893.

Koren, S., and M.A. Persinger (2002). Possible disruption of remote viewing by complex weak magnetic fields around the stimulus site and the possibility of accessing real phase space: A pilot study. *Perceptual and Motor Skills,* 95 (3), 989–998.

Kottmeyer, M. (2006). Letters to ye olde editor, *Saucer Smear,* 53 (2), 25/2/2006.

Kottmeyer, M.S. (2001). Grays. In R.D. Story (ed.), *The Mammoth Encyclopedia of Extraterrestrial Encounters* (273–281). London: Constable and Robinson.

Krippner, S., and J. Achterberg (2000). Anomalous healing experiences. In E. Cardeña, S.J. Lynn, and S. Krippner (eds.), *Varieties of anomalous experience: Examining the scientific evidence* (353–395). Washington, D.C.: American Psychological Association.

Krippner, S.C. (2002). Conflicting perspectives on shamans and shamanism: Points and counterpoints. *American Psychologist,* 57 (11), 3–66.

Kuhlmann, F. (1906). On the analysis of the memory consciousness: A study in the mental imagery and memory of meaningless visual forms. *Psychological Review,* 13 (5), 316–348.

Lachman, G. (2002). Waking sleep. *Fortean Times,* 163.

Lampe, P. (1993). Instrumental communication with the dead. *Journal of Religion and Psychical Research,* 16 (2), 143–148.

Lange, R., and J.M. Houran (1997). Death anxiety and the paranormal: The primacy of belief over experience. *Journal of Nervous & Mental Disease,* 185 (9), 584–586.

Lange, R., and J. Houran (1998). Delusions of the paranormal: A haunting question of perception. *Journal of Nervous and Mental Disease,* 186 (10), 637–645.

Lange, R., and J. Houran (1999). The role of fear in delusions of the paranormal. *Journal of Nervous and Mental Disease,* 187, 159–166.

Lange, R., J. Houran, and T.M. Harte (1996). Contextual mediation of perceptions in hauntings and poltergeist-like experiences. *Perceptual and Motor Skills*, 82 (3/1), 755–762.

Law, S., and L.J. Kirmayer (2005). Inuit interpretations of sleep paralysis. *Transcultural Psychiatry*, 42 (1), 93–112.

Lawrence, T.R. (1995). How many factors of paranormal belief are there? A critique of the paranormal belief scale. *Journal of Parapsychology*, 59, 3–25.

Lawson, A.H. (1984). Perinatal imagery in UFO abduction reports. *The Journal of Psychohistory*, 12 (2), 211–239.

Lawson, A.L. (2001a). In R.D. Story (ed.), *The Mammoth Encyclopedia of Extraterrestrial Encounters* (368–369). London: Constable and Robinson.

Lawson, A.L. (2001b). Alien roots. In R.D. Story (ed.), *The Mammoth Encyclopedia of Extraterrestrial Encounters* (39–53). London: Constable and Robinson.

Lawson, A.L. (2001c). Birth memories hypothesis. In R.D. Story (ed.), *The Mammoth Encyclopedia of Extraterrestrial Encounters* (129–132). London: Constable and Robinson.

Lazar, S.G. (2001). Knowing, influencing, and healing: Paranormal phenomena and implications for psychoanalysis and psychotherapy. *Psychoanalytic Inquiry*, 21 (1), 113–131.

LeDoux, J.E. (1994). The amygdala: Contributions to fear and stress. *Seminars in the Neurosciences* 6, 231–237.

Lee, A., and R.L. Lee (1972). Evaluation of the status inconsistency theory of UFO sightings. *Catalog of Selected Documents in Psychology*, Spring, 66.

Loftus, E.F. (1975). Leading questions and the eyewitness report. *Cognitive Psychology*, 7, 560–572.

Luke, D.P. (2008). Psychedelic substances and paranormal phenomena: A review of the research. *Journal of Parapsychology*, 72 (1), 77–107.

Luke, D.P., and M.A. Kittenis (2005). Preliminary survey of paranormal experiences with psychoactive drugs. *Journal of Parapsychology*, 69 (2), 305–327.

Lynn, S.J., and J.W. Rhue (1986). The fantasy-prone person: Hypnosis, imagination, and creativity. *Journal of Personality and Social Psychology*, 51 (2), 404–408.

Lysenko, N., and G. Barilo (1983). Dermo-optic sensitivity of human beings in the long-wave range of the visible spectrum. *Psi Research*, 2 (4), 39–43.

Mach, Q.H., and M.A. Persinger, (2009). Behavioral changes with brief exposures to weak magnetic fields patterned to stimulate long-term potentiation. *Brain Research*, 1261, 45–53.

MacRae, A. (2004). A means of producing the electronic voice phenomenon based on electro-dermal activity. *Journal of the Society for Psychical Research*, 68 (1), 35–50.

MacRae, A. (2005). Report of an electronic voice phenomenon experiment inside a double-screened room. *Journal of the Society for Psychical Research*, 69 (4), 191–201.

Maduro, R.J. (1987). The initial dream and analysability in beginning analysis. *Journal of Analytical Psychology*, 32 (3), 199–226.

Maher, B.A. (1974). Delusional thinking and perceptual disorder. *Journal of Individual Psychology*, 30, 98–113.

Maher, M.C. (1999). Riding the waves in search of the particles: A modern study of ghosts and apparitions. *Journal of Parapsychology*, 63, 47–80.

Maher, M.C. (2000). Quantitative investigation of the General Wayne Inn. *Journal of Parapsychology*, 64 (4), 365–390.

Maher, M.C., and G.P. Hansen (1992). Quantitative investigation of a reported haunting using several detection techniques. *Journal of the American Society for Psychical Research*, 86 (4), 347–374.

Maher, M.C., and G.P. Hansen (1995). Quantitative investigation of a "haunted castle" in New Jersey. *Journal of the American Society for Psychical Research*, 89 (1), 19–50.

Maher, M.C., and G.R. Schmeidler (1975). Quantitative investigation of a recurrent apparition. *Journal of the American Society for Psychical Research*, 69 (4), 341–351.

Mahowald, M.W., S.R. Woods, and C.H. Schenk (1998). Sleeping dreams, waking hallucinations, and the central nervous system. *Dreaming*, 8 (2), 89–102.

Maillard, L., J-P. Vignal, M. Gavaret, M. Guye, A. Biraben, A. McGonigal, P. Chauvel, and F. Bortolomei (2004). Semiologic and electrophysiologic correlations in temporal lobe seizure subtypes. *Epilepsia*, 45 (12), 1590–1599.

Maleval, C., and N. Charraud (2003). The "alien abduction" syndrome. In N. Totton (ed.), *Psychoanalysis and the paranormal: Lands of darkness* (104–142). London: Karnac.

Manford, M., and S.D. Shorvon (1992). Prolonged sensory or visceral symptoms: An under-diagnosed form of non-convulsive focal (simple partial) status epilepticus. *Journal of Neurology, Neurosurgery and Psychiatry*, 55 (8), 714–716.

Mansfield, V., S. Rhine-Feather, and J. Hall (1998). The Rhine-Jung letters: Distinguishing parapsychological from synchronistic events. *Journal of Parapsychology*, 62, 3–25.

Markwick, B. (1978). The Soal-Goldney experiments with Basil Shackleton: New evidence of data manipulation. *Proceedings of the Society for Psychical Research*, 56 (211), 250–277.

Martin-Del Pozzo, A.L., G. Cifuentes-Nava, E. Cabral-Cano, G. Sánchez-Rubio, M. Reyes, A. Martínez-Bringas, E. Garcia, and C. Arango-Galvan (2002). Volcanomagnetic signals during the recent Popocatépetl (México) eruptions and their relation to eruptive activity. *Journal of Volcanology and Geothermal Research*, 113 (3–4), 415–428.

Maso, I. (2006). Toward a panpsychistic foundation of paranormal phenomena. *European Journal of Parapsychology*, 21 (1), 3–26.

Mason, O.J., and F. Brady (2009). The psychotomimetic effects of short-term sensory deprivation. *Journal of Nervous and Mental Disease*, 197 (10), 783–785.

May, E.C. (2001). Towards the physics of psi: Correlation with physical variables. *European Journal of Parapsychology*, 16, 42–52.

May, E.C., and N.D. Lantz (2010). Anomalous cognition technical trials: Inspiration for the target entropy concept. *Journal of the Society for Psychical Research*, 74 (4), 225–243.

McClenon, J., M. Roig, M.D. Smith, and G. Ferrier (2003). The coverage of parapsychology in introductory psychology textbooks: 1990–2002. *Journal of Parapsychology*, 67 (1), 167–179.

McLeod, C.C., B. Corbisier, and J.E. Mack (1996). A more parsimonious explanation for UFO abduction. *Psychological Inquiry*, 7 (2), 156–168.

McNally, R.J., and S.A. Clancy (2005). Sleep paralysis, sexual abuse and space alien abduction. *Transcultural Psychiatry*, 42 (1), 113–122.

Menon, G.J., I. Rahman, S. Menon, and G.N. Dutton (2003). Complex visual hallucinations in the visually impaired: The Charles Bonnet syndrome. *Survey of Ophthalmology*, 48 (1), 58–72.

Merla-Ramos, M. (1999). Belief and reasoning: The effects of beliefs on syllogistic reasoning. *Dissertation Abstracts International*, 61 (1), 558-B.

Milton, J. (1988). Critical review of the displacement effect: I. The relationship between displacement and scoring on the intended target. *Journal of Parapsychology*, 52 (1), 29–55.

Milton, J., and R. Wiseman (1999). Does psi exist? Lack of replication of an anomalous process of information transfer. *Psychological Bulletin*, 125 (4), 387–391.

Monaco, F., M. Mula, and A.E. Cavanna (2005). Consciousness, epilepsy and emotional qualia. *Epilepsy and Behavior*, 7, 150–160.

Munakata, Y. (2004). Computational cognitive neuroscience of early memory development. *Developmental Review*, 24 (1), 133–153.

Mundle, C.W. (1974). The Soal-Goldney experiments. *Proceedings of the Society for Psychical Research*, 56 (209), 85–87.

Murdie, A. (2010). Case note: The case of the ghostly bailiff. *Journal of the Society for Psychical Research*, 74 (9), 244–245.

Murphy, G. (1943). Psychical phenomena and human needs. *The Journal of the American Society for Psychical research*, 37, 163–191.

Musch, J., and K. Ehrenberg (2002). Probability misjudgment, cognitive ability and belief in the paranormal. *British Journal of Psychology*, 93, 169–177.

Needham, W.E., and R.E. Taylor (2000). Atypical Charles Bonnet hallucinations: An elf in the woodshed, a spirit of evil, and the cowboy malefactors. *The Journal of Nervous and Mental Disease*, 188 (2), 108–115.

Nelson, A. (1976). Orgone (Reichian) therapy in tension headache. *American Journal of Psychotherapy*, 30 (1), 103–111.

Neppe, V.M. (1983). Anomalies of smell in the subjective paranormal experient. *Psychoenergetics*, 5, 11–27.

Newman, L.S., and R.F. Baumeister (1996a). Towards an explanation of the UFO abduction phenomenon: Hypnotic elaboration, extraterrestrial sadomasochism, and spurious memories. *Psychological Inquiry*, 7 (2), 99–126.

Newman, L.S., and R.F. Baumeister (1996b). Not just another false memory: Further thoughts on the UFO abduction phenomenon. *Psychological Inquiry*, 7 (2), 185–197.

Nickell, J. (2005). Mystical experiences: Magnetic fields or suggestibility? *Skeptical Inquirer* 29 (5), 14–15.

Nishino, S., J. Riehl, J. Hong, M. Kwan, M. Reid, and E. Mignot (2000). Is narcolepsy a REM sleep disorder? Analysis of sleep abnormalities in narcoleptic dobermans. *Neuroscience Research*, 38, 437–446.

Norenzayan, A., and I.G. Hansen (2006). Belief in supernatural agents in the face of death. *Personality and Social Psychology Bulletin*, 32 (2), 174–187.

Noyes, R. (1989). Entities: Is there a pecking order? *Journal of the Society for Psychical Research*, 55 (814), 278–281.

Nunn, C.M.H. (1998). Archetypes and memes: Their structure, relationships and behavior. *Journal of Consciousness Studies*, 5 (3), 344–354.

Ogata, A., and T. Miyakawa (1998). Religious experiences in epileptic patients with a focus on ictus-related episodes. *Psychiatry and Clinical Neurosciences*, 52, 321–325.

Ohayon, M.M., J. Zulley, C. Guilleminault, and S. Smirne (1999). Prevalence and pathologic associations of sleep paralysis in the general population. *Neurology*, 52, 1194–1200.

Okami, P., R. Olmstead, P.R. Abramson, and L. Pendleton (1998). Early childhood exposure to parental nudity and scenes of parental sexuality ("primal scenes"): An 18-year longitudinal study of outcome. *Archives of Sexual Behavior*, 27 (4), 361–384.

Olkinuora, M. (1984). Psychogenic epidemics and work. *Scandinavian Journal of Work, Environment and Health*, 10 (6), 501–504.

Page, J. (1935). Superstition and personality. *Journal of Educational Psychology*, 26, 59–64.

Palmer, J., and V.M. Neppe (2003). A controlled analysis of subjective paranormal experiences in temporal lobe dysfunction in a neuropsychiatric population. *Journal of Parapsychology* 67, 75–97.

Palmer, J., C.A. Simmonds-Moore, and S. Baumann (2006). Geomagnetic fields and the relationship between human intentionality and the hemolysis of red blood cells. *Journal of Parapsychology*, 70 (2), 275–301.

Paltry, A.L., and L.C. Pelletier (2001). Extraterrestrial belief and experiences: An application of the theory of reasoned action. *Journal of Social Psychology*, 141 (2), 199–217.

Parker, A. (1991). Book review. *The Journal of Parapsychology*, 55, 90–95.

Parnell, J. (1988). Measured personality characteristics of persons who claim UFO experiences. *Psychotherapy in Private Practice*, 6 (3), 159–165.

Parra, A. (2006). "Seeing and feeling ghosts": absorption, fantasy proneness, and healthy schizotypy as predictors of crisis apparition experiences. *Journal of Parapsychology*, 70 (2), 357–372.

Parra, A., and L.E. Paul (2010). Extrasensory experience and hallucinatory experience:

Comparison between two non-clinical samples linked with psychological measures. *Journal of the Society for Psychical Research*, 74 (3), 145–155.

Partridge, C. (2004). Alien demonology: The Christian roots of the malevolent extraterrestrial in UFO religions and abduction spiritualities. *Religion*, 34, 163–189.

Pauli, G., J.C. Badcock, and M.T. Maybery (2006). The multifactorial structure of the predisposition to hallucinate and associations with anxiety, depression and stress. *Personality and Individual Differences*, 41 (6), 1067–1076.

Pelizzon, L., M.A. Brandimonte, and R. Luccio (2002). The role of visual, spatial, and temporal cues in attenuating verbal overshadowing. *Applied Cognitive Psychology*, 16 (8), 947–961.

Perez-Navarro, J.M., T. Lawrence, and I.R. Hume (2009). Personality, mental state and procedure in the experimental replication of ESP: A preliminary study of new variables. *Journal of the Society for Psychical Research*, 73 (1), 17–32.

Persinger, M.A. (1975). Geophysical models for parapsychological experiences. *Psychoenergetic Systems*, 1, 63–74.

Persinger, M.A. (1979). Possible infrequent geophysical sources of close UFO encounters: Expected physical and behavioral-biological effects. In R.F. Haines (ed.), *UFO phenomena and the behavioral scientist* (396–433). New Jersey: Methuen.

Persinger, M.A. (1990). The tectonic strain theory as an explanation for UFO phenomena: A non-technical review of the research 1970–1990. *Journal of UFO Studies*, 2, 105–137.

Persinger, M.A. (1991). Subjective pseudocyesis (false pregnancy) and elevated temporal lobe signs: An implication. *Perceptual and Motor Skills*, 72 (2), 499–503.

Persinger, M.A. (1993). Vectorial cerebral hemisphericity as differential sources for the sensed presence, mystical experiences and religious conversions. *Perceptual and Motor Skills*, 76 (3), 915–930.

Persinger, M.A. (1996). Subjective pseudocyesis in normal women who exhibit enhanced imaginings and elevated indicators of electrical lability within the temporal lobes: Implications for the "missing embryo syndrome." *Social Behavior and Personality*, 24 (2), 101–112.

Persinger, M.A. (2001). The neuropsychiatry of paranormal experiences. *Journal of Neuropsychiatry and Clinical Neurosciences*, 13 (4), 515–523.

Persinger, M.A. (2003). The sensed presence within experimental settings: Implications for the male and female concept of self. *Journal of Psychology*, 137 (1), 5–12.

Persinger, M.A., (2004). Sense of a presence and suicidal ideation following traumatic brain injury: Indications of right-hemispheric intrusions from neuropsychological profiles. *Psychology Reports*, 75, 1059–1070.

Persinger, M.A., and R.A. Cameron (1986). Are earth faults at fault in some poltergeist-like episodes? *Journal of the American Society for Psychical Research*, 80, 49–73.

Persinger, M.A., and K. Makarec (1986). Temporal lobe epileptic signs and correlative behaviours displayed by normal populations. *Journal of General Psychology*, 114, 179–195.

Persinger, M.A., V. Hoang, and L. Baker-Price (2009). Entrainment of stage 2 sleep spindles by weak, transcerebral magnetic stimulation in an "epileptic" woman. *Electromagnetic Biology and Medicine*, 28 (4), 374–82.

Persinger, M.A., and K. Makarec (1987). Temporal lobe epileptic signs and correlative behaviors displayed by normal populations. *Journal of General Psychology*, 114 (2), 179–195.

Persinger, M.A., and K. Makarec (1993). Complex partial epileptic signs as a continuum from normals to epileptics: Normative data and clinical populations. *Journal of Clinical Psychology*, 49 (1) 33–45.

Persinger, M.A., K. Saroka, S.A. Koren, and L.S. St.-Pierre (2010). The electromagnetic induction of mystical and altered states within the laboratory. *Journal of Consciousness Exploration and Research*, 1 (7), 808–830.

Persinger, M.A., S.G. Tiller, and S.A. Koren (2000). Experimental stimulation of a haunt experience and elicitation of paroxysmal electroencephalographic activity by transcerebral complex magnetic fields: Induction of a synthetic "ghost"? *Perceptual and Motor Skills*, 90, 659–674.

Persinger, M., and S. Koren (2005). A response to Granqvist et al. "Sensed presence and mystical experiences are predicted by suggestibility, not by the application of transcranial weak magnetic fields." *Neuroscience Letters*. 379 (1), 346–347.

Phillips, A. (1995). *Terrors and experts*. London: Faber and Faber.

Phillips, G. (2001). Truth behind alien notions. *Sunday Telegraph* (Sydney), 05/13/2001.

Pietikainen, P. (2002). Utopianism in psychology: The case of Wilhelm Reich. *Journal of the History of the Behavioral Sciences*, 38 (2), 157–175.

Pinkney, J. (2003). *Great Australian mysteries: Unsolved, unexplained, unknown*. Rowville, Victoria: Five Mile Press.

Pizzagalli, D., D. Lehmann, L. Gianotti, T. Koenig, H. Tanaka, and J. Wackermann, and P. Brugger (2000). Brain electric correlates of strong belief in paranormal phenomena: Intracerebral EEG source and regional Omega complexity analyses. *Psychiatry Research: Neuroimaging*, 100 (3), 139–154.

Pizzagalli, D., D. Lehmann, and P. Brugger (2001). Lateralized direct and indirect semantic priming effects in subjects with paranormal experiences and beliefs. *Psychopathology*, 34, 75–80.

Pizzagalli, D., D. Lehmann, L. Gianotti, T. Koenig, H. Tanaka, J. Wackermann, and P. Brugger (2000). Brain electric correlates of strong belief in paranormal phenomena: Intracerebral EEG source and regional omega complexity analyses. *Psychiatry Research: Neuroimaging Section*, 100, 139–154.

Plug, C. (1975). An investigation of superstitious belief and behavior. *Journal of Behavioral Science*, 2 (4), 169–178.

Pontius, A.A. (1996). Forensic significance of the limbic psychotic trigger reaction. *Bulletin of the American Academy of Psychiatry and the Law*, 24 (1), 125–134.

Postow E., and M.L. Swicord (1996). Modulated fields and "window" effects. In C. Polk and E. Postow (eds.), *Biological Effects of Electromagnetic Fields* (2nd ed.) (535–580). Boca Raton: CRC Press.

Pratt, J.G. (1978). Prologue to a debate: Some assumptions relevant to research in parapsychology. *Journal of the American Society for Parapsychological Research*, 72, 127–139.

Price, G.R. (1955). Science and the supernatural. *Science*, 122, 359–367.

Puthoff, H., and R. Targ (1978). *Mind-reach*. New York: Delacorte.

Rae, A. (1995). *Quantum physics: Illusion or reality?* (2nd ed). Cambridge, U.K.: Cambridge University Press.

Ramachandran, V.S., and S. Blakeslee (1998). *Phantoms in the brain*. London: Fourth Estate.

Randi, J. (1997). *The supernatural A–Z: The truth and the lies*. London: Brockhampton Press.

Randi, J. (1998). The matter of dowsing. *Skeptic*, 6 (4), 6–8.

Randle, K. (1999). *Scientific Ufology*. New York: Avon.

Randles, J., and P. Hough (1997). *The complete book of UFOs: Fifty years of alien contacts and encounters*. London: Judy Piatkus.

Ranney, T.A. (1994). Models of driving behavior: A review of their evolution. *Accident Analysis and Prevention*, 26 (6), 733–750.

Reed, G. (1972). *The psychology of anomalous experience: A cognitive approach*, Oxford: Hutchinson University Library.

Reiner, A. (2004). Psychic phenomena and early emotional states. *Journal of Analytical Psychology*, 49, 313–336.

Rhead, G. (2001). Evidence for millimeter-wave radiation associated with paranormal activity. *Journal of the Society for Psychical Research*, 65,138–145.

Rhine, J.B. (1934). *Extra-sensory perception*. Boston: Boston Society for Psychic Research.

Ring, K. (1989). Near-death and UFO encounters as shamanic initiations. *ReVision*, 11 (3), 1–22.

Roach, M. (2005). *Spook: Science tackles the afterlife*. New York: W.W. Norton.

Rockney, R.M., and T. Lemke (1992). Casualties from a junior-senior high school during the Persian Gulf War: Toxic poisoning or mass hysteria? *Journal of Developmental and Behavioral Pediatrics*, 13 (5), 339–342.

Rodeghier, M., J. Goodpaster, and S. Blatterbauer (1991). Psychosocial characteristics of abductees: Results from the CUFOS abduction project. *Journal of UFO Studies*, 3, 59–90.

Roe, C.A., R. Davey, and P. Stevens (2003). Are ESP and PK aspects of a unitary phenomenon? A preliminary test of the relationship between ESP and PK. *Journal of Parapsychology*, 67 (2), 343–366.

Roediger, H.L., and K.B. McDermott (1995). Creating false memories: Remembering words not presented in lists. *Journal of Experimental Psychology*, 21 (4), 803–814.

Rogo, D. Scott (ed.) (1980). *UFO abductions: True cases of alien kidnappings*. New York: Signet.

Rogo, D.S. (1983/2001). Rogo hypothesis. In R.D. Story (ed.), *The mammoth encyclopedia of extraterrestrial encounters* (594–605). London: Constable and Robinson.

Rogo, D.S. (1996). Secret language of UFO abductions — a speculation. *International UFO Reporter*, 10 (4), 8–11.

Roig, M., K.R. Bridges, C.H. Renner, and C.R. Jackson (1998). Belief in the paranormal and its association with irrational thinking controlled for context effects. *Personality and Individual Differences*, 24 (2), 229–236.

Roll, W.G., M.A. Persinger, D.L. Webster, S.G. Tiller, and C.M. Cook (2002). Neurobehavioral and neurometabolic (spect) correlates of paranormal information: Involvement of the right hemisphere and its sensitivity to weak complex magnetic fields. *International Journal of Neuroscience*, 112 (2), 197–224.

Rosen, D.H., S.M. Smith, and H.L. Huston (1991). Empirical study of associations between symbols and their meanings: Evidence of collective unconscious (archetypal) memory. *Journal of Analytical Psychology*, 36 (2), 211–228.

Ross, C.A., and S. Joshi (1992). Paranormal experiences in the general population. *Journal of Nervous and Mental Disease*, 180 (6), 357–361.

Ross, M.L., S.A. Koren, and M.A. Persinger (2008). Physiologically patterned weak magnetic fields applied over left frontal lobe increase acceptance of false statements as true. *Electromagnetic Biology and Medicine*, 27, 365–371.

Rudski, J. (2001).Competition, superstition and the illusion of control. *Current Psychology*, 20 (1), 68–85.

Rudski, J. (2004). The illusion of control, superstitious belief, and optimism. *Current Psychology: Developmental, Learning, Personality, Social*, 22 (4), 306–315.

Rullán, A.F. (2000). *Odors from UFOs: Deducing odorant chemistry and causation from available data, preliminary report*. Martinez, CA.

Rutkowski, C.A. (1984). Geophysical variables and human behaviour: XVI Some criticisms. *Perceptual and Motor Skills*, 58, 840–842.

Sadler, R.M., and S. Rahey (2004). Prescience as an aura of temporal lobe epilepsy. *Epilepsia*, 45 (8), 982–984.

Sagan, C. (1996). *The demon-haunted world*. London: Headline Publishing.

Scheidt, R.J. (1973). Belief in supernatural phenomena and locus of control. *Psychological Reports*, 32, 1159–1162.

Schlitz, M., and E. Gruber (1980). Transcontinental remote viewing. *Journal of Parapsychology*, 44 (4), 305–317.

Schnabel, J. (1995). *Dark white: Aliens, abductions and the UFO obsession*. London: Penguin.

Schredl, M. (2009). Home dream recall in children and young adults. *International Journal of Dream Research*, 2, 58–59.

Schulman, C.A., and M. Richlin (1967). Hallucinations and disturbances of affect, cognition, and physical state as a function of sensory deprivation. *Perceptual and Motor Skills*, 25 (3), 1001–1024.

Sebastian, K.A., and G.V. Mathew (2001). Personality correlates of psi experience. *Journal of Indian Psychology*, 19 (1–2), 21–24.

Self, W. (1997). The Edison of the toolshed orgasm. *Spy Magazine*, 11 (5), 34.

Serafetinides, E.A. (1993). Cerebral dominance, sleep and dream phenomena. *International Journal of Neuroscience*, 71 (1–4), 63–70.

Servan-Schreiber, D., W.M. Perlstein, J.D. Cohen, and M. Mintun (1998). Selective pharmacological activation of limbic structures in human volunteers: A positron emission tomography study. *Neuropsychiatry and Clinical Neuroscience*, 10, 148–159.

Shermer, M. (1997). *Why people believe weird things: Pseudoscience, superstition, and other confusions of our time.* New York: W.H. Freeman.

Shermer, M. (2005). Abducted. *Scientific American*, 292 (2), 34.

Sherwood, S.J. (2002). Relationship between the hypnogogic/hypnopompic state and reports of anomalous experiences. *Journal of Parapsychology*, 66 (2), 127–150.

Shiraishi, Y., T. Terao, K. Ibi, J. Nakamura, and A. Tawara (2004). The rarity of Charles Bonnet syndrome. *Journal of Psychiatry Research*, 38 (2), 207–13.

Simmonds-Moore, C.A., and S.L. Moore (2009). Exploring how gender role and boundary thinness relate to paranormal experiences, beliefs and performance on a forced-choice clairvoyance task. *Journal of the Society for Psychical Research*, 73 (3), 129–149.

Skinner, B.F. (1948). "Superstition" in the pigeon. *Journal of Experimental Psychology*, 38, 168–172.

Slawinski, J. (1987). Electromagnetic radiation and the afterlife. *Journal of Near Death Studies*, 6, 79–93.

Snel, F.W.J.J., P.C. van der Sijde, and F.A.C. Wiegant (1995). Cognitive styles of believers and disbelievers in paranormal phenomena. *Journal of the Society for Psychical Research*, 60 (839), 251–257.

Snowden, R.J., and N.S. Gray (2010). Temperament and character as a function of psychopathy: Relationships between the psychopathy checklist-revised and the temperament and character inventory in a sample of personality disordered serious or repeat offenders. *Journal of Forensic Psychiatry and Psychology*, 21 (6), 815–833.

Solomon, P., and J. Mendelson (1962). Hallucinations in sensory deprivation. In L.J. West (ed.), *Hallucinations* (135–145). Oxford: Grune & Stratton.

Sommerhoff, G. (2000). *Understanding consciousness: Its function and brain processes.* London: Sage.

Sorenson, K. (1990). The intelligence behind taped voice phenomena. *Journal of Religion and Psychical Research*, 13 (3), 129–132.

Spanos, N.P., P.A. Cross, K. Dickson, and S.C. DuBreuil (1993). Close encounters: An examination of UFO experiences. *Journal of Abnormal Psychology*, 102 (4), 624–632.

Spanos, N.P., S.A. McNulty, S.C. DuBreuil, M. Piries, and M.F. Burgess (1995). The frequency and correlates of sleep paralysis in a university sample. *Journal of Research in Personality*, 29, 285–305.

Spatt, J. (2002). Déjà vu: Possible parahippocampal mechanisms. *Journal of Neuropsychiatry and Clinical Neurosciences*, 4 (1), 6–10.

Spencer, J. (1991). *The UFO encyclopedia.* New York: Avon Books.

Spiro, M.E. (1953). Ifaluk ghosts: An anthropological inquiry into learning and perception. *Journal of Abnormal and Social Psychology*, 48, 376–382.

Stanislaw, Grof (1975). *Realms of human unconscious, observations from LSD research.* New York: Viking Press.

Steiner, J., and A. Jinks (2006). The effect of the label "UFO" on memory for ambiguous pictorial stimuli. *Journal of UFO Studies*, 9, 31–41.

Steinfeld, G.J. (1967). Concept of set and availability and their relation to the reorganization of ambiguous pictorial stimuli. *Psychological Review*, 74 (6), 505–522.

Stores, G. (1998). Sleep paralysis and hallucinosis. *Behavioral Neurology*, 11, 109–112.

Storm, L. (1999). Synchronicity, causality and acausality. *The Journal of Parapsychology*, 63 (3), 247–270.

Storm, L., P.E. Tressoldi, and L. Di Risio (2010a). Meta-analysis of free-response studies, 1992–2008: assessing the noise reduction model in parapsychology. *Psychological Bulletin*, 136 (4), 471–485.

Storm, L., P.E. Tressoldi, and L. Di Risio (2010b). A meta-analysis with nothing to hide: Reply to Hyman (2010b). *Psychological Bulletin*, 136 (4), 491–494.

Strean, H.S., and M.C. Nelson (1962). A further clinical illustration of the paranormal triangle hypothesis. *Psychoanalysis and the Psychoanalytic Review*, 49 (3), 61–73.

Suedfeld, P., and J. Vernon (1964). Visual hallucinations in sensory deprivation: A problem of criteria. *Science*, 145, 412–413.

Swami, V., T. Chamorro-Premuzic, and M. Shafi (2010). Psychology in outerspace: Personality, individual difference, and demographic predictors of beliefs about extraterrestrial life. *European Psychologist*, 15 (3), 220–228.

Takeda, Y., Y. Inoue, T. Tottoi, and T. Mihara (2001). Acute psychosis during intracranial EEG monitoring: close relationship between psychotic symptoms and discharges in amygdala. *Epilepsia*, 42 (6), 719–724.

Targ, R. (1996). Remote viewing at Stanford Research Institute in the 1970s: A memoir. *Journal of Scientific Exploration*, 10 (1), 77–88.

Tart, C.T. (1998). Six studies of out-of-body experiences. *Journal of Near-Death Studies*, 17 (2), 73–99.

Tatarelli, R. (2010). A woman lost in the cemetery: A case of time-limited amnesia. *Neurocase*, 16 (1), 23–30.

Teguis, A., and C.P. Flynn (1983). Dealing with demons: psychosocial dynamics of paranormal occurrences. *Journal of Humanistic Psychology*, 23 (4), 59–75.

Tenforde, T.S. (1996). Interaction of ELF magnetic fields with living systems. In C. Polk and E. Postow (eds.), *Biological Effects of Electromagnetic Fields* (2nd ed.) (185–230). Boca Raton: CRC Press.

Thalbourne, M. (2010). Some thoughts on the happy schizotype. *The Journal of the Society for Psychical Research*, 74 (3), 246–250.

Thalbourne, M.A. (1996). Belief in life after death: Psychological origins and influences. *Personality and Individual Differences*, 21 (6), 1043–1045.

Thalbourne, M.A. (2001). Measures of the sheep-goat variable, transliminality, and their correlates. *Psychological Reports*, 88 (2), 339–350.

Thalbourne, M.A., K.A. Dunbar, and P.S. Delin (1995). An investigation into correlates of belief in the paranormal. *Journal of the American Society for Psychical Research*, 89, 215–231.

Thalbourne, M.A. and J. Houran (2000). Transliminality, the mental experiences inventory, and tolerance of ambiguity. *Personality and Individual differences*, 28, 853–863.

Tobacyk, J. (1988). A revised paranormal belief scale. (unpublished manuscript, Louisiana Tech University, Ruston, LA).

Tobacyk, J., and G. Milford (1983). Belief in paranormal phenomena: assessment instrument development and implications for personality functioning. *Journal of Personality and Social Psychology*, 44 (5), 1029–1037.

Tobacyk, L. (1993). Death threat, death concerns, and paranormal belief. *Death Education*, 7 (2–3), 115–124.

Tong, F. (2003). Out-of-body experiences: From Penfield to present. *Trends in Cognitive Science*, 7 (3), 104–106.

Totton, N. (2003). Introduction. In N. Totton (ed.), *Psychoanalysis and the Paranormal: Lands of Darkness* (1–14). London: Karnac.

Tressoldi, P.E., and G. Del Prete (2007). ESP under hypnosis: The role of induction instructions and personality characteristics. *Journal of Parapsychology*, 71, 125–137.

Trezza, V., and P. Campolongo (2009). Toward understanding the neurobiology of social attachment: Role of estrogen receptors in the medial amygdala. *Journal of Neuroscience*, 29 (1), 1–2.

Trimble, M., and A. Freeman (2006). An investigation of religiosity and the Gastaut-Geschwind syndrome in patients with temporal lobe epilepsy. *Epilepsy and Behavior*, 9 (3), 407–414.

Truzzi, M. (2001). Essay review. *Journal of Parapsychology*, 65 (2), 161–179.

Turner, D.J. (1998). Ball lightning and other meteorological phenomena. *Physics Reports*, 93, 1–60.

Tuske, J. (1999). Being in two minds: The divided mind in the nyayasutras. *Asian Philosophy*, 9 (3), 229–239.

Twemlow, S.W. (1994). Misidentified flying objects? An integrated psychodynamic perspective on near-death experiences and UFO abductions. *Journal of Near-Death Studies*, 12 (4), 205–233.

Tyrell, G.N.M. (1963). *Apparitions*. New York: Collier Books.

Ullman, M. (2003). Dream telepathy: Experimental and clinical findings. In N. Totton (ed.) *Psychoanalysis and the Paranormal: Lands of Darkness* (15–46). London: Karnac.

Vallee, J., and J. Vallee (1966). *Challenge to science: The UFO enigma*. New York: Henry Regnery.

Vallee, J.F., and E.W. Davis (2003). Incommensurability, orthodoxy and the physics of high strangeness: A 6-layer model for anomalous phenomena. Paper presented at the Forum on Science, Religion and Consciousness, Portugal (23–25 October 2003).

van Erkelens, H. (1991). Wolfgang Pauli's dialogue with the spirit of matter. *Psychological Perspectives*, 24 (1), 34–53.

Van Paesschen, W., M.D. King, J.S. Duncan, and A. Connelly (2001). The amygdala and temporal lobe simple partial seizures: A prospective and quantitative MRI study. *Epilepsia*, 42 (7), 857–862.

Vedat S., I. Serkan, Ö. Erdinç (2009). Childhood emotional abuse and dissociation in patients with conversion symptoms. *Psychiatry and Clinical Neurosciences*, 63 (5), 670–677.

Vernon, J., T. Marton, and E. Peterson (1961). Sensory deprivation and hallucinations. *Science*, 133, 1808–1812.

von Lucadou, W. (1984). What is wrong with the definition of psi? *European Journal of Parapsychology*, 5 (3), 261–283.

Vyse, S.A. (1997). *Believing in magic: The psychology of superstition*. New York: Oxford University Press.

Wagner, G.A., and E.K. Morris (1980). *Acquisition of superstitious behavior with children.* Abstract of paper presented at the 88th annual convention of the American Psychological Association, Montreal, Canada (1–5 September 1980).

Walker, E., L. Kestler, A. Bollini, and K.M. Hochman (2004). Schizophrenia: Etiology and Course. *Annual Review of Psychology*, 55 (1), 401–430.

Waller, N.G., F.W. Putman, and E.B. Carlson (1996). Types of dissociation and dissociative types: A taxometric analysis of dissociative experiences. *Psychological Methods*, 1 (3), 300–321.

Walter, T., H. Waterhouse, and J. Rudski (2003). What does a "superstitious" person believe? Impressions of participants. *Journal of General Psychology*, 130 (4), 431–445.

Warren, D.I. (1970). Status inconsistency theory and flying saucer sightings. *Science*, 170, 599–603.

Wassermann, E.M., T.A. Blaxton, E.A. Hoffman, C.D. Berry, H. Oletsky, A. Pascual-

Leone, and W.H. Theodore (1999). Repetitive transcranial magnetic stimulation of the dominant hemisphere can disrupt visual naming in temporal lobe epilepsy patients. *Neuropsychologia*, 37 (5), 537–544.

Watt, C. (2005). Parapsychology's contribution to psychology: A view from the front line. *Journal of Parapsychology*, 69 (2), 215–231.

Weitz, L.J. (1976). Jung's and Freud's contributions to dream interpretation: A comparison. *American Journal of Psychotherapy*, 30 (2), 289–293.

Wessel-Berg, T. (2003). A proposed theory of the phenomenon of ball lightning. *Acta Physica D*, 182, 223–253.

Westrum, R. (1977). Social intelligence about anomalies: The case of UFOs. *Social Studies of Science*, 10, 271–302.

Wiersbicki, M. (1985). Reasoning errors and belief in the paranormal. *Journal of Social Psychology*, 125, 489–494.

Wilkinson, H.P., and A. Gauld (1993). Geomagnetism and anomalous experiences. *Proceedings of the Society for Psychical Research*, 57, 275–310.

William, G. (1986). A psychical theory for paranormal phenomena. *European Journal of Parapsychology*, 6, 151–165.

Wilson, C. (1971/1983). *The Occult*. St. Albans: Grenada.

Wilson, S., R.L. Morris, and N. Tiliopoulos (1994). PSI and associational processes. *Journal of Parapsychology*, 68 (1), 129–155.

Wilson, S.C., and T.X. Barber (1983). The fantasy-prone personality: Implications for understanding imagery, hypnosis, and parapsychological phenomena (340–390). In A.A. Sheikh (ed.), *Imagery, current theory, research and application*. New York: Wiley.

Windholz, G., and L. Diamant (1974). Some personality traits of believers in extraordinary phenomena. *Bulletin of the Psychonomic Society*, 3, 125–126.

Windschitl, P.D. (1996). Memory for faces: Evidence of retrieval-based impairment. *Journal of Experimental Psychology*, 22 (5), 1101–1122.

Wing, Y., S.T. Lee, and C. Chen (1994). Sleep paralysis in Chinese: Ghost oppression phenomenon in Hong Kong. *Sleep*, 17, 609–613.

Wing, Y-K., H. Chiu, T. Leung, and J. Ng (1999). Sleep paralysis in the elderly. *Journal of Sleep Research*, 8, 151–155.

Wiseman, R. (2010). "Heads I win, tails you lose": how parapsychologists nullify null results. *Skeptical Enquirer*, 34 (1), 36–39.

Wiseman, R., and E. Greening (2002). The mind machine: A mass participation experiment into the possible existence of extra-sensory perception. *British Journal of Psychology*, 93, 487–499.

Wiseman, R., and E. Greening (2005). "It's still bending": Verbal suggestion and alleged psychokinetic ability. *British Journal of Psychology*, 96 (1), 115–127.

Wiseman, R., E. Greening, and M. Smith (2003). Belief in the paranormal and suggestion in the séance room. *British Journal of Psychology*, 94, 285–297.

Wiseman, R., and R. Morris (1995). Recalling pseudo-psychic demonstrations. *British Journal of Psychology*, 86 (1), 113–126.

Wiseman, R., and M. Smith (1998). Can animals detect when their owners are returning home? An experimental test of the "psychic pet" phenomenon. *British Journal of Psychology*, 89, 453–462.

Wiseman, R., C. Watt, E. Greening, P. Stevens, and C. O'Keefe (2002). An investigation into the alleged haunting of Hampton Court Palace: Psychological variables and magnetic fields. *Journal of Parapsychology*, 66, 387–408.

Wiseman, R., C. Watt, P. Stevens, E. Greening, and C. O'Keefe (2003). An investigation into alleged "hauntings." *British Journal of Psychology*, 94, 195–211.

Wiseman, S., and U. Neisser (1974). Perceptual organization as a determinant of visual recognition memory. *American Journal of Psychology*, 4, 675–681.

Wolfradt, U., V. Oubaid, E.R. Straube, N. Bischoff, and J. Mischo (1999). Thinking styles, schizotypal traits and anomalous experiences. *Personality and Individual Differences*, 27, 821–830.

Wooffitt, R. (2007). Epistemic authority and neutrality in the discourse of psychic practitioners: Toward a naturalistic parapsychology. *Journal of Parapsychology*, 71 (1), 69–104.

Wright, B. (1982). Demystifying Reichian therapy. *Issues in Radical Therapy*, 10 (3), 32–39.

Yee, L., A.J. Korner, S. McSwiggan, R.A. Meares, and J. Stevenson (2005). Persistent hallucinosis in borderline personality disorder. *Comprehensive Psychiatry*, 46 (2), 147–154.

Yoakum, C.S. (1912). An hypnogogic hallucination with dream characters. *Journal of Abnormal Psychology*, 7, 167–175.

Youse, K.M., and C.A. Coelho (2005). Working memory and discourse production abilities following closed-head injury. *Brain Injury*, 19 (12), 1001–1009.

Yuksel, F.V., C. Kisa, C. Aydemir, and E. Goka (2004). Sensory deprivation and disorders of perception. *The Canadian Journal of Psychiatry*, 49 (12), 867–868.

Zanarini, M.C., J.G. Gunderson, and F.R. Frankenburg (1990). Cognitive features of borderline personality disorder. *The American Journal of Psychiatry*, 147 (1), 57–63.

Zeman, A. (2005). Neurology: Tales from the temporal lobe. *New England Journal of Medicine*, 352 (2), 119–121.

Zimmer, T.A. (1984). Social psychological correlates of possible UFO sightings. *Journal of Social Psychology*, 123, 199–206.

Ziskind, E., and T. Augsburg (1967). Hallucinations in sensory deprivation: method or madness? *Diseases of the Nervous System*, 28 (11), 721–726.

Zusne, L., and W.H. Jones (1982). *Anomalistic Psychology*. Hillsdale, N.J.: Lawrence Erlbaum.

Index

Numbers in *bold italics* indicate pages with photographs.